Access™ 2007 VBA Programming For Dummies

D0128564

Top VBA-Access Shortcuts

To Do This	Press This
Switch between Access and the VBA editor	Alt+F11
Get help	F1
View Object Browser (VBA Editor)	F2
View properties and events	F4
Close VBA Editor and return to Access	Alt+Q

General VBA Editor Shortcut Keys

Action	Shortcut Key
Get help	F1
View Object Browser	F2
View properties	F4
View Code window	F7
Open Project Explorer	Ctrl+R
Close and return to Access	Alt+Q
Switch to Access	Alt+F11
View Immediate window	Ctrl+G
View shortcut menu	Shift+F10 (or right-click)
View definition	Shift+F2
Go to last position	Ctrl+Shift+F2
Run a Sub/UserForm	F5
Stop code execution	Ctrl+Break

Debug Shortcut Keys

Action	Shortcut Key
Toggle breakpoint	F9
Step into	F8
Step over	Shift+F8
Step out	Ctrl+Shift+F8
Run to cursor	Ctrl+F8
Clear all breakpoints	Ctrl+F9

Common VBA Tasks

Open a form in Form view:

```
DoCmd.OpenForm "formname", acNormal
```

Change a form property on an open form:

```
Forms![formName].propertyName = newValue
```

Get value from a control on an open form:

```
Forms![formName]![controlName].Value
```

Change value of a control on an open form:

```
Forms![formName]![controlName].Value = newValue
```

Change a control property on an open form:

```
Forms![formName]![controlName].propertyName = newValue
```

Close a form, saving design changes:

```
DoCmd.Close acForm, "formName", acSaveYes
```

Print a report:

```
DoCmd.OpenReport "reportName", acViewNormal
```

Run an action query:

```
DoCmd.RunSQL "SQLstatement"
```

Show a simple message:

```
MsgBox "yourMessage"
```

Ask a question on-screen:

```
variable = MsgBox("yourMessage", vbQuestion + vbYesNo)
```

For Dummies: Bestselling Book Series for Beginners

Access™ 2007 VBA
Programming For Dummies®

Code and Immediate Window Shortcuts

Action	Shortcut Key	Action	Shortcut Key
Move cursor right one character	→	Go to bottom of module	Ctrl+End
Select character to right	Shift+→	Select all text to bottom of module	Ctrl+Shift+End
Move cursor right one word	Ctrl+→	Cut selection	Ctrl+X
Select to end of word	Ctrl+Shift+→	Copy selection	Ctrl+C
Move cursor left one character	←	Paste selection	Ctrl+V
Select character to left of cursor	Shift+←	Cut current line to Clipboard	Ctrl+Y
Move cursor left one word	Ctrl+←	Delete to end of word	Ctrl+Delete
Move cursor to start of line	Home	Delete character or selected text	Delete (Del)
Select text to start of line	Shift+Home	Delete character to left of cursor	Backspace
Move cursor to end of line	End	Delete to beginning of word	Ctrl+Backspace
Select text to end of line	Shift+End	Undo	Ctrl+Z
Move cursor up a line	↑	Indent line	Tab
Move cursor down a line	↓	Outdent line	Shift+Tab
Move cursor to next procedure	Ctrl+↓	Find	Ctrl+F
Move cursor to previous procedure	Ctrl+↑	Replace	Ctrl+H
Scroll up one screen	PgUp	Find Next	F3
Scroll down one screen	PgDn	Find Previous	Shift+F3
Go to top of module	Ctrl+Home	Get help with selected word	F1
Select all text to top of module	Ctrl+Shift+Home	Get Quick Info	Ctrl+I

For Dummies: Bestselling Book Series for Beginners

Access™ 2007 VBA Programming

FOR DUMMIES®

by Joseph C. Stockman and Alan Simpson

Wiley Publishing, Inc.

Access™ 2007 VBA Programming For Dummies®

Published by
Wiley Publishing, Inc.
111 River Street
Hoboken, NJ 07030-5774
www.wiley.com

About the Author

Joe Stockman is an independent consultant, software designer, and author who has been using Microsoft Access since its initial release. He's also developed courseware and taught classes in Access and VBA. Joe developed his first application in Access, and then migrated into Visual Basic and VB.NET, where he specializes in creating applications for the Windows Mobile platform. He worked for several software companies before forming his consulting business in 2002, where he deals with all types of clients including healthcare, financial, government, manufacturing, and small business. His ability to turn his customers' wishes into working applications keeps them satisfied. Joe's also writing the fundamentals column for the *Advisor Guide to Microsoft Access* magazine.

Alan Simpson is the author of over 100 computer books on databases, Windows, Web site design and development, programming, and networking. His books are published throughout the world in over a dozen languages and have millions of copies. Alan has also taught introductory and advanced computer programming courses at San Diego State University and the UCSD Extension. He has served as a consultant on high-technology, education-oriented projects for the United States Navy and Air Force. Despite that, Alan has no fancy job title because he has never had a real job.

Dedication

Joe Stockman: To my mom and all my friends and family who supported me — and left me alone — during this project.

Alan Simpson: To Susan, Ashley, and Alec, as always.

Authors' Acknowledgments

Even though only two authors' names appear on the cover, every book is a team project. These authors would like to thank the many people who contributed to this book. To Carole McClendon and everyone at Waterside Productions, thank you for finding this project and making it happen. Also, many thanks to Kyle Looper and Jean Rogers at Wiley for taking a chance on a new author to help with the rewrite. And also, thanks to Microsoft for making Access a wonderful development environment.

Publisher's Acknowledgments

We're proud of this book; please send us your comments through our online registration form located at `www.dummies.com/register/`.

Some of the people who helped bring this book to market include the following:

Acquisitions, Editorial, and Media Development

Associate Project Editor: Jean Rogers

(Previous Edition: Christopher Morris)

Acquisitions Editor: Kyle Looper

Copy Editor: Becky Whitney

Technical Editor: Russ Mullen

Editorial Manager: Kevin Kirschner

Media Development Specialists: Angela Denny, Kate Jenkins, Steven Kudirka, Kit Malone

Media Development Coordinator: Laura Atkinson

Media Project Supervisor: Laura Moss

Media Development Manager: Laura VanWinkle

Media Development Associate Producer: Richard Graves

Editorial Assistant: Amanda Foxworth

Sr. Editorial Assistant: Cherie Case

Cartoons: Rich Tennant (www.the5thwave.com)

Composition Services

Project Coordinator: Jennifer Theriot

Layout and Graphics: Carl Byers, Stephanie D. Jumper, Barbara Moore, Barry Offringa, Alicia B. South

Proofreaders: Techbooks, Brian H. Walls

Indexer: Techbooks

Anniversary Logo Design: Richard Pacifico

Publishing and Editorial for Technology Dummies

Richard Swadley, Vice President and Executive Group Publisher

Andy Cummings, Vice President and Publisher

Mary Bednarek, Executive Acquisitions Director

Mary C. Corder, Editorial Director

Publishing for Consumer Dummies

Diane Graves Steele, Vice President and Publisher

Joyce Pepple, Acquisitions Director

Composition Services

Gerry Fahey, Vice President of Production Services

Debbie Stailey, Director of Composition Services

Contents at a Glance

Table of Contents

Introduction

*W*elcome to *Access 2007 VBA Programming For Dummies*. As you already
know (we hope), Microsoft Access is a huge database management
program, offering lots of ways to manage data (information). Common uses of
Access include managing mailing lists, memberships, scientific and statistical
data, entire small businesses, and just about anything else that involves storing and managing large amounts of information.

As the title implies, this book is about using Visual Basic for Applications
(VBA) to enhance the power of Access databases. If you want Access to print
words on a check, skip mailing labels that you've already used, or manipulate
data behind the scenes, you have to write VBA code.

By the time you finish this book, you should know exactly what VBA is all
about and how it fits into Access. You'll discover the meanings of all those
obscure terms that programmers throw around — code, variable, array, loop,
object — as though they were common knowledge. You'll be able to write and
use your own, custom code, just like advanced programmers do.

This book covers VBA in Access 2007. Although many changes and improve-
ments to Access have occurred in all the versions that Microsoft has
released, the VBA programming language has hardly changed a bit over the
years. Although Access 2007 looks completely different from previous versions, the underlying objects are virtually unchanged. The code that you see
in this book should also work in Access 2000, 2002, and 2003. The vast majority of the code in this book also works just fine even in last century's versions, such as Access 97.

About This Book

We wish we could say that this book is exactly like a coffee-table book, where
you could just pick it up, flip to any page, and have everything make perfect
sense to you. Well, we *could* say that, but we'd be lying if we did. It's not
because we want to break from the coffee-table book idea. It's really more
because some stuff in life doesn't make much sense until after you already
know something else.

Here, it isn't really possible to make much sense of VBA code until you understand what VBA code is and why it exists. And, we are talking about Microsoft Access VBA here. To make sense of much of anything in this book, you have to already be familiar with Microsoft Access tables, queries, forms, and reports. We just don't have enough room in this book to explain all that stuff from scratch and still have enough pages left over to talk about VBA.

On the bright side, we did everything we could to make it easy to find what you need to know, when you need to know it. You certainly don't have to read this book from cover to cover to make sense of things. After you find the topic you're looking for, you should be able to read through the section and be done with it quickly. Often, you can skip reading sections altogether and get all you need to know from looking at the figures.

Conventions Used in This Book

While we're on the topic of using this book without boring yourself to death by attempting to *read* it, we also stuck with some conventions for displaying text in these pages. For example, any VBA programming code appears in a `monospace` font with a gray background, like this:

```
'VBA code to say Hello World on the screen.
Sub Hello()
    MsgBox "Hello World"
End Sub
```

When we have just a little chunk of code to show in text, like this — `Dim Wit As Date` — you can see what is and what isn't VBA code.

The ⇨ symbol that you see in text separates individual menu options (commands) that you choose in sequence. For example, rather than say "Choose New from the File menu" or "Click File on the menu bar and then click New on the drop-down menu," we just say

Choose File⇨New from the menu bar.

When you see something **in bold,** we want you to enter (type) it.

What You're Not to Read

Not many people in the world would put reading a computer book into the Read for Fun category. We think that reading a computer book is more likely to fall into the Read for Work or Don't Read category. To minimize the time you have to spend away from the fun stuff, we put some information in sidebars and beside Technical Stuff icons. That information is definitely optional reading that you're welcome to ignore.

Foolish Assumptions

To stay focused on VBA in this book, we need to assume that you're already familiar with Access and that you're comfortable creating tables, forms, reports, and queries. However, we don't assume that you're a true Microsoft Access expert. Let's face it: Access isn't exactly an easy program for most people to tackle.

Another assumption we make is that you have already created an Access database with at least some tables and forms in it. In fact, writing VBA code is usually the last step in creating a custom Access database.

Finally, we don't assume that you're already an accomplished programmer who is just picking up a new programming language. Rather, we assume that you've never written any programming code in your life — and maybe you aren't even all that sure what programming code means or how it relates to Microsoft Access.

How This Book Is Organized

All books contain a lot of information. That's what makes them books. To break down topics into smaller, more manageable chunks, we split this book into six main parts.

Part I: Introducing VBA Programming

This part has all the information you need to get started. If you've already been using VBA for a few months or years, you can skim this part. If you don't know a VBA procedure from a PTO meeting, you might want to take a closer look at Part I before venturing forth to other parts.

Part II: VBA Tools and Techniques

Here you discover how to write VBA code to make Access do things for you. For example, you'll see how you can make Access open forms, respond to button clicks, change the appearance of objects, and more.

Part III: VBA, Recordsets, and SQL

Here you get friendly with tools and techniques for managing your Access tables by using VBA with SQL (Structured Query Language) and recordsets. All those buzzwords make this process sound more technical than it really is. But as you'll see, if you've done anything at all with queries, you've already been working with SQL recordsets. The idea is the same. We just use fancier terminology in the VBA world.

Part IV: Applying VBA in the Real World

In this part, you get into some more advanced programming tricks, mostly by using techniques presented in earlier parts in new and creative ways. You'll also see how to use the VBA debugging techniques, which can be real life-savers when things go wrong and you just can't figure out why the code you wrote isn't doing what you intended.

Part V: Reaching Out with VBA

VBA isn't a programming language solely for Microsoft Access. You can also use VBA to customize all the Microsoft Office application programs, including Word, Excel, and Outlook. Furthermore, VBA can import data from, and export data to, a variety of formats that extend its reach even beyond Microsoft Access. Part V shows you how that's all done.

Part VI: The Part of Tens

What *For Dummies* book would be complete without a Part of Tens? Ten is such a nice number to work with, given our ten fingers and all. Chapter 15 covers the main strategies that you can adopt to avoid going crazy trying to get VBA to do your bidding. Chapter 16 goes over the top ten nerdy programming tricks you're most likely to want to do almost from your first day of using VBA.

Icons Used in This Book

As you flip through this book, you'll notice little icons sprinkled throughout its pages. These icons, as described here, point out little chunks of text that deserve either a little extra attention or very little attention:

Tips point out handy tricks or techniques that can make things easier for you when you're working with VBA.

These icons point out techniques that, if you do things wrong, might create problems. If you pay attention to the Warnings we give, you can avoid making common blunders.

These icons point out tools and techniques that you'll use often as you work with VBA. Keep them in mind.

These icons point out text that describes how or why a thing works the way it does from a technical standpoint. If you just want to get a thing to work and don't care about how or why it works, you can always skip these.

Web Site for This Book

If you can find a way to copy and paste — rather than type — VBA code into your database, go for it. Much of the sample VBA code shown in this book is the kind of thing you can just drop into an Access database and start using. There's no need to retype the whole thing. Anyway, we post all the useful code at this Web site:

```
www.dummies.com/go/access2007vbaprog
```

When you get to the site, you'll see where to find the code and how to copy and paste it into your own database, and find a link where you can send us your questions.

Where to Go from Here

Now that you know what this book is about and how it's organized, the next question is "Where do I start?" Your best bet, if you're an absolute VBA beginner, is at Chapter 1. Try to slog through the first three (short) chapters to get your bearings.

Experienced VBA users can probably start anywhere that looks interesting. If you get in over your head at some point, watch for cross-references to earlier chapters where you can quickly fill in the knowledge gap that's causing the confusion.

Part I

Introducing VBA Programming

The 5th Wave   By Rich Tennant

"Once I told Mona that Access was an 'argument' based program, she seemed to warm up to it."

In this part . . .

*V*BA lets you do some pretty amazing stuff in an Access database. With VBA, you can make Access do boring, repetitive jobs that you might otherwise have to do on your own. You can even get Access to do things that it couldn't possibly do on its own. Before you dive right in and try to make such things happen, you need to step back a moment and get a feel for how VBA fits into the whole Microsoft Access scheme of things. Then you need to get friendly with the tools available to you for turning ideas into stuff that actually happens when you want it to happen. We lead you through all of that in Chapters 1 and 2.

With your road map and tool kit in hand, you'll be ready to get into what Access VBA is really all about — writing code (also known as programming) — to make Access do exactly what you want it to do. Yes, you write code by simply typing it, unless, of course, you can just copy and paste the code, as is often the case. Chapter 3 talks about both writing and swiping VBA code.

Chapter 1

Where VBA Fits In

*T*his book is about using *Visual Basic for Applications (VBA),* which is a programming language that helps you program, tweak, and squeeze productivity from Access. VBA, which is embedded in Access, is a sophisticated set of programming tools that you can use to harness the power of a packaged application like Access. Just like you need to know how to walk before you can run, you need to know how to use Access before you can start to use Access VBA.

Maybe you want to use Access to manage a large mailing list. Maybe you need Access to manage your whole business, including customers, products, and orders. Perhaps you need to manage enrollments in courses or events. Whatever your reason for using Access, your first step is always to create the tables for storing your data. From there, you can then create queries, forms, reports, and macros to help manage that data. All these steps take place before you even get into VBA, so in this book we have to assume that you're already an experienced Access user who needs more than what queries, forms, reports, and macros can provide. If you're new to Access, this book isn't a good place to start. If you need to brush up on Access, *Access 2007 For Dummies* (by John Kaufeld, Laurie Ulrich Fuller, and Ken Cook; Wiley Publishing) or *Access 2007 All-in-One Desk Reference For Dummies* (Alan Simpson, Margaret Levine Young, and Alison Barrows; Wiley) is a good place to start.

Although Access has progressed through many versions over the years, VBA has remained relatively unchanged. We used Access 2007 to create this book, but the code examples we present should work fine in just about any version of Access. So now, before launching into VBA, take a moment to delve into what tables, queries, forms, and reports are all about, and how VBA fits into the overall scheme of things.

Taking a Look at Access

Access, part of the Microsoft Office suite, is a huge database management system that you work with by using modern object-oriented methods. (The term *object-oriented* stems from the fact that everything you create in Access — a table, form, report, or whatever — is considered an object.

The Access Navigation pane, as shown in Figure 1-1, is the main container in which you store all the main objects that make up a single database. The Navigation pane breaks down the objects into groups — tables, queries, forms, and so on — and each group contains the objects within that group. The following list summarizes the types of objects.

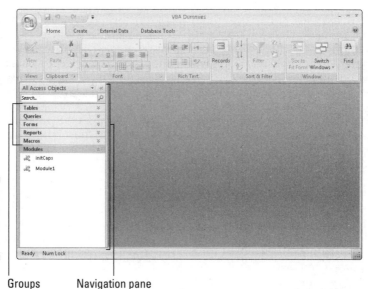

Figure 1-1:
The Access
Navigation
pane.

Groups   Navigation pane

- ✔ **Tables:** *Tables* contain the raw data that all other object types display and manage. Data in tables is stored in *records* (rows) and *fields* (columns).

- ✔ **Queries:** Use *queries* to sort and filter data from one or more tables.

- ✔ **Forms:** Access *forms* are similar to printed fill-in-the-blank forms, but they allow you to view and change data stored in Access tables.

- ✔ **Reports:** *Reports* define how data should be presented on printed pages.

- ✔ **Macros:** *Macros* provide a means of automating certain aspects of Access without programming in VBA.

- ✔ **Modules:** The *Modules* group, as you soon discover, is one of the places where you store VBA code. If you're not already familiar with modules, that's fine. Modules are what this book is really all about.

One of the most important things to understand is that you don't use VBA "instead of" other objects, like tables and forms. You use VBA to *enhance* the capabilities of other object types. Therefore, it makes no sense to even try VBA until you have a firm grasp of the purpose and capabilities of those other object types in Access.

Understanding VBA

Visual Basic is a programming language — a language for writing instructions that a computer can read and process. VBA is a programming language that's specifically designed to work with the application programs in Microsoft Office including Word, Excel, Outlook, and, of course, Access.

When you write text in a programming language (as opposed to writing in plain English), you're writing *code*. Programmers use the term *code* to refer to anything that's written in a computer programming language. For example, Figure 1-2 shows some sample VBA code. The whole trick to mastering VBA is finding out what all the various words in the language mean so that you can write code that tells Access exactly how to perform a task.

```
Public Function PCase(anyText)
    'Custom Access VBA function to fix all uppercase letters.

    PCase = StrConv(anyText, vbProperCase)

    If Left(PCase, 4) = "P.o." Then
        PCase = "P.O." & Mid(PCase, 5)
    End If

    If Left(PCase, 2) = "Mc" Then
        PCase = "Mc" & UCase(Mid(PCase, 3, 1)) & Mid(PCase, 4)
    End If

    If Left(PCase, 3) = "Mac" Then
        PCase = "Mac" & UCase(Mid(PCase, 4, 1)) & Mid(PCase, 5)
    End If

End Function
```

Figure 1-2: Some sample VBA code.

If the sample code shown in Figure 1-2 looks like meaningless gibberish to you, don't worry about it. People aren't born knowing how to read and write VBA code. Programming (writing code) is a skill you have to learn. For now, it's sufficient just to know what code looks like. Knowing what the code means is one of the skills you master in this book.

Because VBA code looks like a bunch of meaningless gibberish typed on a sheet of paper, it begs the question of why anybody would want to figure out how to read and write a dreadful language like that one. The answer to that question lies in the role that VBA plays in an application like an Access database.

Do, not die

Think of the term *execute* in the sense of "to carry out," as when you execute a U-turn or execute a procedure. Don't think of *execute* in the sense of "terminate the life of."

Access does indeed have a ton of tools that let you create a database without any programming. You could easily spend months or years just finding all the things you can do in Access without writing any VBA code. Yet despite the huge number of things you can do without programming, sometimes you want your database to accomplish a task that's not built into Access. That's where VBA comes in. When you want Access to perform a task that it doesn't already know how to perform, you write the steps to be performed in the VBA programming language.

When you're writing VBA code or just looking at some VBA code written by someone else, Access doesn't do anything. Access doesn't start performing the steps described by that code until Access executes the code. When you write VBA code, you're writing a set of instructions that Access can perform at any time, over and over again.

The ability to use the same code over and over again is the key to automating mundane tasks in Access. For example, if you use Access to print checks, you might have to manually type the part of the check where you spell out the amount, like "Ninety-two and 99/100 Dollars" for $92.99 because Access can't make that translation on its own. But if you could write some code to translate a number like $92.99 into words, you wouldn't need to type all those dollar amounts. Access would just print the correct information as it prints each check.

Seeing Where VBA Lurks

In an Access database, VBA code is stored in modules. Despite its fancy name, a *module* is basically an electronic sheet of paper on which VBA code is typed. A module in Access is either of these two types:

- ✔ **Standard:** A page that contains VBA code that's accessible to all objects in the database. A standard module always exists in the Modules group in the Navigation pane.

- ✔ **Class:** A page of VBA code that's attached to every form and report you create. You can also create a class module that appears in the Navigation pane.

The main difference between a standard module and a class module is that you can create an instance of your class module in code. A standard module contains procedures you can run from anywhere in your database. A class module contains code that's either attached to an existing form or report or is its own entity in the Navigation pane.

We talk about the types of modules as they become relevant throughout this book. Right now, they're not terribly important. For now, the main thing to keep in mind is that modules contain VBA code. Now take a look at where modules are stored within an Access database.

Finding standard modules

A *standard module* contains VBA code that's accessible to every table, query, form, report, page, and macro within the current database. Like those other objects, a standard module always gets its own group in the Navigation pane (refer to Figure 1-1). When you open the Modules group, the list shows the names of modules (if any) within the current database, as shown in the example in Figure 1-3. This example contains standard modules and class modules.

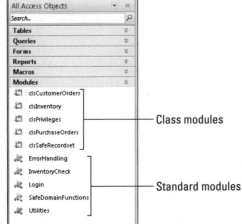

Figure 1-3:
Standard and class modules in a database.

Class modules — clsCustomerOrders, clsInventory, clsPrivileges, clsPurchaseOrders, clsSafeRecordset

Standard modules — ErrorHandling, InventoryCheck, Login, SafeDomainFunctions, Utilities

Don't be surprised if you open the Modules group in a database and the group is empty. These modules don't just happen: You have to create them.

Finding class modules

Like standard modules, *class modules* contain VBA code that tells Access what to do. Unlike standard modules, however, not all class modules are found in the Navigation pane. Class modules are often hidden behind forms and reports in your database. You can also create a class module that appears in the Navigation pane, as shown in Figure 1-3.

It might help to define the term *class* as *a class of objects*. In Access, tables are one class of objects, queries are another class, forms are another class, and reports are another, for example. Or, looking at it from the other direction, a single form is an object within your database. That single form is also a member of the class of objects known as *forms*.

We think that it helps to envision a form or report's class module as literally being hidden behind its form or report, as illustrated in Figure 1-4. This type of class module might be hidden from you if you don't know how to find it.

Class module behind form

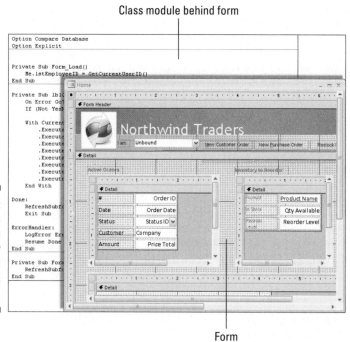

Figure 1-4:
Class
modules
typically
hide behind
forms and
reports.

Form

You have several ways to get to a form's or report's class module, as you discover in upcoming chapters. For now, if you just want to open a class module and have a look, here's one way to do it:

1. In the Navigation pane, open the Forms group or Reports group, depending on which type of object you want to open.

2. **Right-click the name of any form or report and choose Design View.**

3. **To see the class module for the open form or report, click the (Form Design Tools) Design tab, and then click the View Code command in the Tools group (see Figure 1-5).**

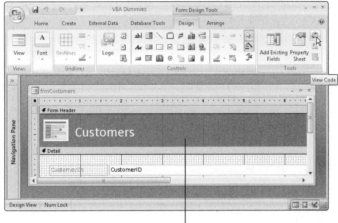

Figure 1-5:
Class modules are accessible from form and report Design views.

Form open in Design view

From VBA to Access

When you open a module, whether it's a standard module or a class module, your screen changes radically. That's because the module opens in the *Visual Basic Editor,* which is a separate program window from Access. In fact, if you look at the taskbar, you still see a taskbar button for Access and another for the Visual Basic Editor. You can switch back and forth between Access and the editor just by clicking their respective taskbar buttons, as shown in Figure 1-6.

Alternatively, you can press Alt+F11 to switch back and forth between Access and the VBA Editor at any time.

If the module you open contains any VBA code, that code is visible in the Code window, also shown in Figure 1-6. If you upgraded a database from a previous version of Access, a class module might contain VBA code, even if you never wrote a line of VBA code in your life, because some of the control wizards in Access 2003 and earlier automatically wrote VBA code for you behind the scenes. In Access 2007, the wizards create embedded macros, which is a new feature that we don't cover in this book.

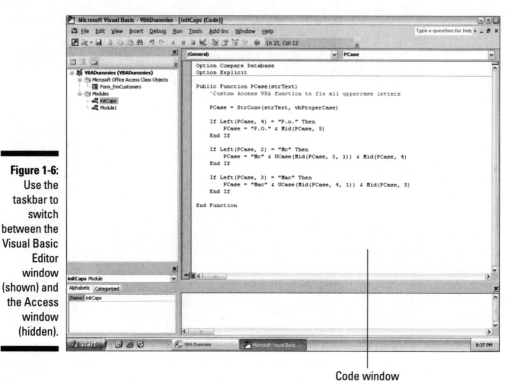

Figure 1-6:
Use the
taskbar to
switch
between the
Visual Basic
Editor
window
(shown) and
the Access
window
(hidden).

Code window

The main thing to keep in mind here is that every time you open a module, you end up in the Visual Basic Editor. You discover how to use that program in upcoming chapters. For now, the most important thing to know is how to close the editor and get back to the more familiar Access program window. Here are two easy ways to close the Visual Basic Editor and get back to the Access program window:

- ✔ Choose File⇨Close and Return to Microsoft Office Access (see Figure 1-7).
- ✔ Press Alt+Q.

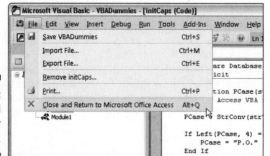

Figure 1-7:
The Visual
Basic Editor
File menu.

The Visual Basic Editor closes, its taskbar button disappears, and you return to the Access program window.

Finding Out How VBA Works

When you open a standard module or class module, there's no telling exactly what you see inside. Some modules are empty; others already contain some VBA code. It all depends on the life history of the module you open. One thing is for sure: If any VBA code is in the module, it's likely organized into one or more procedures.

The term *procedure* in everyday language usually refers to performing a series of steps in order to achieve some goal. For example, the procedure of getting to work every morning requires a certain series of steps. The same definition holds true for VBA code.

Discovering VBA procedures

A VBA *procedure* is a series of instructions written in VBA code that tells an application (like Access) exactly how to perform a specific task. In VBA code, each step in the procedure is a single line of code: a *statement*. When Access executes a VBA procedure, it does so step-by-step, from the top down. Access does whatever the first statement tells it to do. Then it does whatever the second statement tells it to do, and so forth, until it gets to the end of the procedure.

Exactly when Access executes a procedure is entirely up to you. Typically, you want to tie the procedure to some event that happens on-screen. For example, you might want the procedure to perform its task as soon as someone clicks a button. Or perhaps you want your procedure to do its thing whenever someone types an e-mail address into a form. We talk about how that all works in Chapter 6. For now, just realize that you can tie any procedure you create to any event you like.

When the event to which you've tied your procedure occurs, Access *calls* the procedure. What that means is that Access does exactly what the VBA code in the procedure tells it to do. You can envision the process as shown in Figure 1-8 where

1. An event, such as clicking a button, calls a procedure.

2. Access executes the first line in the called procedure; then it executes the second line in the procedure; and so on.

3. When Access encounters the end of the procedure (which is either End Sub or End Function), it just stops executing code and returns to its normal state.

1) Access events calls procedure

        ↓

        `Sub Magic_Click()`

2) Do this step → `Dim Answer As Byte, Msg As String`

3) Do this step → `Answer = MsgBox("Do you eat meat?", vbYesNo, "Question")`

4) Do this step → `Msg = "You are" & IIf(Answer = vbNo, " not", "") & " omnivorous."`

5) Do this step → `Answer = MsgBox(Msg, vbOKOnly, "Info")`

Do no more `End Sub`

Figure 1-8:
Executing a
procedure.

If you think of a line of VBA code as a sentence containing words, a procedure is a paragraph containing more than one sentence.

Recognizing VBA procedures

VBA has two types of procedures. One type is a Sub procedure. A Sub procedure is always contained within a pair of Sub...End Sub statements, like this:

```
Sub subName(...)
    'Any VBA code here
End Sub
```

The *subName* part of the example is the name of the procedure. The (. . .) part after the name can be empty parentheses or a list of parameters and data types. The 'Any VBA code here part stands for one or more lines of VBA code.

When looking at code that has already been written, you see that some Sub procedures have the word Public or Private to the left of the word Sub, as in these examples:

```
Private Sub subName(...)
    'Any VBA code here
End Sub

Public Sub subName(...)
    'Any VBA code here
End Sub
```

`Public` or `Private` defines the *scope* of the procedure. Neither type is particularly important right now. All that matters is that you know that a `Sub` procedure is a chunk of VBA code that starts with a `Sub` or `Private Sub` or `Public Sub` statement and ends at the `End Sub` statement.

If you must know right now, a `Public` procedure has global scope (is available to all other objects). A `Private` procedure is visible to only the module in which it's defined. For example, `Private Sub` procedures in a class module are private to the form or report to which the class module is attached.

The second type of procedure that you can create in Access is a `Function` procedure. Unlike a `Sub` procedure, which performs a task, a `Function` procedure generally does some sort of calculation and then returns the result of that calculation. The first line of a `Function` procedure starts with the word `Function` (or perhaps `Private Function` or `Public Function`) followed by a name. The last line of a `Function` procedure reads `End Function`, as illustrated here:

```
Function functionName(...)
    'Any VBA code here
End Function
```

A module can contain any number of procedures. When you open a module, you might at first think you're looking at one huge chunk of VBA code. But in fact you might be looking at several smaller procedures contained within the module, as shown in the example in Figure 1-9. Notice how each procedure within the module is separated by a black line that's the width of the page.

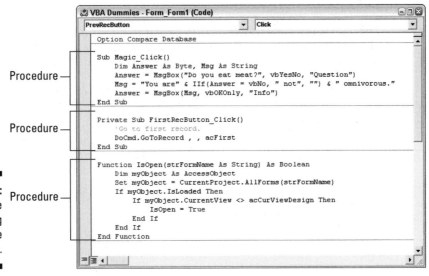

Figure 1-9: A module containing three procedures.

```
VBA Dummies - Form_Form1 (Code)

PrevRecButton                          Click

Option Compare Database

Sub Magic_Click()
    Dim Answer As Byte, Msg As String
    Answer = MsgBox("Do you eat meat?", vbYesNo, "Question")
    Msg = "You are" & IIf(Answer = vbNo, " not", "") & " omnivorous."
    Answer = MsgBox(Msg, vbOKOnly, "Info")
End Sub

Private Sub FirstRecButton_Click()
    'Go to first record.
    DoCmd.GoToRecord , , acFirst
End Sub

Function IsOpen(strFormName As String) As Boolean
    Dim myObject As AccessObject
    Set myObject = CurrentProject.AllForms(strFormName)
    If myObject.IsLoaded Then
        If myObject.CurrentView <> acCurViewDesign Then
            IsOpen = True
        End If
    End If
End Function
```

That's the view of Microsoft Access and VBA from 30,000 feet. Just remember that VBA is a programming language that allows you to write instructions that Access can execute at any time. You can write different sets of instructions for different events. Each set of instructions is a procedure, which is a series of steps carried out in a particular sequence to achieve a goal. You write and edit VBA code in the VBA Editor.

The beauty of it all is that you can write lots of little procedures to handle some of your more mundane tasks automatically and effortlessly. You can also extend Access's capabilities by writing procedures that do the tasks Access can't do on its own.

Chapter 2

Your VBA Toolkit

*A*s we discuss in Chapter 1, any time you want to work with Access VBA code, you need to open (or create) a module. As soon as you open one, you're taken to a program window that's separate from the Access program window. The program that opens and allows you to create or edit VBA code is the Visual Basic Editor (also called the VBA Editor).

It might seem strange that a whole separate program window opens each time you want to write or edit VBA code, but there's a reason: VBA is the programming language for all the programs in Microsoft Office. Whenever you want to create or edit VBA code in any Microsoft Office program window, you use the same Visual Basic Editor. Read through this chapter for all the buzzwords and skills needed to work in the Visual Basic Editor.

Using the Visual Basic Editor

The *Visual Basic Editor* — where you write, edit, and test your VBA code — contains lots of optional tools and panes. There are so many of them, in fact, that we can't even tell you exactly how the editor will look on your screen the first time you open it. However, it will likely contain at least some of the components shown in Figure 2-1.

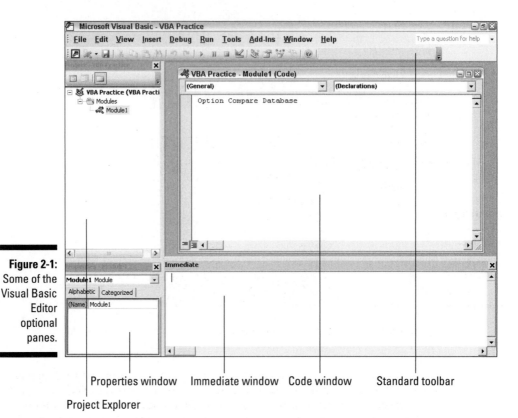

Figure 2-1:
Some of the
Visual Basic
Editor
optional
panes.

Properties window Immediate window Code window Standard toolbar

Project Explorer

Like most program windows, the Visual Basic Editor has a title bar and menu bar at the top. Optional toolbars appear under the menu bar. You can hide or show any toolbar at any time by choosing View⇨Toolbars from the menu bar. Select the check box for the toolbar you want to show; deselect the check box to hide that toolbar.

The View menu also provides options for making the various panes shown in Figure 2-1 visible. For example, if you don't see the Immediate window, choose View⇨Immediate Window from the menu bar to make it visible. To close an open pane or window inside the VBA Editor, click the Close (X) button in the upper-right corner of the pane that you want to close.

In Figure 2-1, the optional panes are *docked* (attached) to the VBA Editor program window. You can undock any pane and change it to a free-floating window. Just drag the item's title bar toward the center of the program window and release the mouse button. For example, Figure 2-2 shows the Project Explorer pane still docked and the Properties window undocked. The title bar for each item is also pointed out in the figure.

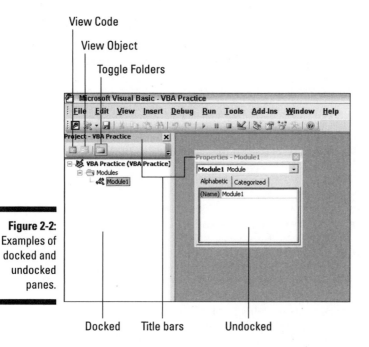

View Code

View Object

Toggle Folders

Docked   Title bars   Undocked

Figure 2-2:
Examples of
docked and
undocked
panes.

If you undock a pane, you can generally re-dock it by dragging it back to any edge of the VBA Editor program window. If the pane refuses to dock, try right-clicking within the pane and choosing Dockable from the contextual menu that appears. Then drag the pane to an edge or border if it doesn't dock right on the spot.

You can size any pane (or free-floating window) by dragging any edge of the item. For example, when both the Project Explorer and Properties panes are docked, you can widen or narrow them both by dragging the right edge of one of those panes. Drag the bottom edge of a pane to make it taller or shorter.

Whether you really need all the panes open depends on what you're doing at the moment within the VBA Editor. You'll probably spend the vast majority of your time in the Code window. Before we discuss that window, take a quick look at the optional Project Explorer and Properties windows.

Using Project Explorer

Project Explorer provides a list of all the modules contained in the current database (which is whatever database happens to be open in Access at the moment). The Toggle Folders button on the Project Explorer toolbar determines how the module names are displayed. When the Toggle Folders button is turned on, module names are shown in these three separate folders:

- ✓ **Microsoft Office Access Class Objects:** Lists the names of all form and report class modules in the current database. The name of the class module is the same as the form or report name, preceded by Form_ or Report_.

- ✓ **Modules:** Lists the names of all standard modules in the current database.

- ✓ **Class Modules:** Lists the names of class modules that appear in the Navigation pane of the current database.

If a folder has a plus sign (+) next to its name, you can click that + to view objects within the folder. Conversely, clicking the minus sign (–) next to either folder name collapses the folder and hides its contents.

To open a module in the VBA Editor, just double-click its name in Project Explorer. Each module that you double-click opens within its own Code window (described a little later, in the section "Using the Code window").

For form and report class modules, Project Explorer also provides quick access to the form or report to which the module is attached. Just right-click any class module name and choose View Object. The form or report opens in Design view in Access. The VBA Editor might then be covered by the Access window. However, the editor is still open, so you can get back to it by clicking its taskbar button.

The buttons to the left of the Toggle Folders button — View Code and View Object — also provide a means of switching between a class module and the object to which it's attached. Press Alt+F11 to switch back and forth between the Access and VBA Editor program windows.

Using the Properties window

The Properties window in the VBA Editor can be quite perplexing because it displays the properties of whatever object is selected in Access. If nothing is selected in Access, the Properties window might show nothing. That's often the case when you're working with standard modules because standard modules aren't tied to any particular object or event.

To illustrate how things tie together, Figure 2-3 shows a portion of a form, in Design view, in Access. A subform on the form is selected. In the VBA Editor window, which also appears in Figure 2-3, the properties for that selected subform appear in the VBA Editor Properties window.

In that same figure, you see an example of how Project Explorer might look in a database that already contains some modules. The modules whose names begin with the word Form_ are all class modules that are attached to forms in that database.

Perhaps the most important thing to remember about Project Explorer and the Properties window is that they're optional, and you really don't need them taking up space in your VBA Editor when you're not using them. Most of the time, you probably won't use them, so feel free to close those panes and forget about them if they just get in the way and confuse matters for you.

VBA Project Explorer lists all
modules in the current database

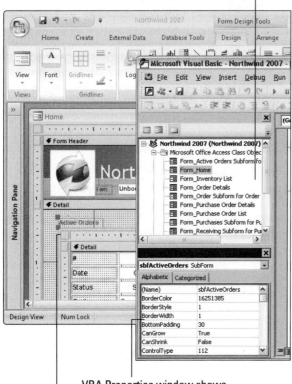

Figure 2-3:
A sample
Properties
window and
Project
Explorer.

VBA Properties window shows
properties of selected Access object

Selected object on Access form

Using the Immediate window

The Immediate window in the Visual Basic Editor allows you to run code at any time, right on the spot. This window is sometimes referred to as the *debug window* because it's mainly used for testing and *debugging* (removing errors from) code. If the Immediate window isn't open in the Visual Basic Editor, you can bring it out of hiding at any time by choosing View⇨ Immediate Window from the editor's menu bar.

When the Immediate window is open, you can anchor it to the bottom of the Visual Basic Editor by dragging its title bar to the bottom of the window. You can optionally make the Immediate window free-floating by dragging its title bar up and away from the bottom of the Visual Basic Editor's program window. You can also dock and undock the Immediate window by right-clicking within the Immediate window and choosing Dockable.

The Immediate window allows you to test expressions, run VBA procedures you created, and more. You see practical examples throughout this book. To get your feet wet, test this simple expression in the Immediate window. Just bear in mind that an Access expression is any formula. For example, the simplest expression in the world is probably 1+1, which (as just about everyone knows) results in 2.

To test an expression in the Immediate window, do the following:

1. **Click inside the Immediate window.**

   You need your cursor in that pane.

2. **Type a question mark (?) followed by a space and the expression you want to test; then press Enter.**

   For example, click in the Immediate window and then type **? 1+1**.

   The Immediate window immediately shows you the result — 2 — as shown in Figure 2-4.

Figure 2-4:
Testing a
simple
expression
in the
Immediate
window.

You might think of the ? character at the start of the line as asking the Immediate window "What is?" For example, if you think of ? 1+1 as meaning "What is one plus one?", it stands to reason that the Immediate window would return 2. After all, 1+1 is 2!

When you start actually writing VBA code, you'll use the Immediate window to test and debug your code. For now, just know that the Immediate window is another optional pane in the Visual Basic Editor that you can show and hide as needed.

Using the Code window

The VBA Editor's Code window is where you write, edit, and view VBA code. The Code window is similar to a word processor or text editor in that it supports all the standard Windows text-editing techniques. For example, you can type text and use the Backspace or Delete keys to delete text. And just like in Word, you can press the Tab key to indent text, select text by dragging the mouse pointer through it, and copy and paste text (to and from the Code window). In short, the Code window is a text editor.

Like all panes in the Visual Basic Editor, the Code window can be docked or undocked. Choosing one view or the other is just a matter of personal preference and doesn't affect how you write and edit VBA code. You can easily switch between docked and undocked views.

When the Code window is undocked, it has its own title bar and can be moved and sized independently. To dock an undocked Code window, click the Code window's Maximize button, as shown in Figure 2-5.

When the Code window is docked, it fills the available space in the VBA Editor window, and its Minimize, Restore, and Close buttons appear near the upper-right corner of the VBA Editor's program window. Clicking the Code window's Restore Window button (also shown in Figure 2-5) undocks the Code window and allows it to float freely.

As we mention earlier, the Code window is really a small word processor or text editor. But word processors tend to be oriented around paragraphs of text, whereas the Code window is built for typing individual lines of code. Unlike a word processor — where you don't press Enter until you get to the end of a paragraph — in the Code window, you press Enter at the end of each line you type.

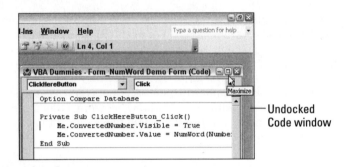

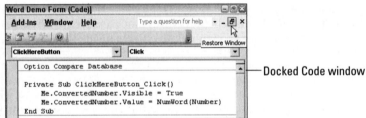

Undocked
Code window

Figure 2-5:
The Code
window
Restore
Window
and
Maximize
buttons.

Docked Code window

When you type a line of VBA code and press Enter, the Visual Basic Editor
compiles that line of code. For now, you can think of compiling as testing the
line of code to see whether it will work. If you just type some line at random in
the Code window — or even if you try to type a legitimate line of VBA code but
make a mistake — you see a compile error message, as shown in Figure 2-6.

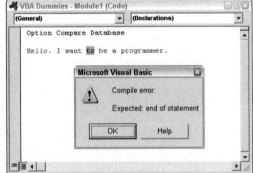

Figure 2-6:
A compile
error in the
Code
window.

We talk about ways of dealing with compile errors when we really get into
telling you how to write code in Chapter 3. For now, just realize that if you
type anything other than a valid line of VBA code into the Code window, you
see a compile error message as soon as you press Enter. So don't waste your
time trying to type text at random into the Code window.

Referring to Objects from VBA

VBA is able to control objects in Access (and other programs in Microsoft Office) because of *Automation* (with a capital *A*) technology. The idea behind Automation is this: A program, database, document, or special capability *exposes* (makes available) its objects through an *object library.* The object library contains an organized set of names that VBA can refer to when it wants to manipulate an object.

Think of an object library as sort of a steering wheel that's sticking out of some database or some program. When the steering wheel isn't available, VBA can't manipulate objects in the program. However, when the steering wheel is exposed, VBA can manipulate objects inside that program. As we discuss in the following section, you control which steering wheels are available by setting references to object libraries.

Figure 2-7 shows a hypothetical example where the Access and Excel object models (steering wheels) are exposed. VBA can therefore manipulate objects in those programs. In the figure, Word and PowerPoint aren't exposing their objects, so VBA can't manipulate objects in those programs.

Figure 2-7:
Object libraries expose objects to VBA.

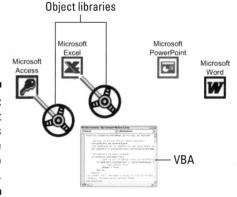

Not all object libraries expose objects in specific Office programs. Some object libraries expose programs; some object libraries expose documents; still others expose technologies that simply help you bridge the gaps between programs. Access, by itself, offers several object models. The important point is, though, that before you start writing VBA code, you need to know what object libraries are available to you.

Setting References to Object Libraries

To manipulate the objects in an object model through VBA, you need to set a reference to the appropriate object library. That part is easy because you just have to put a check mark next to the appropriate object library's name in the References dialog box. To open the References dialog box and choose your object libraries, follow these steps (in the Visual Basic Editor program window):

1. **Choose Tools⇨References from the Visual Basic Editor menu bar.**

   The References dialog box, as shown in Figure 2-8, opens.

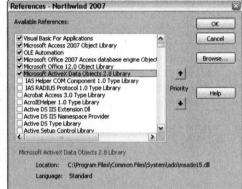

Figure 2-8:
Set object library references here.

2. **To set a reference to an object library, select its check box.**

   Some object libraries are already selected (checked), as shown in Figure 2-8. The selected object libraries shown in Figure 2-8 are typical and are a good starting point for any Access VBA programming.

3. **When all the object libraries you need are selected, click OK to close the dialog box.**

Setting references to object libraries exposes objects to VBA immediately, but it doesn't expose anything to you — at least, not in a way that's readily apparent on-screen. To find out what objects are available to VBA (and you) at the moment — and get help with them all — you need to use the Object Browser.

Using the Object Browser

Every object library provides VBA with a very large set of names that represent objects that VBA can manipulate — so many names that we doubt anybody would even attempt to remember them all. To make it easy to find names of things on an as-needed basis, VBA provides the Object Browser tool.

In this context, *browser* has nothing to do with the Internet or the World Wide Web. Rather, the *Object Browser* is a tool for browsing the contents of all available object libraries. And those object libraries have no connection to the Internet.

While you're in the Visual Basic Editor, you can do any of the following to open the Object Browser:

✔ Choose View⇨Object Browser from the Visual Basic Editor menu bar.

✔ Press F2.

✔ Click the Object Browser button on the VBA Editor's Standard toolbar.

When the Object Browser opens, it doesn't look like it's any big help, but there will be plenty of times when you need to use it. Now is a good time to become familiar with how you work that darn thing. Figure 2-9 points out the names of various tools within the Object Browser.

Project/Library list

Search box

Figure 2-9: The Object Browser.

Classes list   Split bars   Members list

Details pane

Here's a brief description of each tool:

✓ **Project/Library list:** From here, you choose either a single object library to browse or <All Libraries> (where All Libraries means *all object libraries that are selected in the References dialog box*).

✓ **Search box:** Here you type or choose a name to search for.

✓ **Classes list:** This list shows the names of all classes in the selected object library or all available libraries if <All Libraries> is selected in the Project/Library list. A *class* is any class or group of objects, such as `AllForms` (all the forms in the current database).

✓ **Members list:** When you click a name in the Classes list, this pane shows the members (objects, properties, methods, events, functions, and objects) that belong to that class.

✓ **Details pane:** When you click a member name in the Members list, the Details pane shows the *syntax* (rules) for using the item that's selected in the Members list, as well as the name of the library to which the member belongs.

✓ **Split bars:** Drag the split bars left or right (or up and down) to adjust the size of the panes. (Drag any edge or corner of the Object Browser window to size the window as a whole.)

Clicking the Project/Library drop-down list displays the names of all currently loaded object libraries (all the object libraries to which you've set a reference in the References dialog box; refer to Figure 2-8). This list describes the object libraries:

✓ **Access:** The Microsoft Access 2007 Object Library lets you control the Access program programmatically.

✓ **ADODB:** The Microsoft ActiveX Data Objects 2.8 Library allows you to access all data in your database as well as data from outside databases.

✓ **DAO:** The Microsoft Office 2007 Access database engine Object Library is the primary method for working with the Microsoft Jet database engine from code.

✓ **Office:** The Microsoft Office 12.0 Object Library lets you control aspects of Access that are common across all Microsoft Office programs.

✓ **stdole:** The OLE Automation object library (where *stdole* is short for *standard OLE*) provides programmable access to objects that use object-linking and -embedding technologies, such as pictures in tables.

✓ **VBA:** The Visual Basic for Applications object library contains programmable access to objects built into the VBA programming language, such as functions for doing math with dates, times, and dollar amounts.

In addition to listing the names of object libraries selected in the References dialog box, the Project/Library list offers the name of the database you're working in. Consider the name of the current database to be the project on the Project/Library drop-down list. You don't need to set a reference to that object library because it's built into the database that's open in Access.

Searching the Object Library

The real beauty of the Object Browser lies in its ability to help you find information about an object as you need it. Because you probably don't know what library an object resides in, choose <All Libraries> from the Project/Library drop-down list before you begin a search. Then you need to know what name you're searching for.

For example, as you discover a little later in this book, Access offers a DoCmd (do command) object that lets VBA perform a variety of actions, from opening forms to setting the values of controls. Suppose you're writing some code and need some quick information about that object. You could get that information by following these steps to search the Object Browser:

1. **In the Search box in the Object Browser, type the word you're searching for.**

   For example, to search for information on the DoCmd object, type **DoCmd** as the word to search for.

2. **Click the Search button (the binoculars) next to the Search box.**

   The results of your search appear in the Search Results pane under the Search box.

3. **To get help with an item in the Search Results pane, click a name there and then click the Help button (the question mark) on the Object Browser toolbar.**

   The Help text appears in a separate Help window, as shown in the example in Figure 2-10.

 Admittedly, the Help text is technical documentation, written more for programmers than for VBA beginners. But you won't be a beginner for long, and knowing how to search the Object Browser will soon become a valuable skill.

As with other tools that we describe in this chapter, you can close the Object Browser (as well as any open Help window) at any time by clicking its Close (X) button.

Help button

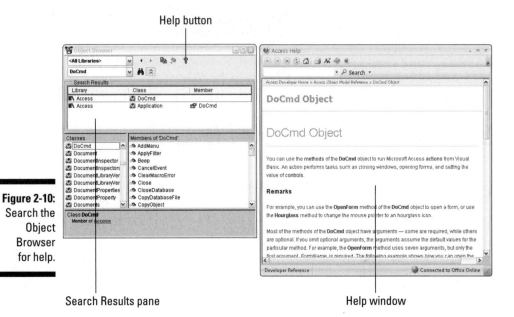

Figure 2-10:
Search the
Object
Browser
for help.

Search Results pane

Help window

We suppose right about now that you're wondering how any of the tools in this chapter will make your life easier. We're working up to that. For now, just being aware of the various panes and windows in the Visual Basic Editor is a good start. Knowing that VBA works by manipulating objects in object libraries is a good thing too. Even just being aware that the Object Browser and Help windows exist is valuable as you start writing code.

Writing code is the actual programming part of VBA. You write VBA code to automate activities, and you automate activities by manipulating objects via object libraries. VBA has a lot of fancy buzzwords, but if you just think of object libraries as steering wheels that VBA can grab onto and steer, you're ahead of the game. Hop to Chapter 3 to start writing code.

Chapter 3

Jumpstart: Creating a Simple VBA Program

In This Chapter

▶ Starting out with a standard module

▶ Creating procedures

▶ Getting help with VBA keywords

▶ Editing existing code

*V*isual Basic for Applications (VBA) is a programming language for writing instructions that tell Office applications — in this book, that means Access — the steps needed to perform a task. You store code in Access modules. The tool that you use to create and edit VBA code is the Visual Basic Editor, which opens automatically whenever you open an Access module. (If you need a refresher on the basics of using the Visual Basic Editor, hop back to Chapter 2.)

In this chapter, we get into some of the nitty-gritty of what's really involved in writing VBA code within Access. You discover how to create a module in Access and how to create procedures within a module. You also read about VBA *syntax,* which defines the rules you need to follow when writing a VBA statement. Finally, this chapter shows you how to use preexisting code in your own modules.

Creating a Standard Module

Before you start writing code, you need a place to put it. Putting your code in standard modules is always a good bet because code in standard modules is accessible to all objects within a database. Creating a new standard module is easy. Just follow these steps:

1. **With your database open in Access, click the Create tab on the Ribbon.**
2. **Click the Macro button and select Module from the drop-down list that appears, as shown in Figure 3-1.**

Click the Create tab...

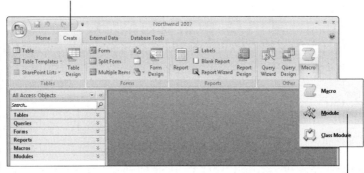

Figure 3-1:
Begin by
creating
a new
standard
module.

...and then select Module.

The new module opens in the VBA Editor. Most likely, it's empty except for the words `Option Compare Database` at the top. That line, a *module-level declaration,* just tells VBA that when comparing values, it should use the same rules as the rest of the database. The module might also contain the words `Option Explicit` on the second line. That line tells VBA to require you to declare variables before using them. If `Option Explicit` appears, just highlight and delete that line. We talk more about that later on.

As we discuss in Chapter 1, a *module* contains VBA code that's organized into one or more procedures. A *procedure* is simply the set of steps needed to perform some task. A new standard module contains no procedures because it's empty. Thus, the first step to writing code is to create a procedure.

Creating a Procedure

Adding a procedure to a module is a fairly simple task. The procedure that you create can be either a `Sub` procedure or a `Function` procedure. For now, it's sufficient to know that a `Sub` procedure is like a command on a menu: When called, it just does its job and doesn't return anything. A `Function` procedure, on the other hand, is more like a built-in function in that it returns a value. However, the steps for creating either type of procedure are the same:

1. **In the Visual Basic Editor, choose Insert⇨Procedure.**

   The Add Procedure dialog box appears.

2. **Type a name for your procedure in the Name text box.**

   The name must begin with a letter and cannot contain any blank spaces or punctuation marks. To create a practice procedure, enter a simple name, like **mySub**.

3. **Choose the type of procedure you want to create (`Sub` or `Function`) by selecting the Sub or Function option button in the Type group.**

   For your first practice procedure, choose Sub. You can ignore the rest of the options in the Add Procedure dialog box; the default settings are fine.

4. **Click OK.**

   The Add Procedure dialog box closes. Your module contains a new procedure with the name that you provided in Step 2.

The two lines of VBA code that are needed to define the new procedure are entered into your module as soon as you click OK. The first line begins with `Public Sub` or `Public Function`, followed by the procedure name and a pair of closed parentheses. For example, if you create (in the Add Procedure dialog box) a `Sub` procedure named `mySub`, the following VBA lines are added to your module:

```
Public Sub mySub()

End Sub
```

The `Public` keyword at the start of each procedure defines the *scope* of each procedure. Because procedures in a standard module are *public* by default, they're visible to all objects in the current database. In a standard module, you can omit the `Public` keyword and just begin the line with the `Sub` or `Function` keyword. Either way, the procedure is public (visible to all objects in the database).

In the module, the procedure name always ends in a pair of closed parentheses, as in `mySub()` or `myFunc()`. The parentheses are required, so they're added automatically when you click OK in the Add Procedure dialog box. Each procedure ends with an `End Sub` or `End Function` statement.

Figure 3-2 shows an example where we used the Add Procedure dialog box (twice) to create a `Sub` procedure named `mySub` and a `Function` procedure named `myFunc`. The module is visible in the Visual Basic Editor's Code window.

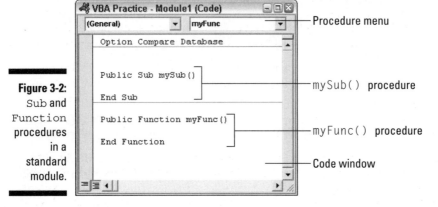

Figure 3-2:
Sub and
Function
procedures
in a
standard
module.

Any code that you type into the procedure must be typed between the two lines that define the procedure. You can easily position the cursor within any procedure by clicking within that procedure. You can also move the cursor into a procedure just by choosing the procedure's name from the Procedure menu in the Code window.

Understanding Syntax

Writing code is the art of programming the computer to perform a specific procedure by defining each step in the procedure as a single VBA statement. For the code to work, every VBA statement must conform to rules of *syntax,* which define exactly how the code is written. The syntax of a VBA statement is the set of rules that define the exact order of words and where spaces, commas, parentheses, and other punctuation marks are required.

Like any written language, the VBA language consists of words *(keywords),* punctuation marks (for example, commas), and blank spaces. Keywords are plentiful, and each has its own specific rules of syntax. The syntax rules are so rigid that you'd never be able to figure them out by guessing. You have to know how to get the information you need, when you need it.

The Visual Basic Editor provides several tools to help with syntax. For example, you use the `MsgBox()` function in VBA to display a custom message on-screen. Imagine that you already know about the `MsgBox()` function and were about to use it in a program, and you type the following line into a procedure:

```
x = MsgBox(
```

As soon as the Visual Basic Editor sees the `MsgBox(` part, it shows a Quick Info screen tip for the `MsgBox` keyword, as shown in the example at the top of Figure 3-3. The Quick Info tip is a small syntax chart showing you the rules for using `MsgBox` correctly. Within the Quick Info, the bold-italic word ***Prompt*** means that you're expected to type a prompt next.

For example, you might type **"Hello World"** (with the quotation marks) and a comma on the line:

```
x = MsgBox("Hello World",
```

The comma lets the Visual Basic Editor see that you typed a valid first argument and are now ready to type the second argument. The second argument in the syntax chart (`[Buttons As vbMsgBoxStyle = vbOKOnly]`) is then boldfaced to indicate that you now should type the second argument. Also, a list of meaningless-looking names (called *constants*) appears, as shown in the bottom half of Figure 3-3.

Okay, you gotta trust us on this one: The Quick Info and list of constants are there to help. Unfortunately, they're helpful only to those people who've used the `MsgBox()` function a zillion times and need only brief reminders on syntax and available constants. For someone who's just starting out, more in-depth information is needed. Fortunately, it's always easy to get.

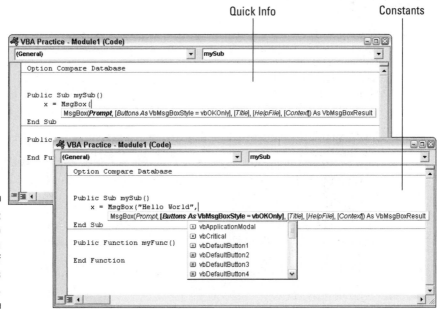

Figure 3-3:
Quick Info (top) and a list of constants (bottom).

Getting keyword help

Whether you're typing your own code or trying to modify someone else's, you can get information on any keyword at any time. Just select (double-click) the keyword right in the Code window where it appears. Then press the Help key (F1) on your keyboard. The Help window that opens describes the command and its syntax.

After you type a keyword into a procedure, you can use the Help window to get detailed information. Just select (double-click) the keyword and press the Help key (F1). Using the Help window is also an excellent way to find out more about code other people have written because you can determine what each line of code does.

When you press F1, the Help window that opens describes whatever keyword you selected in your module. For example, if you double-click MsgBox in a procedure (to select it) and then press F1, the Help page for the MsgBox keyword opens, as shown in the example in Figure 3-4.

Selected keyword

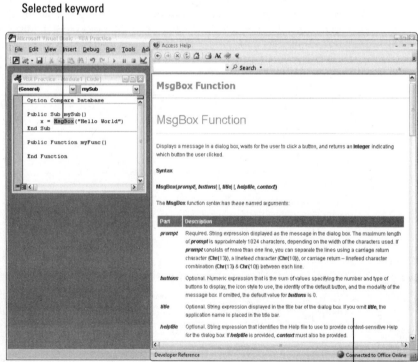

Figure 3-4:
Help for the
MsgBox
keyword.

Help for MsgBox keyword

The Help window shows a ton of information about using the `MsgBox` keyword. The first paragraph describes what the keyword does. Under the heading, the syntax chart shows the same information that the Quick Info screen tip does (namely, the arguments that you can use with the keyboard), as well as the order in which you must use them. For example, the syntax chart for `MsgBox` looks like this:

```
MsgBox(prompt[, buttons] [, title] [, helpfile, context])
```

The first word (`MsgBox`, in this example) is the keyword. The text and symbols enclosed in parentheses represent arguments that you can use with the `MsgBox` keyword. An *argument* is a piece of information that you give to the keyword to use for something. (More on that in the upcoming section "Help with arguments.") The syntax chart uses square brackets, boldface, and italics as described here:

- **Bold:** Represents a required keyword.

- *Italic* or ***bold italic:*** Represents an argument.

- [ ]: Indicates that the argument is optional and can be omitted.

Beneath the syntax chart is a description of each argument that the keyword supports. For example, scrolling down a short way through this Help page reveals a description of each of the argument names that `MsgBox` supports, as shown in Figure 3-5.

Figure 3-5: Find argument info in a keyword Help window.

The description of an argument tells you whether the argument is required or optional. If an argument is required, you must type an acceptable value for that argument into your code (always within the parentheses that follow the keyword). If an argument is optional, you can either type an acceptable value for the argument or just not use the argument.

Never type square brackets into your VBA code: The square brackets in the syntax chart are just there to indicate the optional arguments. If you type the square brackets in your code, the code doesn't work.

The argument acts as a placeholder for some actual value that you'll later pass to the procedure. If you have any experience in using Access expressions, you're familiar with arguments. For example, in the expression Sqr(81), 81 is the *value* being passed to the Sqr() (square root) function. When executed, the function returns 9 because 9 is the square root of 81.

What constitutes an acceptable value for an argument is usually the second item listed in the Help chart. Typically, it's one of these types of expressions:

✔ **String:** Can be literal text enclosed in quotation marks, as in "Hello World", or an expression that results in text.

✔ **Numeric:** Can be a number, like 1 or 10, or an expression that results in a number.

That's a lot to try to understand. Take it one step at a time, though, with an example to try to make sense of it all. First, understand that the arguments of a keyword are typed within parentheses, after the keyword. And multiple arguments are always separated by commas. So the most general view of any keyword that accepts three arguments would be

keyword (argument1, argument2, argument3)

In other words, you don't start typing the first argument until you've typed the keyword and opening parenthesis. After you type the first argument, you have to type a comma before you start typing the second argument, and so forth. The Visual Basic Editor doesn't know that you're ready to type the next argument until you type that comma. Finally, you have to type the closing parenthesis at the end of the statement. If you mess it up, you get a compile error as soon as you press the Enter key. All you can do is click OK and try again (or delete the whole line and start over).

Getting back to the MsgBox() keyword and its arguments, you can see at the top of the first Help page (refer to Figure 3-4) that MsgBox() is a function that returns a value. Although it's not specifically stated in the syntax, to be able to use the command properly in a procedure, you need to use this syntax:

```
x = Msgbox(prompt[, buttons ][, title][,helpfile,
        context])
```

You can see on the Help page that the *prompt* argument is required and must be a string expression. So if you want the message box to display Hello World, you would type those words (remember to enclose them in quotation marks) as the first argument, as in the following example. Because the remaining arguments are optional, you could omit them and just end the whole line with a closing parenthesis, like this:

```
x = MsgBox("Hello World")
```

The Immediate window, which we discuss in Chapter 2, provides a handy means of testing a VBA statement on the fly to see whether it will work when it's executed in your code. For example, if you type (exactly) **x=MsgBox("Hello World")** into the Immediate window and press Enter, VBA executes the statement. The result is a message box containing the words Hello World, as shown in Figure 3-6. (You have to click the OK button in the message box to get back to working in the Visual Basic Editor.)

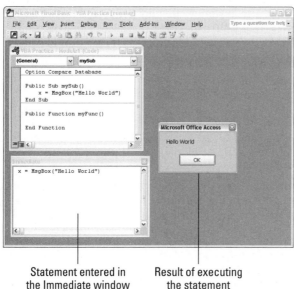

Figure 3-6:
Test VBA statements in the Immediate window.

Statement entered in the Immediate window

Result of executing the statement

Help with arguments

Refer to Figure 3-5 (of the Help page for the MsgBox keyword) to see the Settings section (below the argument descriptions) that provides some specific info on using the *buttons* argument. You can use either the constant or the value in the command. For example, if you want the MsgBox statement to show both an OK button and a Cancel button (rather than just an OK button), use either the value 1 or the constant vbOKCancel as the second argument in the `MsgBox` statement. Arguments are always separated by commas, so the correct syntax is either

```
x = MsgBox("Hello World",1)
```

or

```
x = MsgBox("Hello World",vbOKCancel)
```

A *constant* is a special word in VBA that has been assigned a value that never changes. For example, the constant `vbOKOnly` is always the same as the value 0. You can use `vbOKOnly` (which is easier to remember) in place of 0 in a `MsgBox` statement.

As instructed on the Help page, you can combine values (by using a + sign) in the *buttons* argument to use multiple options. For example, the `vbYesNo` setting (value = 4) displays Yes and No buttons in the message box. The `vbQuestion` setting (value = 32) setting displays a question mark icon in the message box. Thus, if you want to display a message box that displays the question `Are you there?`, a question mark icon, and Yes and No buttons, you can type any of the following statements. (The 36 is allowed because the sum of the two settings' values, 4 and 32, equals 36.)

```
x = MsgBox("Are you there?",vbQuestion+vbYesNo)
```

```
x = MsgBox("Are you there?",32+4)
```

```
x = MsgBox("Are you there?",36)
```

You can test any of these VBA statements by typing one into the Immediate window and pressing Enter. Because all three statements produce the same result, you see a message box with the prompt `Are you there?`, a question mark icon, and Yes and No buttons, as shown in Figure 3-7.

Figure 3-7:
Test a
MsgBox
statement
in the
Immediate
window.

The third optional argument in the `MsgBox` keyword, *title*, allows you to specify a title to display in the dialog box. If you omit that argument in Access, the default title for all Access message boxes — Microsoft Office

Access — appears in the message box. If you include a title (as text in quotation marks), that title replaces the default title. For example, if you test the following command in the Immediate window:

```
x = MsgBox("Are you there?",vbQuestion+vbYesNo,"Howdy")
```

the message box opens with the word Howdy, rather than Microsoft Office Access, on its title bar.

The order of arguments in a VBA statement is critical. For example, the title for a MsgBox must be the third argument in the statement. If you want to use a *title* argument but not a *buttons* argument, you have to still include a placeholder comma for the *buttons* argument and include a similar comma for the *title* argument, as in the following example:

```
x = MsgBox("Hello World", ,"Howdy")
```

In this statement, the first argument (*prompt*) is "Hello World", and the second argument — which acts as a placeholder for the *buttons* argument — is empty. Because you omitted the argument, Access uses the default value for that argument, which is vbOKOnly (0). Thus, when the statement executes, the message box appears with only the default OK button. The third argument is "Howdy", which appears on the message box title bar.

About named arguments

Named arguments provide an alternative to putting arguments in a specific order. With named arguments, you can just type the argument name followed by a colon and an equal sign (:=) and then the value you want for that argument. For example, the following statement is equivalent to x = MsgBox("Hello World", ,"Howdy"), but it uses argument names rather than commas to specify which argument is receiving which value.

```
x=MsgBox(prompt:="Hello World", title:="Howdy")
```

Unfortunately, you can't always easily tell whether a statement supports named arguments. The Quick Info screen tip doesn't provide any clues, and the Help doesn't often show the syntax with the optional names in place. About the only clue you get to whether a statement supports named arguments is from the sentence above the argument descriptions in Help. For example, refer to the Help for the MsgBox function in Figure 3-4: namely, the sentence The MsgBox function syntax has these named arguments, just below the syntax chart for MsgBox(). But because named arguments are entirely optional, you don't have to worry about accidentally excluding them when writing your own code.

Using Existing Code

Just knowing how to read the Help screens is a challenge in itself. It just takes time to practice. Programming isn't the kind of skill you master overnight. It's a skill you acquire gradually by finding out about one keyword, and then another, and then another, and so forth. VBA has so many keywords that it would take years to memorize them all.

Fortunately, you don't have to find out about every keyword before you start writing code. Most programmers discover how to program by example. That is, they look at other people's code and perhaps even use that same code themselves or modify it to suit their own needs.

Using other people's code, when possible, certainly offers some advantages because at least some of the work is done for you. Switch gears for a moment and look at ways in which you can get prewritten code into a module in your own database.

Copy and paste code from the Web

Many programmers start their careers not so much by writing code from scratch but rather by using code that others have written and adapting it to their own needs.

You can use your favorite search engine to find a wealth of code on the Web. For example, to search for code examples for an If...Then statement, type **If Then** in the search engine. You'll probably get all kinds of useless results. To narrow the results to something more useful, add the words **Access VBA** to your search. For example, typing **Access VBA If Then** provides a more useful list of links.

Suppose your search turns up a Web page that gives the code for a sample procedure. Rather than type the whole procedure into your own module, you can copy it from the Web page. First, select the procedure (and nothing but the procedure) by dragging the mouse pointer through the whole procedure — from the starting Sub or Function statement to the ending End Sub or End Function statement. After you select the code, press Ctrl+C or right-click anywhere in the selected text and choose Copy, as shown in Figure 3-8.

After you select and copy the code, just click anywhere in a standard module and press Ctrl+V or right-click and choose Paste. The exact code you selected appears in your module.

You can find most of the code examples from this book at www.dummies.com/go/access2007vbaprog. You can copy and paste any code from that site into any module in your own database.

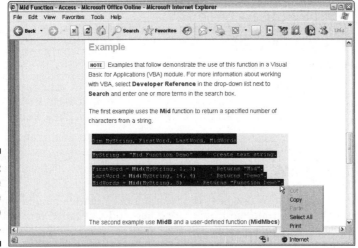

Figure 3-8:
Use sample
VBA code
from a Web
page.

Importing modules

The copy-and-paste method works best with code that's displayed on your screen like plain text, but it's not the only way to get code into your database. You can also import modules from other databases.

Suppose you have a database named myAccessDB.accdb, and within that database is a module named myModule. At the moment, though, some other database is open, and you want to copy myModule from myAccessDB.accdb into the current database. In that case, you can import the module from one database into your current database:

1. **If you're in the Visual Basic Editor, press Alt+F11 to return to the Access program window.**

2. **Click the External Data tab on the Ribbon, and then click the Access command in the Import group.**

   The Get External Data dialog box appears.

3. **Click the Browse button and navigate to the folder that contains the database from which you want to import code (myAccessDB.accdb, in this example).**

4. **When you find the database that contains the code you want to import, double-click the database's icon.**

5. **In the Get External Data dialog box, select the option labeled Import Tables, Queries, Forms, Reports, Macros, and Modules into the Current Database, and click OK.**

   The Import Objects dialog box appears.

6. **Click the Modules tab.**

7. **Click the name of the module — or modules — you want to import; then click OK.**

8. **Click Close to return to Access.**

   When you click Modules in the Navigation pane of your current database, you see the imported module's name. Double-click the module's name, as usual, to open that module in the Visual Basic Editor.

Modifying existing code

After you either copy and paste code or import a module, modifying that code isn't all that different from writing new code, because you still have to know the exact meaning and syntax of every keyword used in the code. In some cases, the existing code might work as-is in your database. In other cases, you might have to edit the code to get it to work.

If you need to modify the code, you can't do so unless you understand what the code is doing and how it works. Thus, you have to know the purposes of each statement. If you need to change a statement, you need to know the correct syntax. Like when you're writing code, you can get more information about existing code by using either of these methods:

 ✔ To see the Quick Info screen tip for a line of code, right-click the line and choose Quick Info.

 ✔ For detailed help with a keyword, select (double-click) that keyword and press F1 to see the Help window.

Modifying existing code takes almost as much skill and knowledge as writing your own code from scratch, so don't expect to be able to get anything accomplished by taking wild guesses. You can see examples of modifying existing code throughout this book. For now, just be aware that you can copy and paste VBA code into a module. Or, if the code is already in some other database's module, you can import that module into your current database.

In Chapter 4, you can pick up more advanced skills for creating procedures. For now, be aware that every VBA keyword has certain rules of syntax, which you must follow to a T if you want your code to work. You can't expect to memorize and master every keyword and its syntax in a short time because VBA has too darn many keywords. However, after you know how to get help with keywords, you always have the information that you need at your fingertips.

Part II
VBA Tools and Techniques

The 5th Wave — By Rich Tennant

"Your database is beyond repair, but before I tell you our backup recommendation, let me ask you a question. How many index cards do you think will fit on the walls of your computer room?"

In this part . . .

The only reason you would ever bother with VBA is to make Access do stuff that it can't do otherwise — either that or to make Access do something you would otherwise have to do yourself over and over again. You coax Access into doing stuff by writing VBA code that manipulates the objects in your database automatically and behind the scenes. That's the short description of how it all works, anyway. More detailed explanations and examples are in the three chapters herein.

Chapter 4

Understanding Your VBA Building Blocks

*M*any programmers begin their careers not so much by writing code from scratch as by acquiring bits of code from books, Web sites, and other resources because that's easier than trying to figure it out from scratch. Plenty of sample code is made available through books and Web sites. Don't worry about "stealing" the code: If folks didn't want you copying their code, they wouldn't have made it accessible to you in the first place!

Whether you plan to write your own code or tweak other people's code, you need to understand some fundamental programming concepts for any of the code to make sense.

You can think of the various programming concepts described in this chapter as the basic building blocks from which all programs are created. As you learn more about Visual Basic for Applications (VBA), you see the same building blocks used to perform many different tasks, in many different settings. The first step, though, is to just be aware that such things exist so that you recognize them when you see them.

The variables, constants, arrays, loops, and decision-making techniques that we present in this chapter are the basic building blocks from which all programs are written. Writing VBA code in Access requires both a basic knowledge of those programming techniques and the ability to work with Access objects (which we cover in Chapter 5).

Commenting Your Code

When you look at existing code, notice that some lines look like plain English while others look like VBA code. The lines that look like English are programmer *comments*. Only humans see comments; the computer sees only the VBA code. Thus, using comments is entirely optional to you, as a programmer and a human.

Programmers add comments to their code for two reasons:

- ✔ **To help others who are trying to understand how the code works**
- ✔ **To jot down notes as you go — to remind yourself of the purpose of different parts of your code**

The first character of a comment must be an apostrophe ('). The comment ends where you press Enter to end the line. After you type the apostrophe, you can type any text you want on that same line because VBA doesn't treat it as code. When viewing existing code, you see the apostrophe at the start of each comment within the code, as shown in the example in Figure 4-1. (In the Code window, comments are also colored green.)

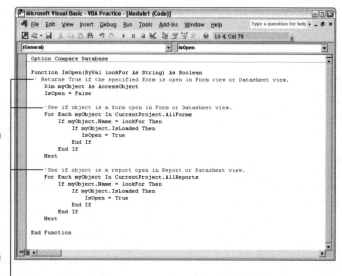

Figure 4-1:
Add comments to make your code understandable.

Comments start with an apostrophe.

When you're modifying existing code, the comments are for human consumption only. Changing a comment doesn't fix code or change how it works. Comments are only notes jotted down within VBA code.

As we mention, writing comments is easy because after you type the initial apostrophe, you can type anything you want. Writing code, though, is a lot harder because of the rules of *syntax* (word order and punctuation). Plus, there are lots of rules concerning the data on which VBA can operate. One of the first things you need to understand is that, like tables in Access, VBA has data types.

Understanding VBA Data Types

When you create a table in Access, you need to define the data type of every field in the table. Data types in tables include things like Text (for storing short strings of text), Memo (larger chunks of text), Number (for numbers), and Date/Time (for dates and times).

VBA can work with data stored in tables. But just like tables, VBA often needs to know the type of information it's working with. As you see shortly, VBA code has a couple of places where you can define data types. You need to know what the various data types mean.

Table 4-1 lists the data types that you work with in VBA. The data type names are listed in the left column, each followed by a brief description. The Storage Size column shows how many bytes each data type consumes. The Declaration Character column shows an optional character that can be used at the end of a name to specify a data type. That's really more information than you need; just knowing the names of the various data types is sufficient for now.

Table 4-1	VBA Data Types		
Data Type	*Acceptable Values*	*Storage Size*	*Declaration Character*
Boolean	True (–1) or False (0)	2 bytes	
Byte	0 to 255	1 byte	
Currency	–922,337,203,685,477.5808 to 922,337,203,685,477.5807	8 bytes	@
Date	January 1, 100 to December 31, 9999	8 bytes	
Double	$-1.79769313486231E308$ to $-4.94065645841247E\text{-}324$ for negative values; $4.94065645841247E\text{-}324$ to $1.79769313486232E308$ for positive values	8 bytes	#

(continued)

Table 4-1 *(continued)*

Data Type	Acceptable Values	Storage Size	Declaration Character
Integer	–32,768 to 32,767	2 bytes	%
Long	–2,147,483,648 to 2,147,483,647	4 bytes	&
Object	Name of any object	4 bytes	
Single	–3.402823E38 to –1.401298E-45 for negative values; 1.401298E-45 to 3.402823E38 for positive values	4 bytes	!
String	Any text from 0 to about 2,000,000,000 characters in length	10 + string length	$
Variant (no text)	Any number up to the range of the Double data type	16 bytes	
Variant (with text)	Any text up to 2,000,000,000 characters long	22 + string length	

In VBA code, you often use data types just to store little bits of information for short periods. The reasons for storing data with VBA code vary. One of the first places you're likely to encounter data types in VBA is when you want to pass data to, or from, your custom procedure.

Passing Data to Procedures

You write a procedure to perform a series of steps. The exact object on which the procedure performs its task can vary. For example, you might inherit a database table of names and addresses, with everything typed in uppercase letters, as in JOHN SMITH. You want to convert all that text to proper case (John Smith), but you don't want to retype it all.

TECHNICAL STUFF

Boring technical stuff on the Decimal data type

When perusing the VBA Help and drop-down menus, you might come across the Decimal data type. We omitted the Decimal data type from Table 4-1 because it just flat-out doesn't work. If we had included the Decimal data type in the table, its acceptable range would be +/–79,228,162,514,264,337,593,543,950,335 with no decimal point; +/–7.9228162514264337593543950335 with 28 places to the right of the decimal; smallest non-zero number +/–0.0000000000000000000000000001. The Decimal data type's storage size would be 14 bytes, and it would have no type declaration character.

The obscure Decimal data type does exist, but you can't declare an item as being of that data type. Instead, you have to declare the item as a Variant data type with a subtype of Decimal. For example, Dim X as Variant defines a variable X as a variant; X = CDec(*value*) stores *value* in X as a Decimal data type.

You could write a procedure to do the conversion for you, but you wouldn't want the procedure to fix just one name or one address. You want the procedure to be flexible enough to fix all the names and addresses in the table with the click of a button. In other words, you want Access to hand over some piece of information, like JOHN SMITH, and then have the procedure return John Smith. However, you want it to do that with any text you pass to it, including JANE DOE and P.O. BOX 123 and HANK R. MCDOUGAL.

If you want a procedure to accept information from the outside world (so to speak), you have to tell the procedure what type of data to expect and where to put the data. You do so within the parentheses that follow a procedure's name within a module. What you type is the *argument list* (or *arglist*, for short). The syntax for each argument is

```
name As type
```

where *name* is any name of your choosing and *type* is one of the data type names listed in Table 4-1. For example, if you want to create a Sub procedure named showMsg() and pass one parameter named msgText to it as text, the first line of the procedure needs to contain msgText As String as an argument, as in the following example:

```
Sub showMsg(msgText As String)

End Sub
```

These lines define a `Sub` procedure named `showMsg()` that accepts one argument: a string (text) named `msgText`. We just made up the `msgText` name — we could have used any name we wanted. The `As String` tells the rest of the procedure to expect text to be passed.

You can pass multiple bits of information to a procedure as long as each has a unique name and you give each a data type. Separate each name and type with a comma. For example, the `Sub()` first line in Figure 4-2 defines a procedure named `showMsg()` that accepts three arguments: `msgText`, `bttns`, and `msgTitle` (all names we made up off the top of our heads). As you can see, `msgText` and `msgTitle` are both declared as the `String` data type, and `bttns` is declared as the `Integer` data type.

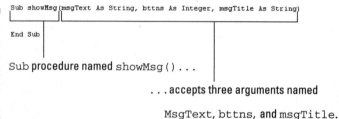

Figure 4-2:
A `Sub`
procedure
can accept
different
arguments.

```
Sub showMsg(msgText As String, bttns As Integer, msgTitle As String)

End Sub
```

Sub procedure named showMsg() . . .

. . . accepts three arguments named

MsgText, bttns, and msgTitle.

Although a `Sub` procedure can accept incoming data through its arguments, it can't return any data to Access or other VBA procedures. A `Function` procedure, on the other hand, can accept incoming data *and* return a value. Thus, a `Function` procedure is like any function that's built in to Access. For example, the built-in `Date()` function always returns the current date.

To see for yourself that `Date()` always returns the current date, type `?` `Date()` in the Immediate window and press Enter. You see today's date.

When you want your own custom procedure to return a value, you have to define the data type of the value being returned. The name of the return value is always the same as the function name, so you don't include a name. And because you're defining a return value, you place the declaration outside the closing parenthesis, as shown here:

```
Function name(arglist) As type

End Function
```

where *name* is the name of the function, *arglist* defines any incoming arguments (exactly as it does in a `Sub` procedure), and *type* is the data type of the value that the function returns. The *type* placeholder must match one of the data type names listed in Table 4-1.

Figure 4-3 shows an example where the first line defines a `Function` procedure named `isOpen()` that accepts a string as an argument and then returns a `True` or `False` value. (***Note:*** Those lines are only the first and last lines. The programmer would have to add more code between them for the procedure to do anything.)

Figure 4-3:
Functions
accept
arguments
and return
values.

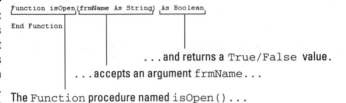

```
Function isOpen(frmName As String) As Boolean
End Function
```

. . . and returns a `True/False` value.

. . . accepts an argument `frmName` . . .

The `Function` procedure named `isOpen()` . . .

From the standpoint of modifying existing code, the argument list inside the parentheses tells you what data is passed to the procedure and as which data type. Code within the procedure can then work on the data that was passed, by simply referring to it by name. Within a procedure, you use variables to store and manipulate little chunks of data, like the values passed to a procedure. Variables are a big part of all programming languages, so spend some time getting to know them.

Storing data in variables and constants

All programming languages, including VBA, have a means of storing little chunks of information (data) in temporary cubbyholes called *variables*. Obviously, the contents of the cubbyhole can vary. For example, a variable named `LastName` might contain Smith, Jones, McDougal, or whatever. The VBA code can operate on whatever value happens to be in the variable at the moment.

Creating a variable is a two-step process:

1. **Declare the variable's name and data type with a Dim statement.**
2. **Assign a value to the variable as needed.**

The syntax usually involves two lines of code that follow this structure:

```
Dim name As type
name = value
```

where *name* is a name of your own choosing, *type* is one of the data types listed in Table 4-1, and *value* is the data you want to store in the variable.

When naming a variable, stick to using short names with no spaces or punctuation. Also make sure the name starts with a letter. You can use either letters or numbers as part of the name after the first character.

Here's an example of creating an `Integer` variable named `x` and storing the number `10` in that variable:

```
Dim x As Integer
x = 10
```

Here's an example of creating a string variable named `LastName` and putting the name `Jones` in it:

```
Dim LastName As String
LastName = "Jones"
```

Note the use of the quotation marks around `Jones`. As in Access expressions, the quotation marks signify a literal text: That is, after the statement `LastName = "Jones"` executes, the variable `LastName` contains (literally) the name `Jones`.

A *constant* is similar to a variable in that it's a name that refers to some value. However, after you assign a value to a variable, you can't change it. Hence, the value remains constant.

Lots of constants are built in to VBA, as you can see in many examples throughout this book. If you ever want to create your own constant, the syntax is

```
Const name As type = value
```

where, once again, *name* is a name of your choosing, *type* is a data type from Table 4-1, and *value* is the data you want to store in the constant. For example, the following VBA statement creates a constant named `pi` that stores the number `3.14159265` as a double-precision number:

```
Const pi As Double = 3.14159265
```

Storing data in arrays

If you think of a variable or constant as one little cubbyhole in which you can tuck away information, a collection of cubbyholes is an *array*. Each cubbyhole is an *element* of the array, although each is just a variable in which you can store information. The cubbyholes in an array, however, all have the same name. You use a *subscript* in parentheses, which defines an element's position in the array, to refer to a specific item in the array.

Declaring an array is a lot like declaring a single variable, but you have to tell VBA how many items are in the array. The syntax looks like this:

```
Dim name(dimensions) As type
```

where *name* is a name that you give the array, *dimensions* specifies how many items are in the array, and *type* is one of the data types listed in Table 4-1. For example, the following VBA statement creates an array named shipOptions that contains five *elements* (each element is one cubbyhole of information):

```
Dim shipOptions(5) As String
```

After VBA executes this statement, five little cubbyholes, each capable of storing any text (string), are available. The first array element is named shipOptions(1) (pronounced "shipOptions sub one"). The second element is named shipOptions(2) (pronounced "shipOptions sub two"), and so forth:

```
shipOptions(1)
shipOptions(2)
shipOptions(3)
shipOptions(4)
shipOptions(5)
```

Because each of those array elements is a string variable, you could assign a value to each by using the same syntax that you use to assign values to individual variables, as shown here:

```
shipOptions(1) = "USPS Media"
shipOptions(2) = "USPS Priority"
shipOptions(3) = "UPS Ground"
shipOptions(4) = "UPS Second Day"
shipOptions(5) = "UPS Overnight"
```

The shipOptions array is a *one-dimensional array* because it has only one dimension: length. Each item in the array contains exactly one subscript, indicating the item's position in the one-dimensional list of items. You can also declare multidimensional arrays. For example, a two-dimensional array has two dimensions — length and width — like a table.

The following VBA statement declares a two-dimensional array named miniTable that contains three rows and two columns:

```
Dim miniTable(3,2) As String
```

Each element in the two-dimensional name has two subscripts. The first subscript represents the row position of the element. The second subscript represents the column position of the element. Hence, you can envision the following variable names (cubbyholes) created by that VBA statement:

```
miniTable(1,1)        miniTable(1,2)

miniTable(2,1)        miniTable(2,2)

miniTable(3,1)        miniTable(3,2)
```

In Access, where you already have tables to store all your data in rows and columns, you rarely need to use multidimensional arrays. However, from the standpoint of modifying existing code, when you see a Dim statement that declares a name followed by a number in parentheses, as in

```
Dim x(10) As String
```

you need to be aware that the statement is creating ten separate variable names: x(1), x(2), x(3), and so forth, up to x(10).

Module-level versus procedure-level

Unlike data stored in Access tables, data stored in VBA variables (including arrays and constants) doesn't last long. Each variable has a *lifetime* that defines how long it exists. Closely aligned with a variable's lifetime is its *scope,* which defines which objects in the database can and cannot access the variable. The scope and lifetime of a variable depend on where you define the variable within a module.

The top of a module, where you typically see Option Compare Database, is the *declarations area.* Here you can *declare* (announce) settings, variables, constants, and arrays to all procedures in the module.

For example, the line Option Compare Database is a *module-level* declaration that announces to all procedures in the module that this code is running within the context of a database. When you're comparing values in code using logic like *equals* or *greater than,* the code should use the same rules as the rest of the database.

You can also declare and assign values to variables, arrays, and constants in the declarations area of the module. Those variables have module-level scope and lifetime. These variables can be *private* — available only to the procedures in the module — or *public* — available to all other procedures in the Access database.

Variables, constants, and arrays declared inside a procedure have *procedure-level* scope and lifetime. Each variable defined within a procedure is visible to only that procedure and exists only while that procedure is running.

The significance of module-level versus procedure-level becomes more apparent as you gain experience coding in VBA. For now, the main thing to keep in mind is that module-level variables, constants, and arrays are declared at the top of a module, before the first procedure. Something that is procedure-level refers to variables, constants, and arrays defined within a procedure. Figure 4-4 illustrates the difference.

Figure 4-4:
Module-
level and
procedure-
level
declarations.

Module-level private

Procedure-level   Module-level public

Naming conventions for variables

Some programmers use naming conventions to identify the data type of a variable as part of the variable's or constant's name. The naming conventions are entirely optional; you don't have to use them. A lot of VBA programmers follow them, though, so you're likely to see them in any code you happen to come across.

The idea behind a naming convention is simple: When you define a new variable, make the first three letters of the name (the *tag*) stand for the type of variable or object. For example, the following line creates an Integer variable named intMyVar, where int is short for *integer:*

```
Dim intMyVar as Integer
```

The tag (int) added to the front of the name doesn't affect how the variable is stored or how you can use it. The tag serves only as a reminder that MyVar is an Integer. Table 4-2 summarizes the tags that you will most likely encounter when reading other people's code. In the Sample Declaration column of the table, *Name* means that you can put in any variable name you choose.

Table 4-2	Naming Conventions Used among VBA Programmers	
Tag	*Stands for This Data Type*	*Sample Declaration*
byt	Byte	Dim byt*Name* As Byte
cur	Currency	Dim cur*Name* As Currency
dtm	Date/Time	Dim dtm*Name* As Date
dbl	Double	Dim dbl*Name* As Double
int	Integer	Dim int*Name* As Integer
lng	Long integer	Dim lng*Name* As Long
sng	Single	Dim sng*Name* As Single
bln	Boolean	Dim bln*Name* As Boolean
str	String	Dim str*Name* As String
var	Variant	Dim var*Name* As Variant

Repeating Chunks of Code with Loops

Occasionally a situation occurs in which you want to execute one or more VBA statements multiple times. Suppose you write some VBA statements that need to operate on each record in a table, and the table holds 1,000 records. You have two choices: Write each set of statements 1,000 times or create a loop that repeats the one set of statements 1,000 times. Needless to say, typing the statements once rather than 1,000 times saves you a lot of time. A *loop* is your best bet.

Using Do...Loop to create a loop

The Do...Loop block is one method of setting up a loop in code to execute statements repeatedly. The loop requires two lines of code: one at the top and one at the bottom. You have a lot of flexibility when defining a Do...Loop. In fact, there are two forms of syntax for creating these loops. The first is the following:

```
Do [{While | Until} condition]
    [statements]
    [Exit Do]
    [statements]
Loop
```

The second form of syntax provides the option of defining the condition at the bottom of the loop, like this:

```
Do
    [statements]
    [Exit Do]
    [statements]
Loop [{While | Until} condition]
```

In both instances, *statements* refers to any number of VBA statements, and *condition* is an expression that can result in either True or False. The vertical bar (also called a *pipe*) indicates that you can use one word or the other. For example, you can use the word While or the word Until, but you can't use both. Other types of loops use similar constructs. So rather than dwell on this type of loop right now, look at some other ways to set up loops.

For now, just realize that when you look at existing code, any statements between the Do and Loop statements are executed repeatedly. Statements outside the loop are still executed once each, from top to bottom. Only the statements inside the loop are executed repeatedly, as illustrated in Figure 4-5.

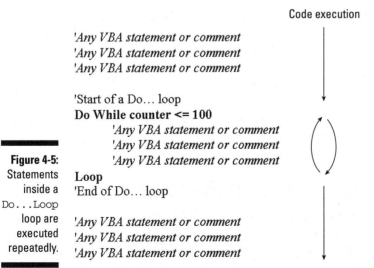

Figure 4-5:
Statements
inside a
Do...Loop
loop are
executed
repeatedly.

Using While...Wend to create a loop

The `While...Wend` loop is similar to `Do...Loop`, but it uses the simpler (and less flexible) syntax shown in the following code:

```
While condition
    [statements]
Wend
```

where `condition` is an expression that results in a `True` or `False` value, and `statements` are any number of VBA statements, all of which execute with each pass through the loop.

The condition is evaluated at the top of the loop. If the condition proves `True`, all lines within the loop execute (down to the `Wend` statement), and then the condition at the top of the loop is evaluated again. If the condition proves `False`, all statements within the loop are ignored, and processing continues at the first line after the `Wend` statement.

Statements within a `While...Wend` loop execute repeatedly, just as they do with a `Do...Loop`, as illustrated in Figure 4-6.

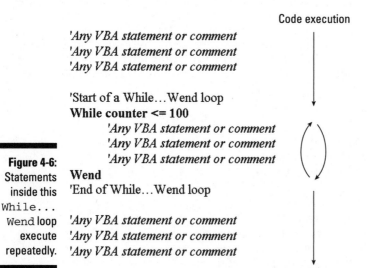

Figure 4-6:
Statements
inside this
`While...`
`Wend` loop
execute
repeatedly.

Using For...Next to create a loop

A third pair of commands for creating loops in code is the `For...Next` block of statements. The syntax for a `For...Next` loop is shown here:

```
For counter = start To end [Step step]
    [statements]
    [Exit For]
    [statements]
Next [counter]
```

where

- ✔ *counter* is any name that you want to give to the variable that keeps track of passes through the loop.

- ✔ *start* is a number that indicates where the loop should start counting.

- ✔ *end* is a number that indicates when the loop should end.

- ✔ *step* is optional and indicates how much to increment or decrement *counter* with each pass through the loop. If omitted, *counter* increments by 1 with each pass through the loop.

- ✔ *statements* are any number of VBA statements that execute with each pass through the loop.

You can see many For...Next examples throughout this book. For now, when you're looking at existing code and see a For...Next pair of statements, realize that the statements inside that loop are executed repeatedly, as illustrated in Figure 4-7.

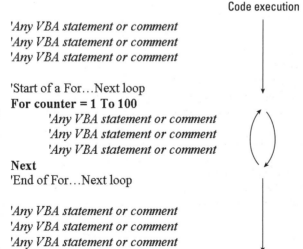

Code execution

'*Any VBA statement or comment*
'*Any VBA statement or comment*
'*Any VBA statement or comment*

'*Start of a For...Next loop*
For counter = 1 To 100
      '*Any VBA statement or comment*
      '*Any VBA statement or comment*
      '*Any VBA statement or comment*
Next
'*End of For...Next loop*

'*Any VBA statement or comment*
'*Any VBA statement or comment*
'*Any VBA statement or comment*

Figure 4-7:
Statements
inside this
For...
. Next
loop are
executed
repeatedly.

Making Decisions in VBA Code

Decision-making is a big part of programming because most programs need to be smart enough to figure out what to do, depending on the circumstances. Often, you want your code to do one thing if such-and-such is true but do something else if such-and-such is false. You use *conditional expressions* to determine whether something is true or false. A conditional expression is one that generally follows this syntax:

```
Value ComparisonOperator Value
```

where *Value* is some chunk of information, and the *ComparisonOperator* is one of those listed in Table 4-3.

Table 4-3	Comparison Operators
Operator	*Meaning*
=	Equal to
<	Less than
<=	Less than or equal to
>	Greater than
>=	Greater than or equal to
<>	Not equal to

For example, the expression

```
[Last Name] = "Smith"
```

compares the contents of the [Last Name] field with the string "Smith". If the [Last Name] field does indeed contain the name *Smith,* the expression is *(returns)* True. If the [Last Name] field contains anything other than *Smith,* the expression returns False.

Another example is the following statement:

```
[Qty] >= 10
```

The contents of the Qty field are compared with the number 10. If the number stored in the Qty field is 10 or greater, the expression returns True. If the number stored in the Qty field is less than 10, the expression returns False.

You can combine multiple conditional expressions into one by using the logical operators summarized in Table 4-4.

Table 4-4	Logical Operators
Operator	*Meaning*
AND	Both are true
OR	One or both are true
NOT	Is not true
XOR	Exclusive or: One — not both — is true

The following conditional expression requires that the [Last Name] field contain *Smith* and the [First Name] field contain *Janet* in order for the entire expression to be True:

```
[Last Name]="Smith" and [First Name]="Janet"
```

 You can include spaces on either side of the equal sign or not. Either way works.

The following example is an expression that returns True if the State field contains either *NJ* or *NY*:

```
[State]="NJ" or [State]="NY"
```

Using If...End If statements

You have a couple of ways to write VBA code that's capable of making a decision. The simplest — and by far the most common — is the If...End If block of code, which uses this syntax:

```
If condition Then
    [statements]...
[Else]
    [statements]...
End If
```

where *condition* is an expression that results in True or False, and *statements* refers to any number of valid VBA statements. If the condition proves True, the statements between Then and Else execute, and all other statements are ignored. If the condition proves False, only the statements after the Else statement execute, as illustrated in Figure 4-8.

Figure 4-8:
The basic
idea behind
the If...
End If
statement.

If *condition* **Then**
    statement1
    statement2   — If *condition* proves True,
    statement3   only these statements are executed.
Else
    statement4   — If *condition* proves False,
    statement5   only these statements are executed.
End If

You have a little bit of flexibility when using If...End If. If only one line of code executes for a True result and only one line executes for a False result, you can put the whole statement on a single line and omit the End If statement, as this line shows:

```
If State="NY" Then TaxRate=0.075 Else TaxRate=0
```

Using a Select Case block

In some situations, you might need to have your code make a decision based on several possibilities. For example, perhaps you need to perform different statements depending on which of ten product types a person ordered. In that case, you can set up a Select Case block of code, which performs a particular set of instructions depending on some value. Typically, the value is stored in a variable or field in a table and is also a number that represents some previously made selection.

The basic syntax of a Select Case block of code looks like this:

```
Select Case value
    [Case possibleValue [To possibleValue]
        [statements]]
    [Case possibleValue [To possibleValue]
        [statements]]...
    [Case Else
        [statements]]
End Select
```

where *value* is some value (like a number), and *possibleValue* is any value that could match the *value*. You can have any number of Case *possibleValue* statements between the Select Case and End Select statements. Optionally, you can include a Case Else statement, which specifies statements that execute only if none of the preceding Case *possibleValue* statements proves True.

Each Case statement can have any number of statements beneath it. When the code executes, only those statements after the Case statement that matches the *value* at the top of the block execute. Figure 4-9 shows the general concept.

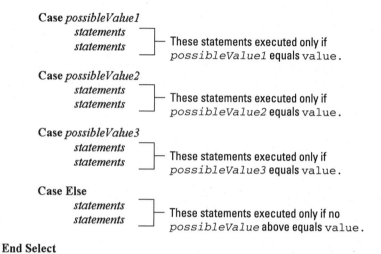

Select Case *value*

> **Case** *possibleValue1*
> > *statements*
> > *statements* ──┐ These statements executed only if
> > *possibleValue1* equals value.

> **Case** *possibleValue2*
> > *statements*
> > *statements* ──┐ These statements executed only if
> > *possibleValue2* equals value.

> **Case** *possibleValue3*
> > *statements*
> > *statements* ──┐ These statements executed only if
> > *possibleValue3* equals value.

> **Case Else**
> > *statements*
> > *statements* ──┐ These statements executed only if no
> > *possibleValue* above equals value.

End Select

Figure 4-9:
A Select Case block runs only certain lines of code.

Chapter 5

Controlling Access through VBA

*U*sing Visual Basic for Applications (VBA) in Access is all about writing code to manipulate Access objects, which is just about everything you see on your screen in Access. Coming up with a simple example is difficult because virtually everything is an object. Every table, query, form, report, macro, and module is an object. Every record and field in every table and query is an object. Every control on every form and report is an object. Even the Access Ribbon is an object that you can manipulate with VBA. (See a pattern here?)

Every object in a database has a unique name. Most objects have properties and methods that VBA can manipulate. The properties and methods exposed by an object are the steering wheels, if you will, that allow VBA to grab hold of an object and take control. The names that define all the objects that VBA can manipulate are organized into an *object model*.

Using VBA in Access is largely a matter of manipulating database objects to achieve a goal. In this chapter, we walk you through the basics of objects that Access exposes to VBA. Access has so many objects, properties, and methods that we have no hope of explaining them all in a single book. You have no real hope of ever memorizing them all, either, because there's just too darn many of them. What you really need is the skill of being able to find the information you need, exactly when you need it. Thus, much of this chapter focuses on that skill.

Understanding Object Models

An *object model* is a road map, or the view from 30,000 feet, of all the objects and properties that VBA can manipulate. Because there are so many thousands of objects, you need a sort of road map to find them, just like you need a map to navigate unfamiliar territory.

When you view an object model (or portion of an object model), all you see are color-coded boxes arranged in a vertical hierarchy. For example, Figure 5-1 shows a graphical representation of the Access object model. Notice the legend in this figure, which points out that some boxes represent an object only, and others represent both an object and a collection.

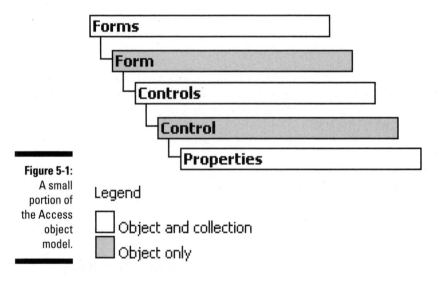

Figure 5-1:
A small portion of the Access object model.

Distinguishing between objects and collections

You're no doubt wondering how (or why) a thing could be both an object and a collection at the same time. Start with a simple, real world example: a can of peas. The can of peas itself is an *object* — a unit — that you can buy at most any store and easily carry in your hand. The can, however, is also a *collection* — a repository — of individual peas. Thus, it's both an object and a collection. The same could be said for a carton of eggs: The carton itself is an object, but it can also be a collection because it holds the eggs inside.

Refer to Figure 5-1, and take a look at what each box refers to. The `Forms` collection is a collection of all the open forms in a database. When your VBA code is running, it can access any form within that collection of open forms. Notice how the word `Form` is indented under the word `Forms`. This illustrates that each object in the `Forms` collection is a `Form`. (Seems reasonable.)

In the object model hierarchy, `Forms` is color-coded as an object and a collection. How can a form (an object) be a collection? If you look at just about any form, you see that it contains controls. In fact, a form is a collection of controls. From a programming standpoint, a form is an object that you can manipulate (open, close, print, and so forth) as a unit (an object). However, it's also a `Controls` collection, which contains smaller individual objects (each called a control) that you can manipulate with VBA.

Wait a minute. According to the object model, `Controls` is both an object and a collection. What collection of things does a control contain? Each control has its own collection of properties that uniquely define its name and many other properties. You can see those properties in form design when you select a single control and view its property sheet. For example, in Figure 5-2, the combo box control named `Company` is selected in the form's Design view. The property sheet in the figure is showing the properties for only that control.

Every form has its own collection of controls.

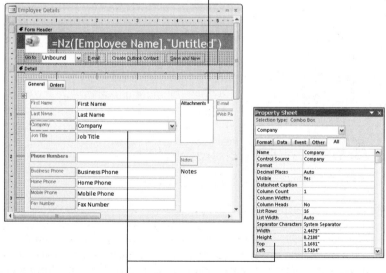

Figure 5-2:
Forms hold controls; controls hold properties.

Every control has its own collection of properties.

When you're in the Access forms Design view, you have several ways to open the property sheet. Use whatever method seems most convenient. Your options are

✔ Double-click the control whose properties you want to view.

✔ Right-click a control and choose Properties.

✔ Press the F4 key.

✔ On the (Form Design Tools) Design tab, click the Property Sheet command in the Tools group.

As you work with VBA in Access, you often see little chunks of object modules (like the example shown in Figure 5-1). The complete Access object model is too big to even fit on-screen and would be a tight squeeze on a printed page in this book. However, you can always browse the Access object model by following these steps:

1. **If you're in the Access program window, press Alt+F11 to switch to the VBA Editor.**

2. **Press F1 or choose Help➪Microsoft Visual Basic Help to show the main Access Developer help screen.**

3. **In the Help window, click Access Object Model Reference.**

   The Help window, shown in Figure 5-3, shows the subcategories of the Access object model. Click one of the subcategories to drill down into each object's specific properties, methods, and collections. (You see a lot of them, so warm up your clicking finger.)

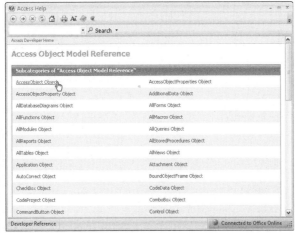

Figure 5-3:
View an object model from Help.

Understanding properties and methods

Every object and every collection exposes at least one property and method to VBA. The difference between a property and a method is described here:

- ✔ **Property:** A characteristic of an object, such as size, color, or font
- ✔ **Method:** An action that can be performed on an object, such as open, close, or copy

The standard syntax for referring to a specific object (or collection) property is to follow the object name or collection name with a period and the property name:

```
ObjectCollectionName.property
```

where *ObjectCollectionName* is a name from the object model, and *property* is a valid property name for that object.

When you type a valid object or collection name followed by a period into the Code or Immediate window of the VBA Editor, it immediately displays a list of properties and methods for that object. For example, if you type

```
Forms.
```

into the Code or Immediate window, Access immediately displays a menu of properties supported by the Forms collection, as shown at the top of Figure 5-4.

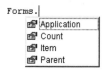

Figure 5-4:
Find menus
of proper-
ties and
methods.

Look at the bottom half of Figure 5-4. DoCmd is another object in the Access object model (which we haven't mentioned yet) that offers many methods. Type its name followed by a period

```
DoCmd.
```

into the Code window or Immediate window, and you see a list of methods supported by the DoCmd object. After the menu is visible, you can just click any property or method name to add it to the command.

The drop-down lists of property and method names, known as IntelliSense, serve as useful reminders for experienced programmers, but beginners need more information than the little lists provide. You can get help with objects and collections by using the same basic techniques that you use for getting help with VBA statements. For example, you can select (double-click) an object or collection name in your code and then click Help (or press F1). Or, you can search the Object Browser for the object name or collection name and get help from there. Here's how:

1. **In the VBA Editor, open the Object Browser by pressing F2 or by choosing View⇨Object Browser from the menu bar.**

2. **In the left column, scroll to and then click the name for which you want help.**

   For example, for help with the DoCmd object, scroll down through the left column and then click DoCmd. Alternatively, you can use the Search tool in the Object Browser to find a specific word. The Members Of pane on the right changes to show only properties, methods, and events for the item you selected in the Classes pane on the left.

3. **Optionally, if you want Help for a name in the right column, click the name for which you want help.**

4. **Press F1 or click the Help button in the Object Browser.**

   For example, if you click DoCmd in the left column and then press F1 or click the Object Browser's Help button, you see the Help page for the DoCmd object, as in the right half of Figure 5-5.

When you're viewing the Help information for an object or collection, be sure to look at the headings under See Also. Those offer help with the specific properties and methods exposed by the object.

Classes and members

Don't let the Classes and Members Of headings in the Object Browser confuse you. This isn't the feudal system, so think of a *class* as anything that can act as a container (an object or a collection). Think of the *members of* as things (properties, methods, other collections) within the collection.

Click for help with methods.

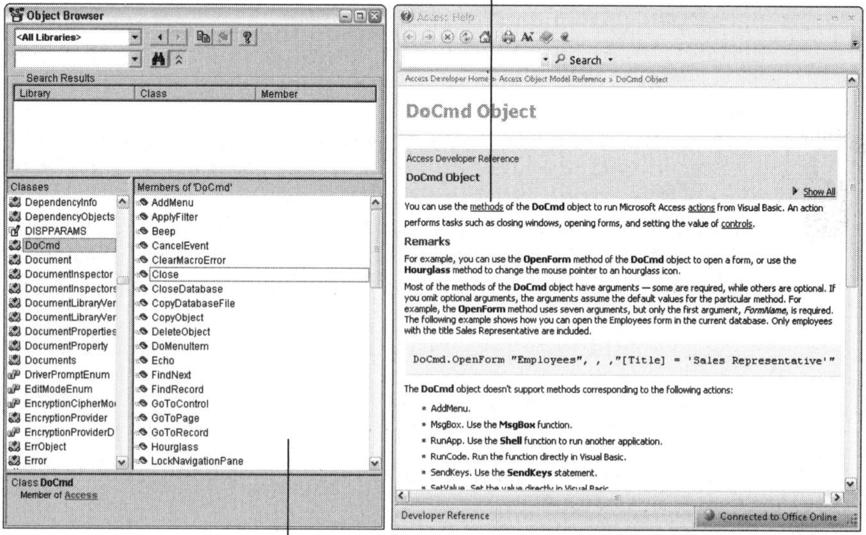

Figure 5-5:
Find help in
the Object
Browser.

Methods of the selected object (DoCmd)

Identifying the icons for objects, properties, and methods

The Object Browser, as well as the menus that appear in the Code and Immediate windows, uses icons to help you visually discriminate between objects, properties, methods, and other items in the object model. Table 5-1 lists each icon. Refer to the Object Browser shown in Figure 5-5 (left side) to see some of the icons in action.

Table 5-1 Icons Used in the Object Browser and the Code Window

Icon	Name
	Property
	Default Property

(continued)

Table 5-1 *(continued)*

Icon	Name
	Method
	Default Method
	Event
	Constant
	Module
	Class (object or collection)
	User Defined Type
	Global
	Object Library
	Project
	VBA Keyword or Data
	Enum

Manipulating Properties and Methods

When you write in any language, your ultimate goal is to be clearly understood. You accomplish this goal by following basic rules of word order and punctuation *(syntax)*. In a sentence in English, for example, nouns, verbs, objects, articles, modifiers, and punctuation fall (usually) in a set way. (The sentence "my the ate. dog homework" is unintelligible; "The dog ate my homework." is correct.)

Likewise, when you write code, you're manipulating the properties and methods exposed by that object and considering the basic rules of syntax for how to refer to objects, properties, and methods. Understanding those rules is critical to being able to write VBA code that works. Knowing how it all works also helps you understand and modify existing code.

Getting the value of a property

The syntax for referring to an object (or collection) property follows this general form:

```
objectCollectionName.property
```

where *objectCollectionName* is any valid object or collection name, and *property* is any valid property for that object. The dot (.) is the delimiter that separates the object name from the property name.

For example, all collections have a `Count` property that contains the number of items in the collection. Remember that the `Forms` collection is an object that contains all open forms in Access. Thus, `Forms.Count` returns the number of open forms in the database. You could see this for yourself by typing the following line in the Immediate window and pressing Enter:

```
? Forms.Count
```

As always in the Immediate window, the question mark asks "What is?" In this case, you're asking the Immediate window, "What is the forms count in this database?" (or, "How many forms are open right now in this database?").

If no forms are open in Access, `Forms.Count` returns 0 (zero). If you open a form (in Form view) in Access and then execute the `? Forms.Count` statement again, it returns 1. In other words, the value returned by `Forms.Count` is equal to the number of forms that are open in Access — 0 (zero) if no forms are open, 1 if one form is open, 2 if two forms are open, and so forth.

Bang (!) versus dot (.) in identifiers

To refer to specific objects in a database, VBA uses the same identifier syntax that's used in Access expressions. An identifier can use two different characters as *delimiters* (separators) between words: either an exclamation point (!) or a period (.). Programmer lingo for these characters is bang and dot, respectively. The general rules for using them are listed here:

✔ ! (bang): Use the bang character to precede any name you made up yourself, such as the name of a form you created or the name of a control you created on the form.

✔ . (dot): Use a dot to precede a property name or any "official" name that you didn't make up yourself.

For example, in `Forms!myForm!myButton.Visible`, both `myForm` and `myButton` are names that we made up. We did so while creating those objects in Access. Both names are preceded by a bang (!) character because they're both names we made up.

The final name in the identifier, `Visible`, is a reference to the object's `Visible` property. We didn't make up the name `Visible` ourselves: Rather, that's the Access name for the property, as you can see in the property sheet shown in Figure 5-6. Because `Visible` is an "official" property name, its name is preceded with a dot (.) rather than a bang (!).

For more information on identifiers, your best bet is to consult an Access book (as opposed to an Access VBA book, like this one). Or you can just search the Access Help (not VBA Help) for the word *identifier*.

To reexecute a statement in the Immediate window, just move the cursor back to the end of the statement that you want to execute and then press Enter. To quickly delete text in the Immediate window, drag the mouse pointer over it and press Delete.

Every control on every form has a `Visible` property that determines whether the control is visible on the form. When `Visible` equals `True` (Yes), the control is visible. Conversely, when the `Visible` property is `False` (No), the control is not visible.

When creating your own forms, you might find instances when you want a control to be visible to the user and instances when you don't want it to be visible. For example, on a form that allows a user to enter payment information for an order, you might want to make controls for entering credit card information visible only when the customer is paying by credit card. If the customer pays by check or cash, you might want to make those same controls invisible so that the user doesn't accidentally choose Cash or Check and then also type in credit card information.

The syntax for referring to the `Visible` property of a control named `myButton` is `myButton.Visible`. However, as with Access expressions, getting to a specific object from outside its container requires using an *identifier*, which provides the complete path to the object. For example, the line

```
Forms!myForm!myButton.Visible
```

refers specifically to the `Visible` property of a control named `myButton` on a form named `myForm`. The `Forms!` part at the beginning refers to the `Forms` collection, which contains all forms that are open in Access. Figure 5-6 illustrates how `Forms!myForm!myButton.Visible` refers to the `Visible` property of the `myButton` control.

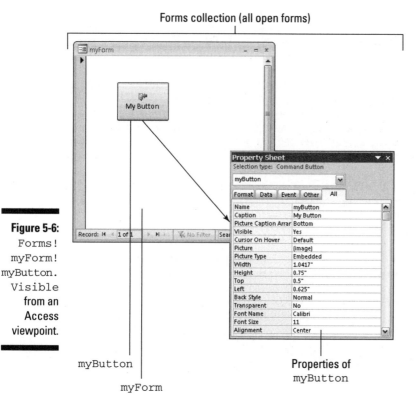

Forms collection (all open forms)

Figure 5-6:
Forms!
myForm!
myButton.
Visible
from an
Access
viewpoint.

myButton

myForm

Properties of
myButton

Changing the value of a property

To change the value of a property, follow the property name with an equal sign and a valid value for the property. For example, the `Visible` property of a control can be `True` (Yes) or `False` (No). For example, the following statement makes invisible a control named `myButton` by setting its `Visible` property to `False` (No):

```
Forms!myForm!myButton.Visible = False
```

To make that same control visible again from VBA, set its `Visible` property back to `True` (Yes), as shown here:

```
Forms!myForm!myButton.Visible = True
```

Using an object's methods

Methods are actions that you can perform on objects. The syntax for referring to an object's methods in VBA varies. In some cases, referring to a method is the same as referring to a property. You simply follow the object or collection name with a period and the method that you want to apply.

For example, the `DoCmd` (do command) object in the Access object model exposes commands on Access menus and other capabilities to VBA. One of the simplest methods exposed by the `DoCmd` object is the `Beep` method. When applied, it simply makes Access sound the default beep sound. In your own code, you might use `DoCmd.Beep` to sound a beep when a form opens — or when the user makes a mistake — to call attention to the screen.

You can try out the `DoCmd.Beep` method right now via the Immediate window. Just type the following line into the Immediate window and then press Enter:

```
DoCmd.Beep
```

The `Beep` method is straightforward in that it's just one word: beep. Some methods support one or more arguments, acting as placeholders for information that you want to pass to the statement later. For example, one of the many methods offered by the `DoCmd` object is `OpenForm`. The syntax for using the `OpenForm` method of the `DoCmd` object looks like this:

```
DoCmd.OpenForm FormName, [View], [FilterName],
        [WhereCondition], [DataMode], [WindowMode],
        [OpenArgs]
```

The first argument, *FormName*, is required. The remaining arguments, enclosed in brackets, are all optional. (As in the syntax charts you see in Help and the Quick Info screen tip, we use square brackets to indicate optional parameters in this book.) For example, if the current database contains a form named `Customers`, the following VBA statement opens it:

```
DoCmd.OpenForm "Customers"
```

Multiple arguments must be separated by commas. For example, the following VBA statement uses the `View` argument and the `acDesign` constant to open the form named `OpenForm` in Design view:

```
DoCmd.OpenForm "Customers", acDesign
```

Single versus double quotation marks

VBA uses the same syntax as Access expressions, where literal numbers are just typed as numbers (like `10`), but literal text and dates must be *delimited* (surrounded by characters). Literal dates need to be enclosed in # characters. For example, the date December 31, 2007, needs to be expressed as `#12/31/07#` in an Access expression as well as in VBA. Literal text, like the name *Smith,* needs to be enclosed in either double quotation marks (`"Smith"`) or single quotation marks (`'Smith'`).

When the syntax of a VBA statement requires its own quotation marks, like the `WhereCondition` argument in `DoCmd.OpenForm`, the literal needs to be contained within the entire argument. For example, the following entire expression `StartDate = #12/31/07#` is an entire `WhereCondition`, enclosed within quotation marks to satisfy the syntax rules:

```
"StartDate = #12/31/07# "
```

It gets tricky when the expression itself contains quotation marks because you need one pair to delimit the literal text and another pair to delimit the entire expression. You need to use single quotation marks for one pair and double quotation marks for the other pair. Otherwise, Access can't tell which quotation mark belongs to which chunk of text. For example, if the `WhereCondition` is `LastName = "Smith"` and that whole part needs to be in quotation marks, the following statement does *not* work:

```
"LastName = "Smith" "
```

The reason it doesn't work is that the computer always reads one character at a time, from left to right. When the computer "sees" the first quotation mark, to the left of `LastName`, it "knows" that this is the start of some chunk of text enclosed in quotation marks. The computer keeps reading one character at a time, left to right. When it then sees the double quotation mark in front of Smith, it "thinks" that's the end of the whole chunk and then gets all befuddled and stops working when it sees more characters after that second quotation mark.

Alternating the single and double quotation marks, as follows, solves the problem:

```
"LastName = 'Smith' "
```

When the computer reads the preceding line, one character at a time from left to right, it "sees," as always, the first quotation mark to the left of `LastName`. When it gets to the first single quotation mark before `Smith`, there's no confusion with the first double quotation mark. Access just "knows" that this single quotation mark is the start of some new literal within the current chunk of text.

As the computer continues from left to right, it sees the second single quotation mark as the end of the first one that started with `Smith`. By the time it gets to the second double quotation mark, it really *is* at the end of the whole chunk of text, so it doesn't get befuddled and fail.

For more information on using literals in Access, refer to a book about Access or search the Access Help (not the VBA Help) for the keyword *literal.* Optionally, you can search the Access Help for the word *expressions* and get more information about literal values from the Help page titled About Expressions.

If you want to use multiple arguments and skip over others, you need to type enough commas to get to the right place. For example, the optional *WhereCondition* argument lets you specify records to display in the form.

The following VBA statement opens the Customers form, displaying only records that have CA in the field named State:

```
DoCmd.OpenForm "Customers", , ,"[State]='CA'"
```

The empty commas leave the optional *View* and *FilterName* arguments empty, ensuring that [State]='CA' is passed as the fourth argument, *WhereCondition*.

Seeking help with properties and methods

When you're typing VBA statements that involve objects, properties, and methods, you get all the usual quick-reminder Help on-screen. You can always get more help, though. For example, as soon as you type **DoCmd.** (remember to type the period as per the syntax for DoCmd), you see a menu of methods that DoCmd provides, as in Figure 5-7. The menu is lengthy, so you have to use the scroll bar to see all the available methods of the DoCmd object.

Figure 5-7:
Menu of valid entries for the first word after DoCmd.

After you type a method name and a blank space, you see the entire syntax for the method in a Quick Info screen tip, as in Figure 5-8. For the lowdown on how to read Quick Info tips (what all the brackets, bold, italics, and other elements mean), check out Chapter 3.

Figure 5-8:
Get Quick Info syntax help.

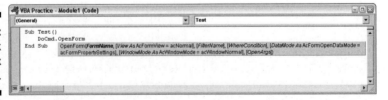

As always, quick reminders don't provide any detail. When you're first finding out how to master VBA, frequent visits to the VBA Help are necessary. VBA has far too many objects, properties, methods, and keywords to list them all in this book (or even a 1,000-page book). The best skill that you can learn in VBA is how to get exactly the help you need, when you need it.

Fortunately, all the Help methods that work with other VBA keywords also work with objects, properties, and methods. For example, for help with the OpenForm method of the DoCmd object, you can do the following:

✔ **In the Code window:** Type **DoCmd.OpenForm** into the Code window, double-click OpenForm to select it, and then press F1 for Help.

✔ **In the Object Browser:** Find DoCmd in the left column, click OpenForm in the right column, and click the Help (?) button in the Object Browser.

As always, a Help window pops up, as in the example shown in Figure 5-9, where you can get more information on the OpenForm method.

Selected keyword

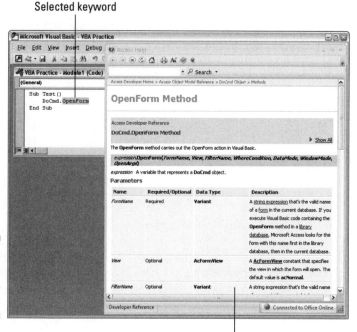

Figure 5-9:
Help for the
OpenForm
method.

Help for selected keyword

Trying to figure out how to write a line of new code, or modify an existing line of code by just guessing, is likely to turn into an exercise in hair-pulling frustration. Nobody was ever born already knowing VBA syntax, and even the experts have to make frequent visits to Help to get specific information when they need it. The Help system in VBA is your best friend. Use it well!

Chapter 6

Programming Access Forms

*O*ne of the most common uses of VBA is to make your Access forms better and easier to use. As a database developer, you always want your forms to make data entry as quick and error-free as possible. Although you can do plenty along those lines in Access without using VBA, you can often make things just a bit better by writing a little VBA code.

In this chapter, we focus on VBA programming techniques that apply specifically to forms. You'll discover how to open forms, change things on a form, and close a form automatically from VBA.

Working with Class Procedures

Every form in a database has a *class module* in which you can store code that's used only by that form. To get to a form's class module, you first have to click the Forms group in the Navigation pane and then open an existing form in Design view or create a new form. Typically, you want to tie your code to an object and event.

For example, a button on a form is an object. Every button has an `On Click` event that occurs whenever a user clicks the button in Form view. If you want to write code that runs every time someone clicks that button, you want to tie the code to that button's `On Click` event.

To see which events an object on a form offers, first select the object. The name of the object appears in the property sheet. In the property sheet, click the Event tab. All the events to which you can tie code appear in the property sheet.

When you click an event name in the property sheet, a Build button (look for an ellipsis) appears to the right (see Figure 6-1). To write code that is executed each time the event occurs, click that Build button. The first time you do, you see a Choose Builder dialog box. Choose Code Builder and then click OK. The form's class module opens in the VBA Editor Code window.

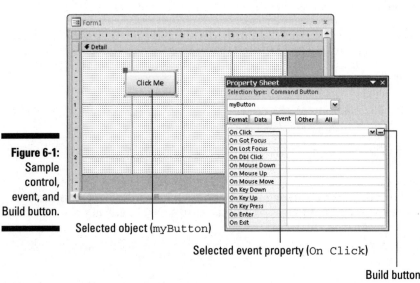

Figure 6-1:
Sample
control,
event, and
Build button.

Selected object (myButton)

Selected event property (On Click)

Build button

The first and last lines of the procedure that will execute in response to the event are already typed into the class module for you. The name of the procedure is a combination of the object and event name followed by a pair of parentheses. For example, the procedure that executes whenever someone clicks a button named myButton is myButton_OnClick(). The first and last lines of VBA code for that procedure look like this in the class module:

```
Private Sub myButton_Click()

End Sub
```

Any VBA code that the event is to execute needs to be typed between those two lines of code. After you write your code, choose File⇨Save and then choose File⇨Close and Return to Microsoft Office Access from the VBA Editor menu bar. The VBA Editor closes, and you're back in the form's Design view. There you see the words

```
[Event Procedure]
```

in the property sheet, next to the name of the property for which you wrote the code. In the future, whenever you click that property and click the Build button, you're taken straight to the form's class module, with the cursor already placed inside the procedure.

Every type of control has a unique combination of events to which you can tie code. When you click a control in the form's Design view, the Event tab in the property sheet shows you all the events the control exposes. Some controls offer quite a few more events than the button control shown in Figure 6-1.

You don't need to memorize all the events supported by all the different controls. There are too many of them, many of which you'll probably never use. Just to give you some examples of events to which you can tie code, we offer the following quick list:

- ✔ On Click (Click): Occurs when the user clicks the control (points to the control and clicks the left mouse button)

- ✔ On Mouse Down (MouseDown): Occurs when the user points to the control and then clicks either the left or right mouse button

- ✔ On Change (Change): Occurs when the contents of a TextBox or ComboBox control change, such as when the user edits the contents of a field

- ✔ Before Update (BeforeUpdate): Occurs after the user makes a change to data in the control but before the new data is inspected and before the underlying record is updated

- ✔ After Update (AfterUpdate): Occurs after the user changes the contents of the control, the new data has passed any data validation rules, and the underlying record has been updated

Here's the reason each item in the preceding list is shown with two names. The first part, outside parentheses, is the name as it appears in the property sheet. The name in parentheses (like Click) is the official VBA name and also the name used in any VBA procedure that you tie to the event. For example, if you tie a procedure to the On Change event property of a control named PaymentMethod, that procedure is automatically named PaymentMethod_Change().

That, in a nutshell, is how you work with class procedures. Examples always help, so your first forays into programming Access forms all use class procedures to illustrate their techniques.

A *module* is a container that contains VBA code, where that code is organized into chunks called *procedures*. A *class module* is a module that contains class procedures. The module and the procedures within it belong to the form (or report) to which the class module is attached.

Enabling or Disabling Form Controls

When you work in most programs and dialog boxes, Windows disables (dims) controls that aren't relevant at the moment. You can add that same capability to your Access databases by using some VBA code. For example, you might create a form that allows a user to choose from among different payment options. When the user chooses Credit Card, you want all the fields for entering credit card information to be enabled. When the user selects any other payment method, you want to disable those same controls, as illustrated in Figure 6-2.

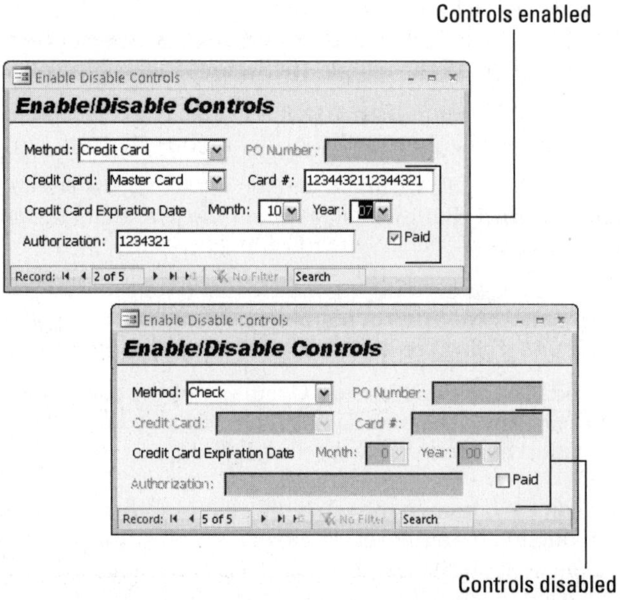

Controls enabled

Figure 6-2: Enabled and disabled controls.

Controls disabled

For the sake of example, assume that the controls in Figure 6-2 are named (from top to bottom) PaymentMethod, PONumber, CCType, CCNumber, CCExpireMonth, CCExpireYear, and CCAuthorization. We refer to those control names in the sections that follow.

Every control on a form has an Enabled property. When that property is True (or Yes), the control looks normal. When the Enabled property is False, the control is disabled and therefore appears dimmed on the form.

To enable or disable a control on a form through VBA, use the general syntax

```
controlName.Enabled = True|False
```

where *controlName* is the name of the control and *True/False* means that you can use `True` to enable the control and conversely use `False` to disable the control.

For example, the following VBA statement enables a control named `CCType`:

```
[CCType].Enabled = True
```

The following VBA statement disables a control named `CCType`:

```
[CCType].Enabled = False
```

In a class module, any field names without identifiers refer to the current form. For example, it's sufficient to use a field name like `[PaymentMethod]` rather than `Forms![formName]![PaymentMethod]` because the current form is assumed.

Note this one catch to enabling and disabling controls from VBA: You can't disable a control if the cursor is in that control. So, in addition to knowing how to enable and disable controls, you need to know how to position the cursor with VBA, as we explain in the following section.

Using VBA to position the cursor

With VBA, you can move the cursor to any control on a form. In programmer lingo, moving the cursor to a control is called giving that control the *focus*. When you type, your text appears in whatever control on a form now has the focus.

Square brackets and field names

VBA itself doesn't use square brackets. In fact, about the only time you see square brackets in VBA is when you're looking at a syntax chart, where square brackets are used to identify optional (as opposed to required) arguments.

Access, however, uses square brackets when an object name — such as a field, query, form, control, or report name — contains one or more blank spaces. Then, square brackets around the name are required. If the name contains no spaces, square brackets are optional.

Most VBA programmers use square brackets around all Access object names even when they're not required, as in the case of the `[CCType].Enabled = False` example. Using the square brackets makes it easier to distinguish between names that refer to Access objects and words that belong to VBA.

You can have VBA automatically move the cursor to any control on your form. This can be handy when your code can anticipate where the user is most likely to type next. You can have VBA position the cursor to the appropriate control automatically so that the user can just keep typing and not move the cursor on his own.

The same technique also lets you avoid error messages caused by trying to disable (or hide or lock) the control that has the focus. The VBA syntax for setting the focus to a specific control is

```
controlName.SetFocus
```

where *controlName* is the name of the control to which you want to move the cursor. For example, the following statement moves the cursor to a control named CCType on the form:

```
[CCType].SetFocus
```

Choosing an object and event for the code

In the example shown in Figure 6-2, assume that you want your code to either enable or disable the various credit-card-related controls (CCType through CCAuthorization) depending on the current contents of the PaymentMethod control. The AfterUpdate event of PaymentMethod occurs whenever a user chooses a valid option from the PaymentMethod control, so you want to tie the code to the PaymentMethod control's AfterUpdate event.

In the form's Design view, click the PaymentMethod control to select it and then click AfterUpdate on the Event tab of the property sheet. The next step is to click the Build button, as shown in Figure 6-3. In the Choose Builder dialog box that opens, choose Code Builder and then click OK.

Figure 6-3:
The
Payment
Method
control's
After
Update
event
property.

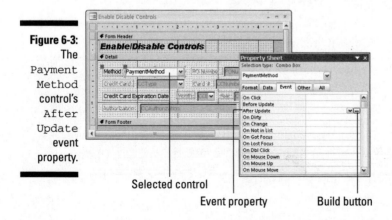

Selected control

Event property   Build button

The form's class module opens, displaying a new, empty Sub procedure named PaymentMethod_AfterUpdate(), based on the object and event names. In the Code window, the empty procedure appears this way:

```
Private Sub PaymentMethod_AfterUpdate()

End Sub
```

Any VBA code that you place between those two lines is executed every time a user changes the contents of the PaymentMethod control.

Every time the PaymentMethod_AfterUpdate() procedure executes, its code needs to make a decision: Should it enable or disable the credit card controls? You can use the VBA If...Else...End If keywords to make the decision.

See Chapter 4 for more information on the VBA If...Then...End If keywords.

Within the If...Else...End If statements, the code positions the cursor and enables or disables controls based on the current contents of the PaymentMethod control. The logic of the procedure (not written in VBA code yet) looks like this:

```
If "Credit Card" is selected in the PaymentMethod Field
          Then
    Enable the various Credit Card Controls
    Move the cursor to Credit Card Type (CCType) control
Else
    Disable the various Credit Card Controls
End If
```

Writing the code

For the procedure to work, that logic needs to be written in VBA language and syntax. Listing 6-1 shows the procedure; the sections that follow look at each step in the procedure more closely.

Listing 6-1: PaymentMethod_AfterUdate() Procedure

```
Private Sub PaymentMethod_AfterUpdate()

    If [PaymentMethod] = "Credit Card" Then
        'Enable controls for entering credit card info.
        CCType.Enabled = True
        CCNumber.Enabled = True
        CCExpireMonth.Enabled = True
        CCExpireYear.Enabled = True
        CCAuthorization.Enabled = True
```

(continued)

Listing 6-1 *(continued)*

```
        'Move the cursor to the CCType control.
        CCType.SetFocus
    Else
        'Disable controls for entering credit card info.
        CCType.Enabled = False
        CCNumber.Enabled = False
        CCExpireMonth.Enabled = False
        CCExpireYear.Enabled = False
        CCAuthorization.Enabled = False
    End If

End Sub
```

The first line of code in the `PaymentMethod_AfterUpdate` procedure compares whatever is now stored in the control named `Payment Method`. That line, on its own, reads

```
If [PaymentMethod] = "Credit Card" Then
```

Translated to English, the line says, "If the control named `PaymentMethod` contains the words *Credit Card,* then do the following lines up to `Else`; otherwise (else), skip the lines under `Else`." The same statement also means, "If the `PaymentMethod` field does not contain the words *Credit Card,* then only do the lines between `Else` and `End If`." Thus, if the `PaymentMethod` control contains the words *Credit Card,* these lines of code execute:

```
        'Enable controls for entering credit card info.
        CCType.Enabled = True
        CCNumber.Enabled = True
        CCExpireMonth.Enabled = True
        CCExpireYear.Enabled = True
        CCAuthorization.Enabled = True
        'Move the cursor to the CCType control.
        CCType.SetFocus
```

Those lines ensure that all the credit card controls are enabled and then position the cursor to the `CCType` control (where the user is most likely to make her next selection).

If the `PaymentMethod` control doesn't contain the words *Credit Card,* only the following lines execute to disable the various credit card controls:

```
        'Disable controls for entering credit card info.
        CCType.Enabled = False
        CCNumber.Enabled = False
        CCExpireMonth.Enabled = False
        CCExpireYear.Enabled = False
        CCAuthorization.Enabled = False
```

Saving the procedure

After you type your procedure, choose File⇨Save and then choose File⇨ Close and Return to Microsoft Office Access. In the form's Design property sheet, the words `[Event Procedure]` appear as the property. To test the procedure, switch to Form view and choose a different option from the `Payment Method` control.

Showing and hiding controls

Just like every control on a form has an `Enabled` property, every control also has a `Visible` property. When the `Visible` property is `True` (Yes), the control is visible on the form. When the `Visible` property is `False` (No), the control is invisible in Form view. You can use this property to make controls on the form appear or disappear, depending on values in other controls.

For example, the earlier `PaymentMethod_AfterUpdate()` procedure uses the `.Enabled` property to make controls either enabled or disabled. You can simply change `Enabled` to `Visible` in that procedure, as shown here:

```
If [PaymentMethod] = "Credit Card" Then
    'Show controls for entering credit card info.
    CCType.Visible = True
    CCNumber.Visible = True
    CCExpireMonth.Visible = True
    CCExpireYear.Visible = True
    CCAuthorization. Visible = True
Else
    'Hide controls for entering credit card info.
    CCType.Visible = False
    CCNumber.Visible = False
    CCExpireMonth.Visible = False
    CCExpireYear.Visible = False
    CCAuthorization. Visible = False
End If
```

This procedure causes the credit card controls to disappear from the form when Credit Card isn't selected in the `PaymentMethod` field. The controls are visible only when Credit Card is selected as the `PaymentMethod`.

Making controls appear and disappear instead of enabling and disabling them is a matter of preference. Generally, it's bad practice to have things appear and disappear as you change data on a screen. A disabled control lets a user know that they can probably do something (check a check box or change a value, for example) to make that control available. If the control is invisible, the user doesn't know that it's there, which may be desirable in other situations, such as configuring a form when you first open it so that it doesn't change while the form is being used.

Making controls read-only

You can lock and unlock controls on a form by using the `.Locked` property. When a control is *locked,* the user can see the data and place the cursor in the control but cannot change the data. (Hence, you say that the information in the control is *read-only.*) To lock a control from VBA, use the syntax

```
controlName.Locked=True
```

An *unlocked* control is a normal control in which the user can see and change the data (called a *read/write control*). To unlock a control from VBA, use the syntax

```
controlName.Locked=False
```

Lock a control when you don't want users to change the data, but you still want to give them the ability to select and copy text from the control. If you just disable a control, users cannot select and copy text.

Responding to Form Events

Your code isn't limited to responding to events that happen in form controls. You can also write code that responds to things that happen to the form as a whole. A common example is writing code that executes as soon as a form opens or each time a user scrolls from one record to the next in a table. Things that happen to the event as a whole are *form events.*

You can see all the form event properties whenever you're designing a form in Design view. Choose Form from the drop-down list near the top of the property sheet (as shown in Figure 6-4) and then click the Event tab. The On Current event (also shown in Figure 6-4) occurs each time the user moves to another record in the form. To write a procedure that executes each time the On Current event occurs, click the On Current event property and click the Build (ellipsis) button that appears to the right. In the Choose Builder dialog box, choose Code Builder and then click OK.

The VBA Editor opens, and you see the form's class module in the Code window. The name of the event procedure that you created is Form_OnCurrent(). The word Form in this context means *the entire form,* and OnCurrent refers to the event. The lines that start and end the procedure look like these:

```
Private Sub Form_Current()

End Sub
```

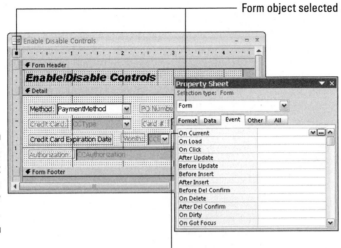

Form object selected

On Current event property

Figure 6-4:
Form event
properties in
the property
sheet.

Any code that you place between those lines is executed each time the user scrolls to a new record in the form. As it turns out, this would be a handy addition to the Payment Methods example described earlier. Only one event now enables and disables credit card controls — changing the contents of the PaymentMethod control. The controls don't change when scrolling through records, even when they should.

To remedy the situation, you can use the same code that you used in the PaymentMethod_AfterUpdate() procedure to enable and disable controls in the Form_Current() procedure. Listing 6-2 shows an example where the Form_Current() procedure moves the cursor to a control named PaymentMethod and then enables or disables credit card controls on the form based on the contents of the PaymentMethod control.

Listing 6-2:   Form_Current() Procedure

```
Private Sub Form_Current()
    'Move cursor to PaymentMethod field.
    PaymentMethod.SetFocus

    If [PaymentMethod] = "Credit Card" Then
        'Enable controls for entering credit card info.
        CCType.Enabled = True
        CCNumber.Enabled = True
        CCExpireMonth.Enabled = True
```

(continued)

Listing 6-2 *(continued)*

```
        CCExpireYear.Enabled = True
        CCAuthorization.Enabled = True
    Else
        'Disable controls for entering credit card info.
        CCType.Enabled = False
        CCNumber.Enabled = False
        CCExpireMonth.Enabled = False
        CCExpireYear.Enabled = False
        CCAuthorization.Enabled = False

    End If
End Sub
```

After you write the code and choose Close and Return to Microsoft Office Access, the On Current event property in the property sheet shows [Event Procedure]. To test the code, switch to Form view (assuming that the form was bound to a table that contains multiple records).

You don't need to study all the details of every event for every control. There are just too many of them. Here's a quick rundown of some of the more commonly used form events for executing VBA code:

- ✔ On Load (Load): Occurs as soon as a form opens in Form view and displays the first record

- ✔ On Current (Current): Occurs when the form is open in Form view and the user scrolls to a different record in the underlying table or query

- ✔ After Insert (AfterInsert): Occurs when the user adds a new record to the underlying table (but not when code or a macro adds a new record to the table)

- ✔ On Delete (Delete): Occurs when a user deletes a record

- ✔ On Close (Close): Occurs after a form is closed and cleared from the screen

The name listed first in these bulleted items (like On Load) is the name as it appears in the property sheet. The second name (like Load) is the VBA name that's added to the procedure name automatically when you tie code to an event. For example, as you can read earlier in this chapter, tying code to a form's On Current event creates a procedure named Form_Current(). If you create a procedure that executes as soon as a form loads, its name is Form_Load().

The event to which you tie a procedure simply defines *when* the procedure runs. You define *what* the procedure does, when it's called, by writing the VBA code within the procedure.

Changing the Appearance of Objects

A form, and each object on a form, contains certain properties that describe the general appearance of the object. Different types of objects have different combinations of appearance properties. When you're working in the form's Design view, the Format tab of the property sheet shows the properties that the selected object (or objects) support. For example, Figure 6-5 shows some of the appearance properties available for the selected TextBox control on the form.

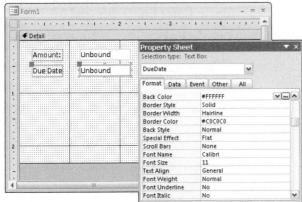

Figure 6-5: Some appearance properties for a TextBox control.

Changing colors

Your VBA code can change the color of objects on forms. Such changes can be handy to use color-coding to call attention to specific items on a form. For example, if a payment is more than 30 days overdue, you might want to choose the amount due to show up in red (to call attention to the value).

The exact color properties available to you depend on the object for which you're writing code. Some common coloring properties include

- BackColor: Defines the background color of a text box, combo box, or form section
- BorderColor: Sets the color of the border surrounding a control (as long as that border isn't transparent)
- ForeColor: Sets the color of text in controls that show text, such as a text box, combo box, or label

When writing code to change the color of any property in the preceding list, use the syntax

```
objectName.property = rgbColor
```

where *objectName* is the name of the object to color, *property* is one of the properties that accepts a color, and *rgbColor* is a color defined as a VBA *ColorConstant* or an expression that defines a color as a mixture of red, green, and blue. ColorConstants are just predefined keywords that specify some of the most basic colors, as shown in Table 6-1.

Table 6-1	Basic Color Constants and RGB Values	
Color	*ColorConstant*	*RGB Equivalent*
Black	vbBlack	RGB(0,0,0)
Blue	vbBlue	RGB(0,0,255)
Cyan	vbCyan	RGB(0,255,255)
Green	vbGreen	RGB(0,255,0)
Magenta	vbMagenta	RGB(255,0,255)
Red	vbRed	RGB(255,0,0)
White	vbWhite	RGB(255,255,255)
Yellow	vbYellow	RGB(255,255,0)

The RGB() function allows you to express any of millions of colors. You can use the Colors dialog box in Access to determine the correct RGB numbers to use to express any color. In the form's Design view, click the BackColor, BorderColor, or ForeColor property, and then click the Build (ellipsis) button that appears next to the property name and choose More Colors from the menu. The Colors dialog box opens, initially showing just the basic colors. Click the Custom tab to define your own colors.

To see the RGB numbers for a color, first click in the large rainbow-looking area and then choose a brightness level to the right of that. The selected color appears in the top half of the New/Current box, and the RGB numbers for that color appear under the rainbow area. Figure 6-6 shows the basic procedure for finding the three numbers necessary to define a color from the Colors dialog box.

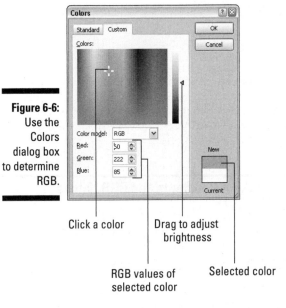

Figure 6-6:
Use the
Colors
dialog box
to determine
RGB.

Click a color   Drag to adjust
brightness

RGB values of   Selected color
selected color

Notice in Figure 6-6 how the selected color is expressed as a mixture of Red
(60), Green (222), and Blue (85). The way to express that color by using the
RGB function is simply RGB(60,222,85).

Be aware that backgrounds and borders can also be *transparent,* or not even
visible, no matter how you color them. Properties that determine whether an
item is transparent or opaque include

- ✔ BackStyle: When set to 0 (zero), the background is transparent. When
  set to 1, the background is opaque and can therefore show color.
- ✔ BorderStyle: When set to 0 (zero), the border is transparent. When
  set to 1, the border is opaque and can therefore show color.

In the following simple example, your form contains a control named DueDate
that contains the date when a payment is due. As you scroll through records
in the table, you want DueDate to appear in red whenever the payment is
more than 30 days past due. Because you want the control to change while
you're scrolling through records on the form, you could attach the code to
the form's On Current event. The code would appear in a class module, as
shown in the following example. (The comment above each line of code tells
what the line beneath it does.)

```
Private Sub Form_Current()
    If Date - [DueDate] > 30 Then
        'Make control background opaque.
        DueDate.BackStyle = 1
        'Make control background color white.
        DueDate.BackColor = vbWhite
        'Make font color red.
        DueDate.ForeColor = vbRed
    Else
        'Make control background transparent.
        DueDate.BackStyle = 0
        'Make font color black.
        DueDate.ForeColor = vbBlack
    End If
End Sub
```

When working with more than the basic colors, many programmers prefer to define colors in advance by storing them in variables. To use this method, you must first declare the variable or constant as a Long (long integer number) and then use the RGB function to assign a value to the variable. For example, the following Dim statements declare a bunch of color names as variables containing Long Integer data. Lines below the Dim statements assign colors to those names:

```
'Declare some color names as Long Integer variables.
Dim Beige As Long, Brown As Long, Chartreuse As Long
Dim DarkBlue As Long, DarkGreen As Long
Dim Fuschia As Long, Gold As Long, Gray As Long
Dim HotPink As Long, Dim Lavender As Long, Maroon As Long
Dim Navy As Long, Olive As Long, Orange As Long
Dim Pink As Long, Purple As Long, Salmon As Long
Dim Silver As Long, Teal As Long

'Assign colors to variables as RGB values.
Beige = RGB(245, 245, 220)
Brown = RGB(165, 90, 33)
Chartreuse = RGB(127, 255, 0)
DarkBlue = RGB(0, 0, 139)
DarkGreen = RGB(0, 100, 0)
Fuschia = RGB(255, 0, 255)
Gold = RGB(255, 215, 0)
Gray = RGB(128, 128, 128)
HotPink = RGB(255, 105, 180)
Lavender = RGB(230, 210, 250)
Maroon = RGB(128, 0, 64)
Navy = RGB(0, 0, 128)
```

```
Olive = RGB(128, 128, 0)
Orange = RGB(255, 165, 0)
Pink = RGB(255, 192, 203)
Purple = RGB(128, 0, 128)
Salmon = RGB(241, 128, 114)
Silver = RGB(192, 192, 192)
Teal = RGB(0, 192, 192)
```

After the color name has been assigned a value, you can use it in your code. For example, the following lines set the background color of the form's Detail section to a Salmon color:

```
Dim Salmon as Long
Salmon = RGB(241, 128, 114)
Forms!Form1.Detail.BackColor = Salmon
```

For details on creating variables, see Chapter 4.

Controlling boldface, italics, and such

If a control displays text or numbers, you can change the font or style of text by using VBA. The property names are self-explanatory, as are most of their settings. As always, *controlName* stands for the name of a control on a form. Wherever you see a pipe (|) separating options, you can use one or the other:

```
controlName.FontBold = True | False
controlName.FontItalic = True | False
controlName.FontName = stringExpression
controlName.FontSize = numberPoints
controlName.FontUnderline = True | False
```

The .ForeColor property described in the earlier section "Changing colors" determines the color of text in a box. In other words, the .ForeColor property defines the font color.

For example, to set the font of a control named Notes to Courier New, 12 point, with boldface, italics, and underline all turned on (and to make the text red, for added overkill), use these statements:

```
Notes.FontName = "Courier New"
Notes.FontSize = 12
Notes.FontBold = True
Notes.FontItalic = True
Notes.FontUnderline = True
Notes.ForeColor = vbRed
```

Changing special effects

Text boxes and some other controls on forms have a `Special Effect` property that defines their general appearance on the form. When you're creating a form in the form's Design view, you set a control's `Special Effect` property in the property sheet. If you want your code to change a control's special effect, use the syntax

```
controlName.SpecialEffect = setting
```

where `controlName` is the name of the control whose effect you want to change, and `setting` is either the number or constant, as shown in Table 6-2.

Table 6-2   Using a Constant or Number As a SpecialEffect Setting

Appearance	Number	Constant
Flat	0	acEffectNormal
Raised	1	acEffectRaised
Sunken	2	acEffectSunken
Etched	3	acEffectEtched
Shadowed	4	acEffectShadow
Chiseled	5	acEffectChisel

As an example, the following line of code sets the special effect of a control named `ContactID` to the flat appearance:

```
ContactID.SpecialEffect = acEffectNormal
```

The following line achieves exactly the same result as the preceding line but uses a number rather than the constant for the setting:

```
ContactID.SpecialEffect = 0
```

Using the With...End With statements

If you want your code to change several properties of a control, you can use a `With...End With` block of code to make your code easier to read. For example, if you want your code to change several properties of a control named `myControl` on a form named `myForm` (and the code isn't in a class

module), you could include that lengthy identifier on every line of code, as
shown here:

```
Forms!myForm.myControl.BackStyle = 1
Forms!myForm.myControl.BackColor = vbWhite
Forms!myForm.myControl.ForeColor = vbRed
Forms!myForm.myControl.SpecialEffect = acEffectNormal
Forms!myForm.myControl.FontBold = True
```

Or, you can use a `With...End With` block of code:

```
With Forms!myForm.myControl
    .BackStyle = 1
    .BackColor = vbWhite
    .ForeColor = vbRed
    .SpecialEffect = acEffectNormal
    .FontBold = True
End With
```

Most programmers prefer to write using the latter format because the code
is easier to read. When executing the code, VBA understands that `With`
`Forms!myForm!myControl` means that all the property settings to follow
(up to the `End With` statement) are to be applied to the object named
`Forms!myForm.myControl`.

Filling form controls with data

Controls that can contain data, like `TextBoxes`, `ComboBoxes`, `CheckBoxes`,
and such, all have a `.Value` property that defines the contents of the control.
To put data into a control, use the following syntax, where `controlName` is
the name of the control, and `value` is the data you want to put in the control:

```
controlName.Value = value
```

If `controlName` refers to a control that's bound to an underlying table, the
field in the current record of that table receives the same value as the control.

Suppose that your form includes controls named `State`, `SalesTaxRate`,
`OrderSubtotal`, `SalesTaxAmt`, and `GrandTotal`, as in Figure 6-7. You
want to write some code that does the following:

1. If `State` is CA, put 0.0725 (7.25%) in the `SalesTaxRate` control.

2. If `State` is not CA, put 0 (zero) in the `SalesTaxRate` control.

3. Calculate and display the `SalesTaxAmt`.

4. Calculate and display the `GrandTotal` amount.

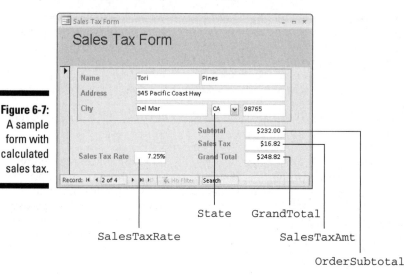

Figure 6-7:
A sample
form with
calculated
sales tax.

You need an `If...Then...Else` block of code to make the decision in your VBA code. For the calculations, just use the * (multiplication) and + (addition) operators, as shown here:

```
If [State] = "CA" Then  'If State is CA then...
    '...Set SalesTaxRate to 7.25% for CA
    [SalesTaxRate].Value = 0.0725
Else
    'Otherwise, set SalesTaxRate to zero.
    [SalesTaxRate].Value = 0
End If

'Calculate and show SalesTaxAmt and GrandTotal
SalesTaxAmt.Value = [SalesTaxRate] * [OrderSubtotal]
GrandTotal.Value = [OrderSubtotal] + [SalesTaxAmt]
```

When assigning values to controls, make sure to use the correct data type. For example, if you want to put text in a `Text`, `Memo`, or `Hyperlink` control, enclose the text in quotation marks, as in the following examples (all of which use completely hypothetical control names):

```
anyTextbox.Value = "Smith"
anyHyperlink.Value = "myname@mycompany.com"
anyHyperlink.Value = "www.dummies.com"
```

To put a check mark into a check box, set the check box's value to `True`, as in *anyCheckbox*.`Value = True`. To clear a check box, set its value to `False`, as in *anyCheckbox*.`Value = False`.

If you want to put a specific date into a Date/Time field on a form (or in a table), enclose the date in pound signs (#). For example, the following line assumes that DateEntered is the control for a Date/Time field named DateEntered. The code places the date 12/31/07 into that control:

```
[DateEntered].Value = #12/31/07#
```

To put today's date into a Date/Time field, use the word Date, alone, to the right of the equal sign, as in DateEntered.Value = Date.

Far be it from us to confuse things, but we should point out that for many controls, the .Value property is assumed if you don't include it in your code. This is because .Value is the *default property* of the text box and combo box controls. you must understand this point when modifying existing code because some programmers might prefer to omit the .Value property name. For example, when you see something like this line in your code:

```
[SalesTaxRate] = 0
```

it means exactly the same thing as

```
[SalesTaxRate].Value = 0
```

Both these VBA statements put the value 0 into a control named SalesTaxRate.

Opening and Closing Forms

VBA doesn't limit you to working with individual controls on forms. You can work with entire forms as objects, too. For example, VBA can open a closed form and display it on-screen. The OpenForm method of the DoCmd *(do command)* object gives you great flexibility in exactly how VBA opens a form. The syntax for using the OpenForm method of the DoCmd object is

```
DoCmd.OpenForm formName, [View], [FilterName],
          [WhereCondition], [DataMode], [WindowMode]
          [OpenArgs]
```

Only the first argument, *formName*, is required. If you omit other arguments, the form opens as it would when you just double-click the form's name in the Navigation pane, with all the property settings that are defined in the form's basic design. The optional arguments that allow you to change how the form opens are described here:

✔ *View*: Specify how you want to open the form that's displayed using any of the constants acDesign, acLayout, acFormDs (datasheet), acFormPivotChart, acFormPivotTable, acNormal (the default), or acPreview.

✔ *FilterName*: If you previously created and named a filter, use this option to filter records that the form displays. If you didn't create and name a filter, you can use the optional *WhereCondition* argument instead to filter records.

✔ *WhereCondition*: Use this option to specify a record or records without using a named filter. For example, the WhereClause "[ContactID]= 1001" displays only records where the ContactID field contains 1001. The WhereClause "[State]='NY'" displays only records that have NY in a field named State.

✔ *DataMode*: Determines how the form opens using the constants acFormAdd (user can add new records but not edit existing records), acFormEdit (users can add or edit data), and acFormReadOnly (users can view, but not change, data). The default argument, acFormProperty Settings, is used if you omit the argument and opens the form in Normal view, honoring the AllowEdits, AllowDeletions, AllowAddItems, and DataEntry properties defined in the form's properties.

✔ *WindowMode*: Specifies the style of the window when opened using one of these constants:

- acDialog: Opens a dialog box with Modal and PopUp properties set to True

- acHidden: Opens the form in Form view but isn't visible on-screen

- acIcon: Opens the form minimized in the Access window

- acWindowNormal: Opens the form with settings defined in its property sheet

Setting a form's Modal and PopUp properties to True makes the form open as a dialog box. When a form is modal, it must be closed before the user can perform any other action. When the PopUp property is enabled, the form stays on top of other open windows on the desktop.

✔ *OpenArgs*: Specifies additional arguments that can be passed to the form and then processed by other code that manipulates the form.

For example, to open a form named MyForm with no special settings (as though you just double-clicked the form's name in the Navigation pane), use this simple syntax:

```
DoCmd.OpenForm "MyForm"
```

The following statement opens the form named MyForm in Design view:

```
DoCmd.OpenForm "MyForm",acDesign
```

The following statement opens the form named MyForm in Form view but limits the display of records to those that have (215) as the first five characters of the Phone field:

```
DoCmd.OpenForm "MyForm",,,"Left(Phone,5)='(215)'"
```

Closing a form

To close a form that's already open, use the Close method of the DoCmd object and the syntax

```
DoCmd.Close objectType, objectName, SaveOptions
```

where

- ✔ objectType: Describes the type of object being closed. Use acForm for forms (acReport for reports).
- ✔ objectName: The name of the form (or other object) to close.
- ✔ SaveOptions: Specifies whether to save changes made to the object by using one of these constants:

  acSaveYes: The current object is saved automatically.

  acSaveNo: Any changes made to the object are discarded and not saved.

  acPrompt: Displays a prompt asking the user whether he wants to save the changes to the object.

As an example, the following VBA statement closes a form named Address Book Form and automatically saves any changes made to the form:

```
DoCmd.Close acForm,"Address Book Form",acSaveYes
```

Adding a related record to another table

One of the most common uses of opening forms from VBA is to allow the user to easily enter a record of information with some data already provided. For example, Figure 6-8 shows a sample form named `Address Book Form`. It displays records from a table of names and addresses, where each customer has a unique `ContactID` number.

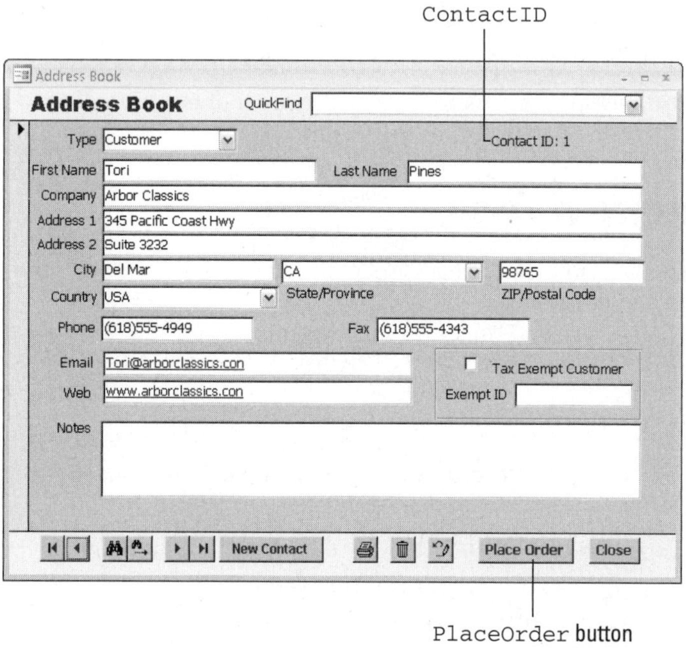

ContactID

Figure 6-8:
Sample
address
book form
and Place
Order
button.

PlaceOrder button

Suppose that a user has just finished entering the name and address and other information for a new customer and now wants to switch over to an order form and enter a new order for that customer. When the order form opens, you want it to have already created a new record for the order, put the current customer's `ContactID` value into that order form, and position the cursor to where the user is most likely to type next, such as the `Payment Method` control, as shown in Figure 6-9.

To make these tasks work, you need to tie some code to the Place Order button's `On Click` event procedure. That code needs to perform these steps:

1. Open the order form so that it's ready to add a new record.

2. Copy the customer's ContactID to the `ContactID` control on the order form.

3. Move the cursor to a convenient control on the order form.
4. Close the address book form and save its record.

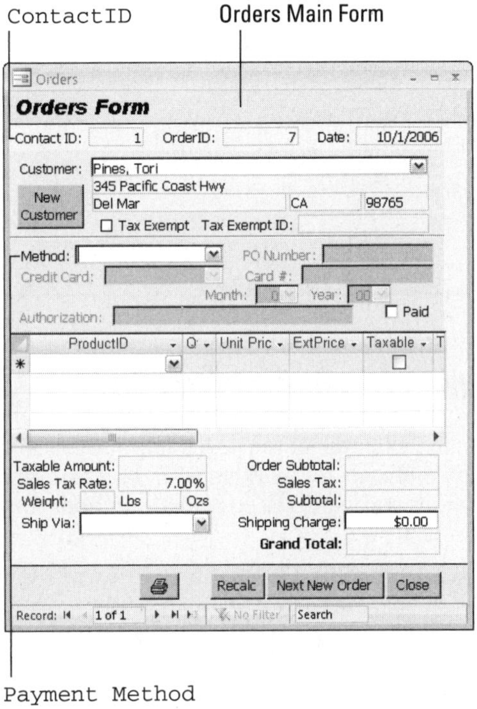
ContactID
Orders Main Form
Orders
Orders Form
Payment Method

Figure 6-9: Sample order form.

To start this programming endeavor, open `Address Book Form` in Design view, click the `PlaceOrder` button, click the Event tab in the property sheet, click the Build button in the property sheet, and choose Code Builder. As always, you're taken to the class module for the form. The cursor is in a new `Sub` procedure whose name reflects the button and the `On Click` event, as shown here:

```
Private Sub PlaceOrder_Click()

End Sub
```

Next, you convert into VBA code the plain-English steps that the procedure needs to take. The complete procedure, as it appears in the VBA Editor Code window, is shown in Listing 6-3.

Listing 6-3: Form_Address Book Form

```
Private Sub PlaceOrder_Click()
    'Open the order form ready to add a new record.
    DoCmd.OpenForm "Orders Main Form", acNormal, , , acFormAdd

    'Copy customer's ContactID to ContactID control on order form.
    Forms![Orders Main Form]!ContactID.Value = Me![ContactID].Value

    'Move cursor to convenient field in order form.
    Forms![Orders Main Form]![Payment Method].SetFocus

    'Close the address book form and save its changes.
    DoCmd.Close acForm, "Address Book Form", acSaveYes

End Sub
```

More DoCmd methods for forms

The DoCmd object used in the example in the preceding section to open and close forms provides many methods for working with data on forms. Table 6-3 summarizes some of the more commonly used DoCmd methods for working with forms and data in forms.

Table 6-3	Commonly Used DoCmd Methods
To Do This	*Use This*
Move cursor to a specific control	DoCmd.GoToControl
Select object	DoCmd.SelectObject
Move to a specific record	DoCmd.GoToRecord
Find a record	DoCmd.FindRecord
Find next matching record	DoCmd.FindNext
Filter records in a form	DoCmd.ApplyFilter
Remove filter	DoCmd.ShowAllRecords
Sound a beep	DoCmd.Beep
Print form (or other object)	DoCmd.PrintOut
Save form (or other object)	DoCmd.Save

To Do This	Use This
Perform a command from the Ribbon	DoCmd.RunCommand
Copy a form (or other object)	DoCmd.CopyObject
Rename a form (or other object)	DoCmd.Rename
Delete a form (or other object)	DoCmd.DeleteObject
Send object electronically	DoCmd.SendObject

You don't need to study and memorize all these methods now because you can easily get detailed information as needed. Just type the beginning of the statement into your code, like this:

```
DoCmd.GoToRecord
```

Just double-click the method name (such as GoToRecord) to select it and then press F1.

The Object Browser, which is always available in the VBA Editor, provides another great resource for getting quick information on methods of the DoCmd object (as well as every other object in your database). To open the Object Browser in the VBA Editor, choose View➪Object Browser from the VBA Editor's menu bar or press F2 while you're in the VBA Editor.

See Chapter 2 for more information on using the Object Browser.

After the Object Browser is open, click DoCmd in the left column. The methods that DoCmd supports are listed down the right pane. For help with a particular method, click its name in the right column and then click the Help button near the top of the Object Browser (see Figure 6-10).

DoCmd selected   Help

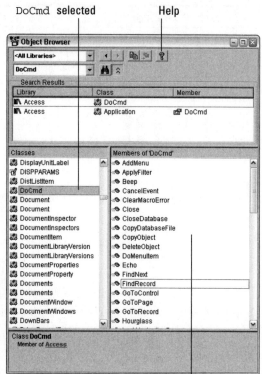

Figure 6-10:
Methods of
the DoCmd
object in the
Object
Browser.

DoCmd methods

Part III
VBA, Recordsets, and SQL

The 5th Wave   By Rich Tennant

"Yes, I know how to query information from the program, but what if I just want to leak it instead?"

In this part . . .

We suppose that the first thing the title of this part brings to mind is "What is a SQL recordset (and why would I care to know)?" If you've been faced with any VBA code in the past, you've probably seen the word *recordset* sprinkled throughout many a VBA procedure. Either way, SQL recordsets are basically a means of letting VBA work directly with the data in your tables, where it can do all kinds of useful work for you. This part is mostly about managing data in Access tables with VBA and recordsets.

Chapter 7

The Scoop on SQL and Recordsets

*Y*ou don't have to be involved with database management for long before the *SQL* acronym starts rearing its head. SQL (most often pronounced "sequel") stands for Structured Query Language. As the name implies, SQL is a language for defining which fields and records you want from a table. Actually, it's not just *a* language: It's more like *the* language for getting data from tables because it can be used in virtually all database management systems.

In this chapter, you discover what SQL is all about, how it applies to Access, and how you can use SQL in VBA to do the jobs that queries do in regular interactive Access. As you'll see, a SQL statement is basically a query that has been converted to words. And although you can't just drop the Query Design screen into code (because it's a screen and not words), you can certainly drop a SQL statement (which is just words) into your code.

What the Heck Is SQL?

Although you might not realize it, every time you create a query in Access, you create a SQL statement. This is a good thing because as a rule, creating a query in Access is a lot easier than writing a SQL statement from scratch.

To illustrate how every query is really a SQL statement in disguise, Figure 7-1 shows a basic Access Select query that displays (in Datasheet view) some fields and records from a table.

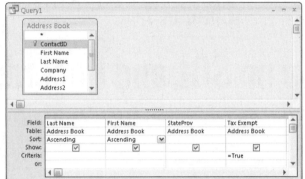

Figure 7-1:
Simple,
sample
select
query.

So where's the SQL statement in Figure 7-1? Well, it's not visible when you're looking at the query in Design view. To see the SQL statement that defines a query, right-click the title bar of the query Design screen and choose SQL View. The whole window changes, by hiding the QBE (Query By Example) grid and displaying the SQL statement that the query performs, as in Figure 7-2.

Figure 7-2:
SQL
statement
for the
query
shown in
Figure 7-1.

At first glance, the SQL statement and query might seem to be unrelated. However, if you look closely at the SQL statement, you see that it is indeed a reflection of what the query says. The syntax of a SQL statement generally looks like this:

```
SELECT fieldnames FROM tableName WHERE condition ORDER BY
          field(s)
```

where

- ✔ SELECT *fieldnames* lists the fields from the underlying table to be displayed by the query (or SQL statement).

- ✔ FROM *tableName* specifies the name of the table from which the data is being drawn.

- ✔ WHERE *condition* is an expression specifying which records to include in the query.

✔ ORDER BY *field(s)* lists the names of fields used for sorting (alphabetizing) records in the query results.

If we take the repetitive table name [Address Book] out of the sample SQL statement shown in Figure 7-1 (just to make the statement a little easier to read), the SQL statement looks like this:

```
SELECT [Last Name], [First Name], [StateProv], [Tax
        Exempt]
FROM [Address Book]
WHERE ((([Tax Exempt])=True))
ORDER BY [Last Name], [First Name];
```

Figure 7-3 shows how the various parts of the QBE grid correspond in fact to text in the SQL statement. Note the following:

✔ The fields listed across the Field row specify the fields to display (for example, SELECT [Last Name], [First Name], [StateProv], [Tax Exempt]).

✔ The table name in the top half of the grid specifies where the fields and records come from (for example, FROM [Address Book]).

✔ The WHERE clause gets its expression from the Criteria rows of the QBE grid (for example, WHERE [TaxExempt] = True).

✔ The ORDER BY fields come from the Sort row in the grid (for example, ORDER BY [Last Name], [First Name]).

SELECT   FROM

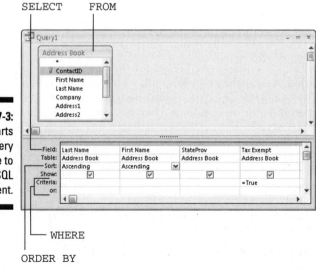

Figure 7-3:
How parts
of a query
translate to
a SQL
statement.

WHERE

ORDER BY

Writing SQL without knowing SQL

The example we show you in the preceding section illustrates that every query has a corresponding SQL statement. You can prove this by opening any query in any Access database, anywhere. Right-click that query's title bar and choose SQL View, and there you see that query's SQL statement. Right-click the title bar again and choose Design View, and you're back to the Query Design grid.

The beauty of it all is that you really don't need to master SQL in order to write SQL statements. If you know how to create an Access query, you know how to write SQL statements because you can just create your query to do whatever you want it to do, right-click the title bar, and choose SQL View — and there's your SQL statement. Drag the mouse pointer through that statement to select it, and press Ctrl+C to copy it, and then you can just paste the SQL statement wherever you want.

You can even discard the original query after you have the SQL statement because the SQL statement and query are essentially one and the same. The only real difference is in how you use them. To perform a query in Access, you create the query and switch to Datasheet view to see the results. To perform the query from VBA, you execute the SQL statement instead.

The bond between Access queries and SQL is a two-way street. Suppose that the current database has a table, such as Address Book shown in earlier figures in this chapter, and you type the following SQL statement into a text editor, such as Notepad:

```
SELECT [Last Name], [First Name], [City], [StateProv]
FROM [Address Book]
WHERE (((StateProv)="CA"))
ORDER BY [Last Name], [First Name];
```

Now suppose that you create a new query in Access but don't add any tables to it. You just have a blank QBE grid to start with. In that query, you right-click the title bar and choose SQL View. Then you copy and paste (or type) the preceding SQL statement into the window that displays the SQL statement. Intuitively, this process might seem weird because, normally, building the query creates the SQL statement, not the other way around. Given the two-way street of SQL and Access queries, however, going back to Query Design view after entering the SQL statement almost miraculously translates the SQL statement into a QBE grid, as in Figure 7-4.

It's a lot easier to create a query in the Query Design grid and convert it to SQL than it is to write a SQL statement and convert it to a query. If you put an incorrectly written SQL statement into the query, it doesn't translate. In truth, we doubt that anyone would ever go to the trouble of writing out a SQL statement first to create a query. The point is that a SQL statement *is* an

Access query. It's just that a SQL statement is a query expressed in words (which can be placed in VBA code) rather than a query expressed as information in a QBE grid (which can't be dropped into VBA code).

Figure 7-4:
Sample SQL
statement
translated to
an Access
query.

Exactly how you use SQL in VBA is a long story, which this chapter and the next describe in detail. Also, not all SQL statements contain exactly the words SELECT, FROM, WHERE, and ORDER BY. Although you can use lots of different words in SQL to perform different kinds of tasks, the first thing you need to realize is that a SQL statement is just an Access query expressed as words rather than graphically on a grid.

Select queries versus action queries

To this point in this chapter, we talk only about Access select queries. That type of query gets its name from the fact that it only *selects* fields and records from a table. A select query never alters the contents of a table.

An action query is different from a select query in that an action query changes the contents of a table. In Access, you create action queries in much the same way you create select queries. You start off by creating a new, regular query so that you're at the Query Design grid. Then you choose the type of action query you want to create from the Query Type group on the (Query Tools) Design tab, shown in Figure 7-5.

Figure 7-5:
The (Query
Tools)
Design tab
in Access.

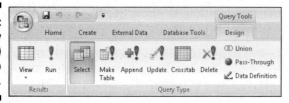

The main types of action queries that you can create and their purposes and relevant SQL buzzwords (described in the sections that follow) are summarized in Table 7-1.

Table 7-1	Access Action Query Types and Corresponding SQL Keywords	
Action Query Type	**Purpose**	**Relevant SQL Keywords**
Make-Table	Create a new table by using data from an existing table.	`SELECT...INTO`
Update	Change multiple fields and records within a table.	`UPDATE...`
Append	Add records from one table to another table.	`INSERT INTO...`
Delete	Remove multiple records from a table.	`DELETE`

The changes that an action query makes to a table can be extensive and permanent! Never test or play around with action queries on data you need. It would be a shame (to put it mildly) to test out a delete query on your only copy of 10,000 names and addresses, only to realize that it worked — and now you have 11 names and addresses in your table and no backup. Always make a copy of your database, and test your action queries on the copy.

After you create an action query in Access, you still have to run the query before it makes any changes to your database. To run an action query in Access, the action query must be open and visible on-screen in Design view. From there, you click the Run (!) button in the Results group on the (Query Tools) Design tab to run the query.

Every action query that you create is also a SQL statement, just like when you create select queries. You get to an action query's SQL statement just like you get to a select query's — by right-clicking the title bar in Query Design and choosing SQL View. For example, Figure 7-6 shows an update query that changes the value of a field named `SentWelcome` to `True` wherever that `City` field contains `"Houston"`. (Note the Update To row in the QBE grid.)

Right-clicking the title bar shown in Figure 7-6 and choosing SQL View reveals the SQL version of the query. Because this is an update query, the SQL statement doesn't start with `SELECT`. Rather, it starts with `UPDATE`, as shown here:

```
UPDATE [Address Book] SET SentWelcome = True
WHERE (((City)="Houston"));
```

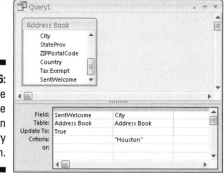

Figure 7-6:
Sample
update
query in
Query
Design.

Still, the SQL statement is perfectly valid and runs just fine as VBA code. You can select and copy the SQL statement just as you could any other.

Getting SQL into VBA

The bottom line (again) is that if you know how to create queries in Access, you know how to write (most) kinds of SQL statements. We mention earlier that you can copy and paste a SQL statement just like you can copy and paste any other hunk of text that you see on-screen. But we would be lying if we said that you just have to drop the SQL statement into your VBA code to make it work. Here are the reasons that it's not that simple:

✔ You need to get rid of the semicolon (;) at the end of the SQL statement in SQL view. (VBA doesn't like that last semicolon.)

✔ If the SQL statement is broken into multiple lines, unbreak it back to a single line. (Make sure to place a blank space where the line breaks used to be.)

✔ The whole statement needs to be placed inside quotation marks (alternating single and double quotation marks).

✔ If the SQL statement represents an action query, the whole SQL statement needs to be preceded by DoCmd.RunSQL in your code.

Look at an example starting with the UPDATE SQL statement shown earlier. When you copy and paste the statement into VBA code, the entire statement turns red, indicating a problem. The only real problem, though, is that things need to be reformatted a bit.

1. Move the cursor to the end of the top line, press Delete (Del) to unbreak the line, and then press the spacebar to insert a blank space where the line break used to be.

Repeat this step as necessary until the whole SQL statement is on one, long line in the code.

2. **Delete the semicolon at the end of the statement and put the whole statement into quotation marks.**

   You can use either single (`'`) or double (`"`) quotation marks. However, if any quotation marks are already in the statement, you can't use the same type. For example, the sample SQL statement has a pair of double quotation marks around the word `"Houston"`, as shown here:

   ```
   (City) = "Houston"
   ```

   To avoid a conflict with the embedded quotation marks, you have to either use single quotation marks to enclose the whole SQL statement:

   ```
   'UPDATE [Address Book] SET SentWelcome = True WHERE
        (((City)="Houston")))'
   ```

   or change the inner quotation marks to single quotes and then use double quotation marks around the whole statement — which is the preferred method:

   ```
   "UPDATE [Address Book] SET SentWelcome = True WHERE
        (((City)='Houston')))"
   ```

3. **Tell VBA that the statement is SQL and that you want VBA to execute the statement by adding `DoCmd.RunSQL` to the start of the line:**

   ```
   DoCmd.RunSQL "SELECT [City], [StateProv] FROM [Address
        Book] WHERE ((([StateProv])='CA'))"
   ```

   Adding `DoCmd.RunSQL` to the SQL statement is necessary because, otherwise, VBA doesn't recognize the SQL as being different from any other code in the procedure.

The final statement in the VBA Editor, after making all the necessary changes, looks like this:

```
Sub whatever()

    'Set SentWelcome field to True for all Houston addresses.
    DoCmd.RunSQL "UPDATE [Address Book] SET SentWelcome = True WHERE
          (((City)='Houston'))"

End Sub
```

Hiding warning messages

Typically when you run an action query — whether from Access or VBA — you get a warning message about what the query is about to do. That gives you a chance to change your mind before the query executes. However, when you're running action queries from VBA, you might want them to just "do their thing" without displaying any warnings or asking the user for permission.

The DoCmd object provides a simple means of hiding those warning messages. To prevent a warning message from appearing when your code runs an action query, place the following line anywhere above the line that runs the action query:

```
DoCmd.SetWarnings False
```

To get warning messages back to normal after the query runs, use this statement in your code:

```
DoCmd.SetWarnings True
```

The following example shows the sample procedure from the end of the preceding section with appropriate code added to hide warning messages just before the query runs and then set the warnings back to normal:

```
Sub whatever()

    'Hide warning messages presented by action queries.
    DoCmd.SetWarnings False

    'Set SentWelcome field to True for all Houston addresses.
    DoCmd.RunSQL "UPDATE [Address Book] SET SentWelcome = True WHERE
            (((City)='Houston'))"

    'Get warning messages back to normal.
    DoCmd.SetWarnings True

End Sub
```

You might be wondering whether select queries show warnings, because they don't change data. The answer is a definite no. In fact, if you just run a select query by using DoCmd.RunSQL in code, absolutely nothing happens on-screen. That's because, to use select queries in VBA, you have to store the results of the query in a *recordset*. We talk about how recordsets work in Chapter 8. In this chapter, we stay focused on action queries (and SQL statements) that make changes to data stored in tables.

Storing SQL statements in variables

You can store SQL statements in variables, just as you can store text in variables. This can help with those extremely long SQL statements that seem to extend forever past the right margin of the Code window. Many programmers use this technique of building a long SQL statement from smaller chunks and storing the statement in a variable. As an example, here's a series of VBA statements that build and execute a single lengthy SQL statement from smaller chunks:

```
'Create string variable (storage place) named mySQL.
Dim mySQL As String

'Add lengthy SQL statement to mySQL in chunks.
mySQL = "UPDATE Orders SET"
                'Leading spaces below ensure spaces between words.
mySQL = mySQL & " InvRecPrinted = True, LabelPrinted = True"
mySQL = mySQL & " WHERE (((PONumber) Is Null)"
mySQL = mySQL & " AND ((CCType)='MC'))"
'Line above uses single quotation marks inside double quotation marks.

'Now, mySQL contains the complete SQL statement,
'so hide warnings and execute the SQL statement.
DoCmd.SetWarnings False
DoCmd.RunSQL mySQL

'Update query has now been performed. Back to normal warnings.
DoCmd.SetWarnings True
```

For the goods on variables, read about storing data in variables and constants in Chapter 4.

As daunting as the preceding code looks, it's not so bad if you read it as it would execute, one step at a time from top to bottom. The first statement, `Dim mySQL As String`, sets aside a cubbyhole of storage space in which you can store some text. In code, refer to the contents of that cubbyhole as `mySQL` (although we could have used any name here).

The next statement, `mySQL = "UPDATE Orders SET"`, stores the chunk of text in the quotation marks in the `mySQL` variable. So now the cubbyhole contains `"UPDATE ORDERS SET"`.

The next statement changes the contents of that variable by creating a new string that consists of the current contents of the variable (`mySQL`) concatenated with (`&`) the string `" InvRecPrinted = True, LabelPrinted = True"`. By the time that line is finished being executed, the `mySQL` variable contains this line:

```
UPDATE Orders SET InvRecPrinted = True, LabelPrinted =
           True
```

Notice the addition of the blank space at the start of the second string. That blank space is added to make ensure that a blank space appears between `SET` and `InvRecPrinted`.

The ampersand (`&`) is used to concatenate — or join — two strings. Use the ampersand when you want to join one or more smaller string values into one string value. This character is especially useful when you're creating SQL statements in code because these statements can get quite long.

The following two lines of code do the same as the previous line in that each adds more text to the string stored in `mySQL`. The `mySQL = mySQL & "` `WHERE (((PONumber) Is Null)"` statement tacks part of a `WHERE` clause (criterion) onto the string (again preceded by a blank space). Then the statement `mySQL = mySQL & " AND ((CCType)='MC'))"` tacks on a blank space and its chunk of text.

The single quotation marks inside the string are required in order to avoid conflict with the double quotation marks surrounding the whole string.

By the time the final `mySQL = mySQL & ...` statement has executed, the variable named `mySQL` contains the following SQL statement, which exactly matches all the syntax required of a valid SQL statement:

```
UPDATE Orders InvRecPrinted = True, LabelPrinted = True WHERE (((PONumber) Is
            Null) AND ((CCType)='MC'))
```

The statement is too lengthy to show on one line in this book, but in the `mySQL` variable, it's definitely one long, valid SQL statement. (Like most SQL statements that you see in this book, this example is just a copy-and-paste job from a query's SQL view.)

The next statement in the code, `DoCmd.SetWarnings False`, just hides the warning message that action queries otherwise show. Then comes the execution of the SQL statement in this statement:

```
DoCmd.RunSQL mySQL
```

By the time VBA gets to this statement, it knows that the name `mySQL` refers to a cubbyhole that we told it to create earlier. So it knows that it really needs to replace the name `mySQL` with the contents of the variable named `mySQL` before it does anything else. First, it does a quick substitution, by replacing the variable name with its contents, as shown here:

```
DoCmd.RunSQL "UPDATE Orders SET InvRecPrinted = True, LabelPrinted = True WHERE
            (((PONumber) Is Null) AND ((CCType)='MC'))"
```

The preceding statement is what VBA does when it executes the statement. It runs the update query specified in the SQL statement. (Technically, it's all executed as one long line — it's just too wide to show it that way in this book.)

When the action query is finished, the next statement — `DoCmd.SetWarnings True` — sets the warning messages to their normal status.

Because code is building the SQL statement, the code can also make decisions about how to build the statement along the way. Thus, a VBA procedure could customize a SQL statement to a particular need or situation. In short, a procedure can make decisions about how to "write itself" before it executes itself. (Funky but true.)

Creating Tables from VBA

As you know (we hope), you can create tables in Access interactively, by using Table Design. If you've ever created a Make-Table action query, you know that you can build a new table from any existing table or query. VBA can also create new tables, either from existing tables and queries or from scratch.

Creating new tables from existing tables

The easiest way to use VBA to create a new table from an existing table is to first design a Make-Table query in Access. [In Query Design view, click the Make Table command in the Query Type group on the (Query Tools) Design tab, and then specify the name of the table to create. Refer to Figure 7-5.] Figure 7-7 shows an example of a Make-Table query that selects fields from a couple of related tables, where the `Paid` field contains `False`. This query creates a new table named `UnpaidOrdersSummaryTable`, which is set in the query's `Destination Table` property.

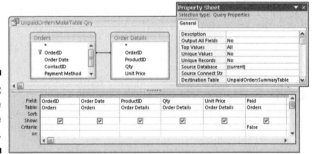

Figure 7-7:
Sample
Make-Table
query.

Viewing the SQL statement for the Make-Table query shown in Figure 7-7 reveals the following:

```
SELECT Orders.OrderID, Orders.[Order Date], [Order Details].ProductID, [Order
        Details].Qty, [Order Details].[Unit Price], Orders.Paid
        INTO UnpaidOrdersSummaryTable FROM Orders INNER JOIN [Order
        Details] ON Orders.OrderID = [Order Details].OrderID WHERE
        (((Orders.Paid)=False));
```

Even in the SQL statement, the only indication that this is a Make-Table query are the words `INTO UnpaidOrdersSummaryTable`, which tell the query to store a copy of the records that the query produces into a table named `UnpaidOrdersSummaryTable`.

When a Make-Table query executes, it first checks whether the destination table (UnPaidOrdersSummaryTable, in this example) exists. If that table exists, it's deleted before the new table is created. If you want to add new records to an existing table, use an Append query rather than a Make-Table query.

Of course, the Make-Table query shown here is just an example. The technique for converting the Make-Table query to code is the same for any query — it's simply a matter of copying the SQL statement to the Code window and tweaking the statement so that it works in VBA. The following code shows how the Make-Table query shown in Figure 7-7 looks after being properly formatted to work in a VBA procedure:

```
'Declare a variable to store SQL statement.
Dim mySQL As String

'Build mySQL string from query's SQL statement.
mySQL = "SELECT Orders.OrderID, Orders.[Order Date], [Order Details].ProductID,"
mySQL = mySQL & " [Order Details].Qty, [Order Details].[Unit Price],
                Orders.Paid"
mySQL = mySQL & " INTO UnpaidOrdersSummaryTable"
mySQL = mySQL & " FROM Orders INNER JOIN [Order Details]"
mySQL = mySQL & " ON Orders.OrderID=[Order Details].OrderID"
mySQL = mySQL & " WHERE (((Orders.Paid)=False))"

'Now turn off warning and execute the SQL statement.
DoCmd.SetWarnings False
DoCmd.RunSQL mySQL
DoCmd.SetWarnings True
```

Creating a new, empty table from VBA

You can also create tables programmatically from VBA by using a SQL CREATE TABLE statement with the syntax

```
CREATE TABLE tableName (field type (size)) [, ...]"
```

where

- *tableName* is the name of the table to create.
- *field* specifies the name of one field in the table.
- *type* specifies the data type of the field.
- *size* indicates the size of the field.
- ... indicates that you can repeat the field type (size) combination for each field you want to define in the table.

For example, the following SQL statement creates a new, empty table named myTable that contains a Text field named ProductID that's 5 characters wide and a Text field named VendorList that's 255 characters wide:

```
CREATE TABLE myTable ([ProductID] text (20), [VendorList] text (255))
```

To create that table from within a procedure, use DoCmd.RunSQL to execute the CREATE TABLE statement

```
DoCmd.RunSQL "CREATE TABLE myTable ([ProductID] text (20), [VendorList] text
    (255))"
```

as one long line in your code. As always, if the SQL statement is lengthy, you can break it into chunks, as shown here:

```
Dim mySQL As String
mySQL = "CREATE TABLE myTable"
mySQL = mySQL & " ([ProductID] text (20),"
mySQL = mySQL & " [VendorList] text (255))"

DoCmd.RunSQL mySQL
```

Closing and deleting tables through VBA

In some situations, you might want your VBA code to close a table if it's open, or even delete an entire table from the database. (You can't delete an open object, so if you want to delete a table, you have to close it first.) Suppose that you want to write a procedure that checks whether a table named myTable already exists in the current database. If that table already exists and is open, you want the procedure to close it. Finally, assuming that the table exists, you want your code to delete the table.

You could write the procedure as follows. In your own code, replace the table name myTable with the name of the table you want to close and delete. The rest of the code will work as it stands:

```
'Look at each object in All Tables collection.
Dim obj As AccessObject
For Each obj In Application.CurrentData.AllTables

    'If the current table is named myTable...
    If obj.Name = "myTable" Then
        'and if MyTable is open (loaded)...
        If obj.IsLoaded Then
'...close myTable
            DoCmd.Close acTable, "myTable", acSaveNo
        End If
```

```
       'Now delete the closed myTable table.
       DoCmd.DeleteObject acTable, "myTable"
       End If
Next obj

'By the time execution gets here, the table named
'myTable no longer exists in the current database.
```

To close the open table, the code uses the `Close` method of the `DoCmd` object. To delete the table, the code uses the `DeleteObject` method of the `DoCmd` object. All the rest of the code is really about finding out whether the table already exists and is open to make sure that the code doesn't attempt to close an open or a nonexistent table. Those steps are necessary because if the code attempts to close an open or nonexistent table, the code fails and throws an error message on-screen.

Adding Records to a Table

VBA can also *append* (add) records to any table that already exists in the database without deleting or changing any records that might already be in the table. If the records to be appended to the table already exist in some other table, you can use a simple append query (in Access) to generate the appropriate SQL statement.

For example, Figure 7-8 shows an append query that selects several fields and records from two related tables in a database. The name of the destination table, `PaidOrderSummary`, is visible in the query's `Destination Table` property. You specify the destination table's name after choosing Append Query from the Query Type group on the (Query Tools) Design tab. When you view the SQL statement for the query, you also see the destination table's name there, as shown here:

```
INSERT INTO PaidOrderSummary ( OrderID, [Order Date], ProductID, Qty, [Unit
        Price] ) SELECT Orders.OrderID, Orders.[Order Date], [Order
        Details].ProductID, [Order Details].Qty, [Order Details].[Unit
        Price] FROM Orders INNER JOIN [Order Details] ON Orders.OrderID =
        [Order Details].OrderID WHERE  (((Orders.Paid)=True));
```

Because an append query is an action query, you can execute it by using `DoCmd.RunSQL` just as you can execute other action queries shown in this chapter. You can add the various portions of the lengthy SQL statement to a variable and then execute the statement in the variable:

```
'Declare a string variable named mySQL.
Dim mySQL As String

'Put a lengthy SQL statement into mySQL (in chunks).
mySQL = "INSERT INTO PaidOrderSummary"
mySQL = mySQL & " (OrderID, [Order Date], ProductID, Qty, [Unit Price] ) "
mySQL = mySQL & " SELECT Orders.OrderID, Orders.[Order Date], "
mySQL = mySQL & " [Order Details].ProductID, [Order Details].Qty,"
mySQL = mySQL & " [Order Details].[Unit Price]"
mySQL = mySQL & " FROM Orders INNER JOIN [Order Details]"
mySQL = mySQL & " ON Orders.OrderID = [Order Details].OrderID"
mySQL = mySQL & " WHERE (((Orders.Paid)=True))"

'Turn off warnings and append the records as specified in the SQL.
DoCmd.SetWarnings False
DoCmd.RunSQL mySQL
DoCmd.SetWarnings True
```

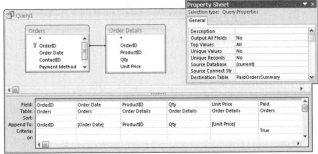

Figure 7-8:
A sample
append
query in
Access
Query
Design.

Appending a single record with SQL

You can also use the `SQL INSERT INTO` statement to add a single record to a table. However, the syntax is a little tricky, as are the rules that determine how you do it. For example, you can't append an entirely blank record to a table that contains required fields because the table doesn't accept the record until all requirements have been met.

The basic syntax for inserting a single record into a table in SQL is

```
INSERT INTO tblName [(fldName [,...]) VALUES (value
         [,...])
```

where

- ✔ *tblName* is the name of the table to which the record should be appended.

- ✔ *fldName* is the name of the field that is assigned a value.

✔ *value* is the value you want to store in the field.

✔ [, ...] means that you can list multiple fields and values, if you want, as long as you separate their names with commas.

The order of values being assigned to fields must match the order of the field names in the statement. For example, the database might contain a table named Stats that contains a Date/Time field named Submitted, a Yes/No field named Paid, and a Text field named Status (among other fields). The following SQL statement adds one record to that table, by placing the current date in the Submitted field, False in the Paid field, and No Reply in the Status field:

```
INSERT INTO Stats ( Submitted, Paid, Status ) VALUES (Date(), False, 'No Reply')
```

To execute the statement from VBA, just put the whole SQL statement in quotation marks next to a DoCmd.RunSQL statement, as usual. Or you can build it from shorter lines, as shown here:

```
Dim mySQL As String
mySQL = "INSERT INTO Stats ( Submitted, Paid, Status )"
mySQL = mySQL & " VALUES (Date(), False, 'No Reply')"
DoCmd.RunSQL mySQL
```

Query to append one record

You can create a query that appends a single record to a table, although the way you create the query is a little weird. The resulting SQL statement doesn't exactly match the syntax that we described earlier, either. But it all works and would definitely be easier than trying to write a lengthy SQL statement by hand.

The trick is to create a new query that doesn't have any tables at the top of the Query design window. Or, if a table is at the top of the query, right-click the table and choose Delete so that no tables are at the top. Click the Append button on the (Query Tools) Design tab to change the query to an append query, and specify the name of the table into which the query should append its record.

In the Field row of the QBE grid, you need to provide a value for at least one field in the table. The syntax is *name: value*, where *name* can be any name, and *value* is the value that you want to store in a field. Then, in the Append To row, choose the field into which you want to place the value. For example, the query in Figure 7-9 appends a single record with the current date in the Submitted field, False in the Paid field, and No Reply in the Status field. The figure also shows the SQL statement for the query.

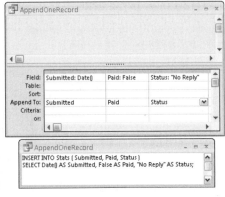

Figure 7-9:
Sample
append
query and
its SQL
view.

Even though the syntax of the SQL statement for the query doesn't look like the syntax that we describe earlier, the statement executes just fine in VBA. Here's how you can write the code to execute that statement (and temporarily turn off warning messages):

```
Dim mySQL As String
mySQL = "INSERT INTO Stats ( Submitted, Paid, Status )"
mySQL = mySQL & " SELECT Date() AS Submitted, False AS Paid,"
mySQL = mySQL & " 'No Reply' AS Status"
'Note single quotation marks inside double quotation marks above.

DoCmd.SetWarnings False
DoCmd.RunSQL mySQL
DoCmd.SetWarnings True
```

Changing and Deleting Table Records

Any Access update query or delete query also converts nicely to VBA. For example, you might keep track of which new customers you've sent e-mail to by using a `Yes/No` field named `SentWelcome` in a table. Customers who have been sent the message have `SentWelcome` set to `True`; customers who haven't been sent the message have `SentWelcome` set to `False`. For the sake of example, say that this table also has a field named `Email` that's either the `Text` or `Hyperlink` data type that contains each customer's e-mail address.

Now suppose that you want to write some code that automatically changes the contents of the `SentWelcome` field to `True` for all AOL customers. You create an update query that includes the `SentWelcome` field and set its `Update To` row to `True` to change the contents of that field to `True`. Then you also need a criterion to prevent the change from occurring in all records. In this case, where you want to update only records that have `@aol.com` in the Email field, the criterion expression is InStr([Email],'@aol.com')>0. The entire update query would look like Figure 7-10. (Because it's a small query, we managed to fit both the Query Design and SQL views of the query into one figure.)

Figure 7-10:
A sample update query (two views).

Don't experiment with a delete query or an update query against a table that contains data that you can't afford to lose or ruin. Your best bet is to work in a copy of your database so that you don't have to worry about losing any important information.

When you use the standard method of getting a SQL statement into a variable and executed from VBA, the code that's needed to turn off warnings, do the update, and turn warnings back on looks like this:

```
'Build SQL statement into string variable named mySQL.
Dim mySQL As String
mySQL = "UPDATE Customers"
mySQL = mySQL & " SET Customers.SentWelcome = True"
mySQL = mySQL & " WHERE (InStr([Email],'@aol.com')>0)"

'Hide warning and do the update.
DoCmd.SetWarnings False
DoCmd.RunSQL mySQL
DoCmd.SetWarnings True
```

If you want your code to delete records from a table, just create a delete query that specifies the records to be deleted and put its SQL statement into VBA code. For example, Figure 7-11 shows an Access delete query in both Query Design view and SQL view. That particular query deletes all records from a table named PaidOrderSummary.

Figure 7-11:
Sample
delete
query.

As with any action query, to get the SQL statement to execute from VBA and delete all records from the table, you need to execute the SQL statement with DoCmd.RunSQL. Because this particular SQL statement is so short, there's no need to store it in a variable in chunks. The following statement is sufficient:

```
DoCmd.RunSQL "DELETE PaidOrderSummary.* FROM PaidOrderSummary"
```

Performing an Action Query on One Record

No rule says that an action query must work on multiple records in a table. Any action query can perform its task on just one record in the table, as long as there's a way to uniquely identify the record. If the table has a primary key, isolating a record by a value in that field is simple.

Suppose that you have a table named Customers that contains an AutoNumber field named CustID that acts as the primary key. You can easily isolate any customer in the table by using the customer's CustID value as the Criteria entry for the CustID field. Figure 7-12 shows a delete query that uses such a criterion to delete only Customer #14 from the Customers table. The SQL statement reflects the criterion that the CustID field equals 14 by the addition of WHERE (((Customers.CustID)=14)) to the SQL statement.

Not all the parentheses in that WHERE clause are necessary, nor is the table name Customers. The WHERE clause could be written more simply as WHERE CustID=14 or with the field name in square brackets, as in WHERE [CustID]=14.

Figure 7-12:
Sample
query to
delete one
record.

Working with Select Queries and Recordsets

To this point in this chapter, we focus mainly on Access action queries that you execute from VBA by using DoCmd.RunSQL. Select queries, which only display data (and never change the contents of a table), are a completely different story. In Access, you don't run a select query. You simply switch from Query Design view to Datasheet view to see the records returned by that query. And in VBA, you don't use DoCmd.RunSQL to execute a select query. Rather, you store the results of the query in a weird, invisible thing called a *recordset*.

When you click Queries in the Access Navigation pane, icons for saved action queries generally include an exclamation point (!), and icons for saved select queries have no exclamation point.

Look at an example, starting in Access. The left side of Figure 7-13 shows a fairly simple select query (in Query Design view) that displays the fields named FirstName, LastName, and Email from a table named Customers. The criteria expression, Like "*@aol.com*" , limits the display to those records that have the characters @aol.com somewhere in the e-mail address. Switching that query to Datasheet view shows the query results, as in the lower-right half of that same figure.

In VBA, that Datasheet view of the query shows exactly what a recordset that uses the same SQL statement of the query produces. As with any query, you can easily view (and copy) a select query's SQL statement by right-clicking the query's title bar and choosing SQL View. However, unlike in the Datasheet view of a query, which is plainly visible on-screen, a recordset is visible only to VBA, not to humans.

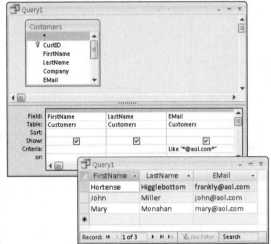

Figure 7-13:
Simple
select query
and its
datasheet
results.

Creating a recordset in VBA usually takes several lines of code. As always, you have a ton of options for how to write the code. The syntax of statements that you need in order to create a recordset from one or more tables in the current database generally looks like this:

```
Dim cnnX As ADODB.Connection
Set cnnX = CurrentProject.Connection
Dim myRecordSet As New ADODB.Recordset
myRecordSet.ActiveConnection = cnnX

myRecordSet.Open SQLstatement
```

where

- *cnn* is a variable name of your choosing that defines the connection.

- *myRecordSet* is the name that you want to give to your recordset. (You use whatever name you put here to refer to the recordset from elsewhere in the procedure.)

- *SQLstatement* is a valid SQL statement that isn't an action query (for example, the SQL from any select query's SQL view, or the name of a table or query in the current database).

If the code shows you an error message stating that it doesn't know what the ADODB.Connection is, you have to tell VBA where to look for it. Choose Tools⇨References from the VBA Editor menu bar, scroll down to Microsoft ActiveX Data Objects 2.8 Library in the Available References list, and check the box next to it. Click OK and VBA knows what an ADODB.Connection is, even if you don't.

Start with a simple example. Suppose that you want to create a recordset named myRecordSet that contains all the fields and records from a table named Customers. In that case, you don't need SQL because using the table name in the myRecordSet.Open statement is sufficient, as shown here:

```
Dim cnn1 As ADODB.Connection
Set cnn1 = CurrentProject.Connection
Dim myRecordSet As New ADODB.Recordset
myRecordSet.ActiveConnection = cnn1

myRecordSet.Open "[Customers]"
```

If you want the recordset to contain only some fields and records from the Customers table, use a valid SQL statement in place of the whole table name. For example, the SQL statement SELECT FirstName, LastName FROM Customers creates a recordset that contains only the FirstName and LastName fields from the Customers table. Using that SQL statement in place of the table name in the code looks like this:

```
Dim cnn1 As ADODB.Connection
Set cnn1 = CurrentProject.Connection
Dim myRecordSet As New ADODB.Recordset
myRecordSet.ActiveConnection = cnn1

myRecordSet.Open "SELECT FirstName, LastName FROM Customers"
```

As with action queries, the SQL statement for a select query can be very long. To prevent super-wide lines in your code, you can store the SQL statement in a variable in chunks. Then use the variable name in place of a table name or SQL statement in the myRecordSet.Open statement. For example, the following SQL statement is from a query that shows the CustID, FirstName, LastName, and Email fields from a table named Customers but only for records where the Email address field is now empty (or *null*, in programmer lingo):

```
SELECT Customers.CustID, Customers.FirstName,
         Customers.LastName, Customers.Email
FROM Customers
WHERE (((Customers.Email) Is Null));
```

To use that SQL statement in VBA, you could write the code this way:

```
Dim cnn1 As ADODB.Connection
Set cnn1 = CurrentProject.Connection
Dim myRecordSet As New ADODB.Recordset
myRecordSet.ActiveConnection = cnn1
```

```
'We'll put lengthy SQL statement in variable named mySQL.
Dim mySQL As String
mySQL = "SELECT Customers.CustID, Customers.FirstName,"
mySQL = mySQL & " Customers.LastName, Customers.Email"
mySQL = mySQL & " FROM Customers"
mySQL = mySQL & " WHERE (((Customers.Email) Is Null))"

'Now we use mySQL variable name in statement below.
myRecordSet.Open mySQL
```

We suppose that any way you slice it, the code needed in order to create a
recordset is just plain ugly and intimidating. All those `Dim` and `Set` statements at the top of each example shown to this point in this section need to
be executed before the recordset is created with the `.Open` method. You
wouldn't have to use those *exact* lines: They're just the standard lines that
you use to build a recordset from a table or query in the current database.
However, you do have to define a connection and name for a recordset before
you can open it.

Defining a connection

Although a recordset is invisible to a human, it's a real object that VBA can
manipulate. You can think of a recordset as sort of an invisible, ghost image
of a datasheet that invisible VBA can manipulate (at lightning speeds, we
might add). But before VBA can even create such a ghost, it needs to know
where the tables for the ghost reside. That's where the first two statements,
shown as follows, come in:

```
Dim cnn1 As ADODB.Connection
Set cnn1 = CurrentProject.Connection
```

The first line declares to all VBA statements to all lines of code that follow
that it is creating a thing named cnn1 that will be an ADODB connection.
ADO, which stands for ActiveX Data Objects, is the object model we use to
create recordsets throughout this book. ADO isn't built into Access: It's an
object library that many programs use to manipulate data in Access tables.
For example, you could write VBA code in a Microsoft Excel or Word macro
to grab data from an Access table, if you use ADO.

To use ADO in VBA, you need to set a reference to Microsoft ActiveX Data
Object Library in the References dialog box. Like all object libraries, ADO is a
highly organized collection of objects, properties, and methods that you can
boss around with VBA to make databases do things. And, like all other things
you can manipulate with VBA, ADO objects, properties, and methods are
found in the Object Browser and also in the VBA Help.

DAO is not DOA, but ADO is A-OK

Originally, Access offered only one way to create a recordset: DAO (Data Access Objects). DAO used different words, like `DBEngine` and `WorkSpace`, to create recordsets. You might still see that in other code examples (but not in this book). In this book, we use the ADO (ActiveX Data Objects) technology to create and manipulate recordsets.

Ever since the introduction of ADO, a battle has taken place over which one is best to use. Some developers swear by ADO; others prefer DAO. Many developers thought that DAO would eventually go away as ADO grew in popularity, but Microsoft has added functionality to DAO for Access 2007. You can do a lot of the same things with ADO and DAO — just be aware that their syntax in VBA code is different.

So, what the heck does `Dim cnn1 As ADODB.Connection` mean? Well, the `Dim` statement is declaring to the rest of the code, "From this point on in this procedure, the name *cnn1* shall refer to an ActiveX Data Objects Database connection." The `cnn1` part is just a name we made up. It can be any valid variable name, including `X`, `myConnection`, `Connection01` — whatever you want it to be.

The next line of code, `Set cnn1 = CurrentProject.Connection`, gets more specific about what `cnn1` is all about. It says, "More specifically, *cnn1* is the connection to that data in the database we're working on." Both lines are required because there are lots of other things to which you can set a connection (none of which is particularly relevant to this book, though).

Defining the recordset and data source

Referring to most of the previous recordset examples, the second two lines of code declare what the recordset is and where it gets its data, as shown here:

```
Dim myRecordSet As New ADODB.Recordset
myRecordSet.ActiveConnection = cnn1
```

The first line declares to all the code that follows (within the current procedure) that the name `myRecordSet` refers from here on out to an ActiveX Data Objects Database recordset. That tells the rest of the code a lot about what `myRecordSet` is, but it doesn't say anything about where this `myRecordSet` thing will find data from which it can create recordsets. The next line of code, `myRecordSet.ActiveConnection = cnn1`, takes care of that problem, though, by setting the `myRecordSet` active connection to the connection we already defined as `cnn1`.

Filling the recordset with data

With the VBA statements that define a connection and name for the recordset out of the way, you can finally write the code that adds data to the table. That's where the `.Open` method comes into play. In all our earlier examples, we use a relatively simple statement to open the recordset. The full syntax for creating an ADO recordset looks like this:

```
myRecordSet.Open SQLStatement [,Connection] [,CursorType] [,LockType]
```

All the arguments after SQL statements are optional, so that's why you don't see them used in any of the preceding `myRecordSet.Open` statements in this chapter. Chances are that if you omit those arguments in your own `myRecordSet.Open` statements, your recordsets will work just fine, too. We bring them up here just so you know that other options are available, which can be particularly useful when modifying code written by other people. Here's what each of the optional arguments allows you to specify:

✔ *Connection* is the connection (not required if you already defined the connection by using `myRecordSet.ActiveConnection` in code).

✔ *CursorType* defines how VBA can access records in the recordset, and how simultaneous changes to the recordsets underlying data affect the contents of the recordset by using any of the following constants:

  • `adOpenDynamic`: Code can freely move the cursor through the records. Other users' additions, changes, and deletions carry over to the recordset.

  • `adOpenKeyset`: Code can freely move the cursor through the records. Other users' additions, changes, and deletions don't carry over to the recordset.

  • `adOpenStatic`: The recordset contains a snapshot of data that's no longer connected to the live data in any way, so other users' changes to the underlying table or query have no effect on the recordset. VBA can move the cursor freely through the recordset.

  • `adOpenForwardOnly`: The cursor can scroll down through records only; additions, changes, and deletions from other users are ignored. This is preferred when VBA just needs quick, brief access to a table to search for something or to count things (and also the default setting if you don't include this argument in your `.Open` statement).

✔ *LockType* determines how other users' simultaneous changes to the table or query are handled. The more commonly used constant names and lock types are listed here:

  • `adLockOptimistic`: Indicates *optimistic locking,* where records are locked only when you call the `.Update` method in your VBA code.

- adLockPessimistic: Indicates *pessimistic locking,* where records are locked automatically after a change (without calling the .Update method).

- adLockReadOnly: Indicates read-only records, whereby no changes are allowed to data in the recordset.

As an example of using a couple of arguments in a recordset's .Open method, the following code creates a forward-only, read-only recordset that gets its records from a table named Customers:

```
Dim myRecordSet As New ADODB.Recordset
myRecordSet.Open "[Customers]", CurrentProject.Connection, adOpenForwardOnly,
        adLockReadOnly
```

The syntax for ADO recordsets also allows you to specify optional arguments individually, using the syntax recordSetName.*property* = *value.* For example, the following lines create a recordset that connects to the current database (CurrentProject.CurrentConnection), sets the cursor type to adOpenDynamic, and sets the LockType to adLockOptimistic:

```
'Set up the connection, name it cnn1.
Dim cnn1 As ADODB.Connection
Set cnn1 = CurrentProject.Connection

'Define a new recordset and pre-define optional arguments.
Dim myRecordSet As New ADODB.Recordset
myRecordSet.ActiveConnection = cnn1
myRecordSet.CursorType = adOpenDynamic
myRecordSet.LockType = adLockOptimistic

'Fill recordset with data from Customers table
myRecordSet.Open "SELECT * FROM Customers"
```

Managing recordsets

After a recordset's .Open method has been executed, the recordset contains the fields and records specified by the table or SQL statement in the .Open statement. You don't see this recordset anywhere on-screen, but your VBA code can see and move through the records in the recordset.

For example, assuming that the current database contains a table named Customers — which in turn contains fields named LastName, FirstName, and Email (among other fields) — the following statements create a recordset of records from that table that have @aol.com in the Email field.

```
Dim cnn1 As ADODB.Connection
Set cnn1 = CurrentProject.Connection

Dim myRecordSet As New ADODB.Recordset
myRecordSet.ActiveConnection = cnn1

'Store the SQL statement in a variable.
Dim mySQL As String
mySQL = "SELECT FirstName, LastName, Email"
mySQL = mySQL & " FROM Customers"
mySQL = mySQL & " WHERE ([Email] Like '*@aol.com*')

myRecordSet.Open mySQL
```

Assume that the table named `Customers` contains three records that have `@aol.com` in the recordset. The invisible recordset named `myRecordSet` that's created in the preceding code would look something like Figure 7-14 (if you could see it).

Figure 7-14:
What a
recordset
would look
like if you
could see it.

FirstName	LastName	EMail
Hortense	Higglebottom	frankly@aol.com
John	Miller	john@aol.com
Mary	Monahan	mary@aol.com

After the recordset exists in code, you can use numerous methods of the ADODB recordsets to move the cursor through the recordset. (Like the recordset itself, the cursor is invisible, but VBA can still move that invisible cursor into any record in the recordset.) The syntax is generally *myRecordSet*.*method* where *myRecordSet* is the name of the recordset on which the method should be performed followed by a dot (.) and a valid method.

The cursor type of the recordset puts severe restrictions on which methods you can use. For maximum flexibility, use the `adOpenDynamic` cursor type option, described earlier in this chapter.

- ✔ *myRecordSet*.`MoveFirst`: Moves the cursor to the first record in the recordset

- ✔ *myRecordSet*.`MoveNext`: Moves the cursor to the next record in the recordset

- ✔ *myRecordSet*.`MovePrevious`: Moves the cursor to the previous record in the recordset

✔ *myRecordSet*.MoveLast: Moves the cursor to the last record in the recordset

In addition to the preceding methods, you can use the BOF (Beginning of File) and EOF (End of File) properties to determine whether the cursor is pointing at a specific record. For example, the following statement returns True only if the cursor is sitting above the first record in the recordset:

```
myRecordSet.BOF
```

The following statement returns True only if the cursor is already past the last record in the set (pointing at nothing):

```
myRecordSet.EOF
```

You often see these properties used in code that loops through records in a set one record at a time. For now, it's sufficient to know that the properties exist. Take a look next at how you can refer to fields in a record from VBA.

Referring to fields in a recordset

The columns (fields) in a recordset all have names, just as they do in tables. However, in VBA, each record is also a collection of fields, with the first (leftmost) field numbered 0; the next field, 1; the next, 2; and so forth. The full reference to a field by its number is *myRecordSet*.Fields(*x*) where *x* is a number. For example, VBA can refer to the columns in the recordset named myRecordSet as myRecordSet.Fields(0), myRecordSet.Fields(1), and myRecordSet.Fields(2), as illustrated in Figure 7-15.

```
myRecordSet.Fields(0)
```

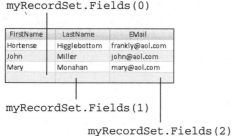

Figure 7-15: Referring to recordset fields by position.

```
myRecordSet.Fields(1)
```

```
                    myRecordSet.Fields(2)
```

Each field has properties and methods, too — for example, the Name property. When used as follows, it returns the name of the field at that position:

```
myRecordSet.Fields(0).Name
```

The Value property of a field, when used as follows, returns the field's contents:

```
myRecordSet.Fields(0).Value
```

You can refer to a field in a recordset by its name rather than by its number. To refer to a field by its name, replace the number in the preceding syntax with the name of the field enclosed in quotation marks. For example, the following statement returns the value of the field named Email in the current record in the recordset:

```
myRecordSet.Fields("Email").Value
```

Closing recordsets and collections

To close an open recordset, use the Close method with the recordset name. For example, to close an open recordset named myRecordSet, use the statement

```
myRecordSet.Close
```

You should also close the connection — after you close the recordset because the recordset uses the connection object — with the similar statement

```
cnn1.Close
```

The preceding statements close the recordset and connection only in terms of being able to manipulate data from VBA. The recordset and its connection, which you originally defined by using Dim and Set statements, should be cleared from memory too. Anytime you use a Set keyword to define something, you should clear it from memory after you're done using it by setting it to the keyword Nothing. For example, the following statements remove the recordset myRecordSet and the cnn1 connection from memory:

```
Set myRecordSet = Nothing
Set cnn1 = Nothing
```

Recordsets aren't the easiest things in the world to create and manipulate. Fortunately, you can often avoid creating and using recordsets to get a job done just by creating an action query to perform the job and executing the query's SQL statement by using DoCmd.RunSQL.

When an action query just doesn't cut it, you can always fall back on creating and manipulating table data through a recordset. You see a practical example of using recordsets in the next chapter.

Chapter 8

Putting Recordsets to Work

· ·

In This Chapter

▶ Working with objects and collections

▶ Making reading and modifying existing code easier

▶ Creating a procedure to skip over used mailing labels

▶ Tying a Sub procedure to a form event

· ·

*I*n this chapter, you put to work many of the concepts and techniques from earlier chapters by creating a custom procedure named SkipLabels(). This procedure is handy for anyone who prints mailing labels on individual label sheets by printing on sheets that are missing some labels.

Before you get into writing SkipLabels(), though, you need to know a few more general techniques. In particular, you need to discover what programmers call *looping through collections,* or *enumerating,* for short. You also look at some general info on reading and modifying existing code.

Looping through Collections

As we mention in Chapter 5, Access contains objects and collections whose properties and methods can be controlled through VBA. Each collection has a specific name. For example, the CurrentProject.AllForms collection contains the names of every form in the current database.

Every collection has a .Count property that describes how many objects are in the collection. For example, CurrentProject.AllForms.Count represents the number of forms in the current database. For example, if you type **? CurrentProject.AllForms.Count** into the VBA Editor's Immediate window and press Enter, you see the number of forms contained within the database.

Objects within a collection are always *enumerated* (numbered), starting with 0 (zero). For example, the first item in the `AllForms` collection is `AllForms(0)` (pronounced "all forms sub zero"); the second item in the `AllForms` collection is `AllForms(1)`; the third is `AllForms(2)`; and so on. In the collection shown in Figure 8-1, Address Book Form is `AllForms(0)`; Email Messages Form is `AllForms(1)`; EmailWarningDialog is `AllForms(2)`; and so on.

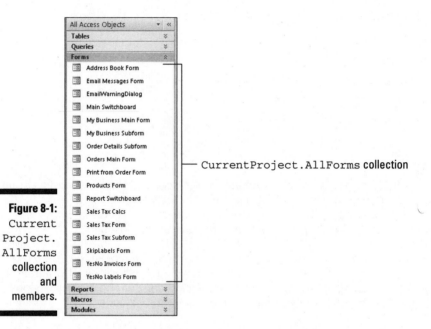

`CurrentProject.AllForms` collection

Figure 8-1:
`Current`
`Project.`
`AllForms`
collection
and
members.

As discussed in Chapter 5, an object can also be a collection. That is, it can be both an object and a collection at the same time. For example, a form is an object, but a form is also a collection of controls. From VBA (or an Access expression), you refer to an open form's `Controls` collection by using the syntax

```
Forms!("formName").Controls
```

where *formName* is the name of an open form. As with any collection, the controls in a form are enumerated (numbered starting with zero). For example, the first control on a form is *formName*`.Controls(0)`, the next is *formName*`.Controls(1)`, and so forth. Figure 8-2 shows an example using a form named `MyForm` that contains nine controls, numbered this way:

BizName text box	`MyForm.Controls(0)`
Biz Name label	`MyForm.Controls(1)`
BizPhone text box	`MyForm.Controls(2)`
Phone label	`MyForm.Controls(3)`
BizURL text box	`MyForm.Controls(4)`
Web Site label	`MyForm.Controls(5)`
BizEmail text box	`MyForm.Controls(6)`
Email label	`MyForm.Controls(7)`
Close button	`MyForm.Controls(8)`

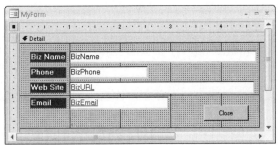

Figure 8-2:
A form as a
collection of
controls.

Using For Each loops

The specific number assigned to each item in a collection isn't terribly important. What is important is that VBA provides some special commands for looping through (or *enumerating*) a collection, where the code looks at each object in a collection either to get information about it or to change it. The special code is a slight variation on the `For...Next` loop called a `For Each...Next` loop. The basic syntax for the `For Each...Next` loop is

```
For Each objectType in collectionName
    '...code to be performed on each object
Next
```

where *objectType* is one of the object type names listed in Column 2 of Table 8-1, and *collectionName* is the name of a collection from Column 3. Note that some collections are specific objects, too. For example, in Table 8-1, *formName* needs to be replaced with the name of an open form, and *ctrlName* needs to be replaced with the name of a specific control on an open form.

Table 8-1	Object Types and Collection Names for For Each...Next Loops	
Object	*Object Type*	*Collection Name*
Table	`AccessObject`	`CurrentData.AllTables`
Query	`AccessObject`	`CurrentData.AllQueries`
Form	`AccessObject`	`CurrentProject.AllForms`
Report	`AccessObject`	`CurrentProject.AllReports`
Open form	`Form`	`Application.Forms` (Open forms)
Open report	`Report`	`Application.Reports` (Open reports)
Control	`Control`	`Forms!("`*`formName`*`").Controls`
Property	`Property`	`Forms![`*`formName`*`]![`*`ctrlName`*`].Properties`
Recordset field	`ADODB.Field`	*`recordsetName`*`.Fields`

The `Forms` collection refers to all forms that are open. The `AllForms` collection refers to all forms in the current database, whether they're open or not.

For example, this `For Each...Next` loop looks at each object in the `Forms` collection:

```
For Each AccessObject in CurrentProject.AllForms
    '...code to act on each form goes here
Next
```

Here's a `For Each...Next` loop that looks at each control on an open form named `MyForm`:

```
For Each Control in Forms!MyForm.Controls
    '...code to act on each control goes here
Next
```

For an example you can try out, open a database that already contains some tables and forms. Within that database, click the Create tab, and then select the Module command from the Macro drop-down menu to create a new, empty module. Now you're in the VBA Editor.

From the menu bar in the VBA Editor, choose Insert⇨Procedure. In the Add Procedure dialog box that opens, type a simple name (like **test**), choose Sub as the function procedure type, and click OK. You see the lines `Public Sub test()` and `End Sub` in the Code window.

Within the procedure, type some code to test. For example, you could type the following `For Each` loop to try out looping through the `AllForms` collection:

```
For Each AccessObject In CurrentProject.AllForms
    Debug.Print AccessObject.Name
Next
```

When executed, the `For Each...Next` loop repeats once for each form that's contained within the current database. Within the loop, the `Debug.Print` statement just prints the name of the current object in the collection (using the AccessObject's `Name` property).

As you can read in Chapter 12, `Debug.Print` is often used as a debugging tool. Here, you use `Debug.Print` just to see the name of each object that the `For Each...Next` loop encounters.

Whenever you add a `Sub` procedure to a module, you can test it out just by typing its name (without the following parentheses). In this case, the procedure is named `test`. After you get the whole procedure typed into the Code window, as in the top of Figure 8-3, type **test** into the Immediate window and press Enter to run the code. With each pass through the loop, the code prints the name of the next form in the database; you see the results in the Immediate window. For example, Figure 8-3 shows the results of running the test procedure in one of our databases.

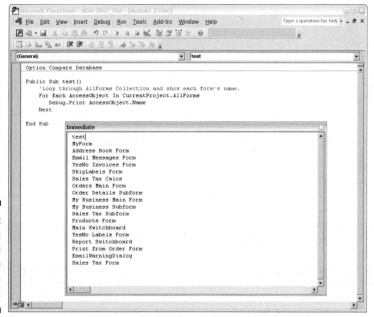

Figure 8-3:
Testing
some code
in the
Immediate
window.

If you change the name `CurrentProject.AllForms` to `CurrentData.AllTables` in the test procedure shown in Figure 8-3 and then run the procedure again, the code lists the name of every table in the current database. Likewise, changing `CurrentData.AllTables` to `CurrentData.AllQueries` lists all the queries in the current database.

Assume now that you want to create a `For Each` loop that looks at each control on an open form named `Products Form`. (This code works only in a database that has a form named `Product Form` and when that form is open.) In this case, `Forms![Products Form].Controls` is the name of the collection, and each object in the collection is a control. Thus, a `For Each` loop to display the name of each control in the Immediate window looks like this:

```
For Each Control In Forms![Products Form].Controls
    Debug.Print Control.Name
Next
```

All objects in Access have a `.Name` property that returns the name of that particular object. All collections have a `.Count` property that reflects the number of items in the collection.

Using shorter names for objects

When you look at code written by other people, you often see a slight variation on the `For Each` loop where programmers use `Dim` statements to assign an object to a short variable name. Then the programmer uses that short name in the `For Each` loop. This helps prevent long lines of code that are hard to read.

Even though you use a `Dim` statement to create a short name, you don't assign a data type to the variable. Rather, you assign an object type. For example, each of the following `Dim` statements is perfectly valid. The comment after each `Dim` statement describes what that `Dim` statement declares:

```
Dim myObject As AccessObject    'MyObject is a placeholder for any object
Dim myForm As Form              'MyForm is a placeholder for any form
Dim myReport As Report          'MyReport is a placeholder for any report
Dim myControl As Control        'MyControl is a placeholder for any control
Dim MyProp As Property          'MyProp is a placeholder for any property
```

Each `Dim` statement in the preceding list is declaring an *object variable*. The difference between a regular variable and an object variable is that a regular variable just stores a number or some text in a cubbyhole. An object variable refers to an entire object. The syntax for assigning an object to an object variable is

```
Set name = object
```

For example, the following lines of code declare the short name `Ctrl` as a placeholder for any control object and the short name `Frm` as a placeholder for any form. The `Set` statement then assigns the open form named `Products Form` to the `Frm` object variable name:

```
Dim Ctrl As Control
Dim Frm As Form
Set Frm = Forms![Products Form]
```

In a loop that looks at each control of the form, you can use the short name `Ctrl` where you would have used the full word `Control`. And you can use `Frm` where otherwise you would have had to type **Forms![Products Form]**, as shown here:

```
For Each Ctrl In Frm.Controls
    Debug.Print Ctrl.Name
Next
```

Suppose that you have an open form named `Products Form` and on that form is a control named `Selling Price`. Remember that every control has its own, unique set of properties. To create a `For Each` loop that lists the name of every property for the `Selling Price` control on `Products Form`, you could either use this syntax

```
For Each Property In Forms![Products Form].[Selling Price].Properties
    Debug.Print Property.Name
Next
```

or write the code this way:

```
Dim ctrl As Control
Dim prp As Property
Set ctrl = Forms![Products Form].[Selling Price]
For Each prp In ctrl.Properties
    Debug.Print prp.Name
Next
```

The result is the same either way — the name of each property for the control named `Selling Price` appears in the Immediate window.

In real life, you wouldn't create such loops just to have them print names of objects in the Debug window. More likely, you'll do other types of operations on objects in a collection. You can place as many statements as you want between the `For Each` and `Next` statements. Any code between those statements is executed once for each object in the collection, just like the `Debug.Print` statement is executed once for every object in each preceding collection example.

One main reason we even mention all this business with `For Each` loops and `Dim` statements is that when you try to modify existing code, you're likely to come across many situations where the programmer uses a `For Each` loop to look at each object in a collection. While we're on the topic of reading other people's code, look in the next section at some more VBA rules and how you can use those rules to make more sense of any VBA code that you ever choose to read or modify.

Tips on Reading and Modifying Code

Many programmers start their careers by trying to modify existing code rather than trying to write their own code from scratch. Before you can modify existing code to suit your purposes, though, you need to be able to read and understand what the existing code is doing.

When you're viewing existing code in the Code window, you can easily get help with any keyword in that code. Just select (double-click) the keyword with which you need help. Then press F1 to summon the Help window. However, not every single word in VBA code is a VBA keyword. For example, variable names and field names — which you make up on your own — aren't part of the VBA language, so you can't get any help with those in the VBA Editor. For example, in the statement

```
Dim X As String
```

X is just a made-up variable name, not a keyword that's built into VBA. You could, though, select either the `Dim` or `String` term and press F1 to get help with either of those keywords.

Square brackets represent names

The rules for referring to field names in VBA are the same rules used in Access expressions. When referring to a field name that contains blank spaces, you must enclose the field name in square brackets, like this: [Sales Tax Rate]. If the field name contains no blank spaces, the square brackets are optional. For example, the name SalesTaxRates in VBA refers to a field named SalesTaxRates, even without the square brackets.

Many programmers put square brackets around all field names for a couple of reasons. For one, it's a good habit to get into so that you don't forget to use the square brackets when you need them. Second, the square brackets visually identify which parts of a statement are names, thus making the code easier to read. For example, you can tell that SalesTaxRate and State are names of things just by looking at the following example:

```
If [State]="CA" Then
    [SalesTaxRate] = 0.0775
Else
    [SalesTaxRate] = 0
End If
```

The square brackets around names apply to form names and object names, too. For example, in the following statement, `Products Form` is the name of a form, and `Selling Price` is the name of a field on that form. Both names are enclosed in square brackets because each name contains a blank space:

```
Forms![Products Form].[Selling Price]
```

Some programmers put square brackets around every part of an identifier, even parts of the name that don't require square brackets. For example, neither the following form name nor field name contains a space — nor does the word `Forms`. But because square brackets are optional when there's no space in the name, you can include them or not. Because none of the following hypothetical names contains a space, either version of the statement is perfectly okay (as long as an open form named `ProdForm` really contains a control named `SellPrice` in the current database):

```
[Forms]![ProdForm].[SellPrice]
```

```
Forms!ProdForm.SellPrice
```

Use the exclamation point (!), also called a *bang operator* by programmers, to separate object names in an identifier. For example, `Me!MyCombo` refers to the object named `MyCombo` on the current form. Use the period to precede a property or method name, such as `Controls.Count`. For more information, search the Access Help (not VBA Help) for *identifier*.

Other ways to refer to objects

You don't always have to refer to an object by its specific name. You can use some special names in code to refer to objects in Access, as listed here:

- `Me`: In a class module, the term `Me` refers to the form or report to which the class module is attached. For example, `Me![Selling Price]` is short for "the control named Selling Price on the form to which this code is attached."

- `CodeContextObject`: This refers to the name of the object in which the code is running. (In a class module, it's always the same as the form or report to which the class module is attached.)

- `Screen.ActiveControl`: This refers to whatever control has the focus right now.

Each of the preceding names supports a Name property, which you can use to determine the name of the control. For example, take a look at the sample form named MyForm in Figure 8-4. Note the names of the controls on the form.

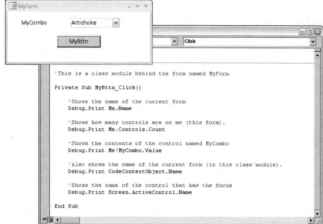

Figure 8-4:
A form,
some
controls,
and a class
procedure.

The class module shown in Figure 8-4 is the class module for that tiny MyForm form in the same figure. Note the use of various names in the code. Here's what each of those names returns when the module is run:

✔ Me.Name: Displays MyForm because MyForm is the name of the form to which the module is attached.

✔ Me.Controls.Count: Displays 3 because there are three controls on MyForm:

  • MyCombo label

  • MyCombo combo box

  • MyBttn button

Note that Me.Controls refers to the current form's Controls collection. The .Count property returns the number of items in the collection.

✔ Me!MyCombo.Value: Displays Artichoke, which is the value of the control named MyCombo on the current form.

✔ CodeContext.Name: Returns MyForm in this example because the class module always runs within the context of the current form, whose name in this case is MyForm.

✔ Screen.ActiveControl.Name: When executed in this example, returns MyBttn because the user clicks MyBttn to execute the code. MyBttn gets the focus when the user clicks it.

`Screen.ActiveControl.Value` returns whatever value is stored in whatever control on-screen now has the focus. Be careful when you're using `Screen.ActiveControl.Value` because not every control has a `Value` property.

The continuation character

When writing VBA code, you can break a long line into two or more lines by using a *continuation character,* which is just an underscore (_). Many programmers use continuation characters to break lengthy VBA statements into two or more lines, especially in code you see printed in books and such because the code needs to fit within the margins of the book.

For example, this fairly long line of code barely fits within the margins in this book:

```
Public Sub MySum(anyName As String, anyNum as Number)
```

Here's the same line broken into two lines by using a continuation character:

```
Public Sub MySum(anyName As String, _
    anyNum as Number)
```

When VBA sees the continuation character at the end of a statement, it knows that the line to follow is a continuation of the current statement, so it treats the two (or however many) lines as one long line.

If you want to use the continuation character when writing your own code, be aware that the continuation character never inserts blank spaces. If you need a blank space before the next word in a broken line, put a blank space in front of the continuation character. For example, the preceding example ends with a blank space and *then* the continuation character.

Also, be aware that you can't use a continuation character within a literal string in code. A *literal string* is any text that's enclosed in quotation marks. For example, the following line assigns a fairly long line of literal text to a control named `MyCombo` on the current form:

```
Me!MyCombo.Value = "Literal text in quotation marks"
```

It's perfectly okay to break the preceding line as follows because the continuation character isn't inside the literal text:

```
Me.MyCombo.Value = _
    "Literal text in quotation marks"
```

However, if you try to break the line within the literal text this way:

```
    Me.MyCombo.Value = "Literal text _
in quotation marks"
```

the code fails when executed, and you get a syntax error.

We should mention, though, that you can break long strings of literal text in code in a couple of ways. One is to just keep adding chunks of text to a string variable by using

```
variableName = variableName & "nextString"
```

You can see an example of that when building the `mySql` variable in Chapter 7.

The other way in which you can use an alternative to building a variable is to break the large literal into smaller literals, each surrounded by quotation marks. Concatenate (join) the strings by using the `&` sign, and break the line with a continuation character immediately after the `&` sign. For example, you could break the long literal, shown in the previous example, like this:

```
Me.MyCombo.Value = "Literal text" & _
    " in quotation marks"
```

Don't forget to include any blank spaces between words inside your quotation marks. For example, in the preceding line, the space before `in` is the blank space between the words `text` and `in`.

When VBA "unbreaks" the line, like this:

```
Me.MyCombo.Value = "Literal text" & " in quotation marks"
```

the whole line still makes sense and executes perfectly, by placing the words `Literal text in quotation marks` inside a control named `MyCombo` on the open form.

The first line in the following code example declares a string variable named `SomeString`. The next four lines are actually one long line that stores a lengthy chunk of text in the variable. Again, notice how each portion is contained within its own quotation marks. Each broken line ends with an `&` sign (to join strings) and an underscore (to continue the same line):

```
Dim SomeString As String
SomeString = "You can break VBA statements using" & _
    " an underscore, but not inside a literal. If" & _
    " you want to break a long literal, you have to" & _
    " enclose each chunk in its own quotation marks."
```

Okay, that's enough talk about general VBA stuff. The title of this chapter is "Putting Recordsets to Work," and you do that in the next section. It shows you how to create a real solution to a real problem (for some people, anyway) by using VBA, some recordsets, and a little bit of everything else described in previous chapters.

Skipping Over Used Mailing Labels

Suppose that you often use Access to print mailing labels on individual sheets. Each time you print a partial sheet of labels, you end up with some extra, unused labels on the sheet. If you reuse that sheet of labels in the printer, Access prints right on the missing labels. Basically, you can't reuse a sheet of labels that's already partially used. That's not good because labels aren't cheap.

A solution to the problem is to pop up a dialog box like the one shown in Figure 8-5 just before Access is about to print the labels. There, the user can specify how many empty places are on the first sheet. Then the user clicks the Print button. Access prints the labels and skips over the places left behind by used labels. No more wasted labels!

Figure 8-5:
Skip
Labels
Form form.

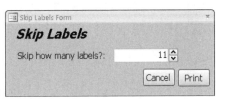

The solution to the problem requires a form and some VBA code. The form is needed because you need some way of telling the procedure how many labels to skip. In the example shown in Figure 8-5, the form itself is named `SkipLabelsForm`. The control in which the user types the number of labels to skip is named `LabelsToSkip`. The form also contains a Cancel button and a Print button named `CancelBttn` and `PrintBttn`, respectively, to which you can tie code later. Figure 8-6 shows the exact name of the form and controls in Design view.

The procedure you're about to create doesn't print labels. Your database needs a report for that. You can easily create a report for printing labels via the Access Label Wizard. In Access, click a table or query in the Navigation pane from which the report gets names and addresses. Click the Create tab, and then click Labels in the Reports group to start the Label Wizard. Follow the instructions to create a report for the desired labels, which fields you want on the labels, and how you want them to appear on each label. Don't forget to put spaces between the fields as you add them.

Figure 8-6:
The Skip
Labels
Form
shown in
Design
view.

For this example, we created a label format report named `Avery 8462 Labels` that's bound to a query named `SkipLabelsSampleQry`. However, you don't use those names in the VBA code because you want your `SkipLabels` procedure to work with any label-printing report, regardless of which table or query that report is bound to. So within the VBA code, refer to the report that prints the labels as `ReportName` and to the report's underlying table or query as `RecSource` (see Figure 8-7).

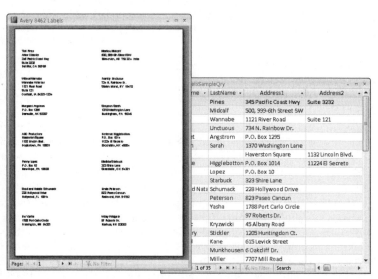

Figure 8-7:
The Label
report
(Report
Name; left
window)
and record-
source
(Rec
Source;
right
window).

For `SkipLabels` to work, it needs to pad the top of the recordsource for the report with one blank record for each label to be skipped over. For example, if `SkipLabels` needs to skip over seven empty spots on a sheet of labels, it inserts seven blank records at the top of the label report's recordsource. That way, when the sheet prints, the empty records get "printed" first (on the empty spots), and real data starts printing on the first available label. Figure 8-8 illustrates the basic idea.

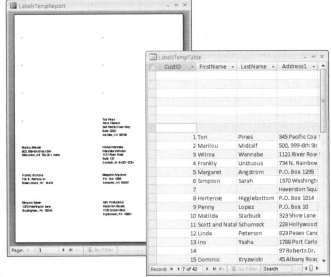

Blank records equal skipped-over labels.**Figure 8-8:**

Getting those blank records to the top of the report's recordsource is no small feat. Plus, you don't want `SkipLabels` to insert blank records into any real tables or make changes to any real reports in your database. `SkipLabels` creates and works with copies of the necessary objects: It always creates a report named `TempLabels` report that prints data from a table named `LabelsTempReport`. It creates both those objects, on-the-fly, each time.

Of course, you can't write `SkipLabels` in such a way that it always skips the same number of labels on the same report. You need to make it flexible enough to work with any number of empty labels on any label report. To provide flexibility, treat the number of labels to skip and the report names as *parameters* (values that get passed to an argument). In other words, write the `SkipLabels` procedure so that it can be executed at any time, using the syntax

```
SkipLabels(ReportName, LabelsToSkip)
```

where *ReportName* is the name of the report to print, and *LabelsToSkip* is a number indicating the number of blank labels at the top of the page. For example, the following statement tells `SkipLabels` to print the report named `Avery 8462 Labels` and skip over the first seven used labels on the first page:

```
SkipLabels("Avery 8462 Labels",7)
```

The code required to meet all these goals isn't brief, but you don't even need to look at it if you don't want to. All you need to really know about `SkipLabels` is how to get it into a standard module in your own database and how to call it to work with your own labels. You can skip to the section "Calling a Procedure from an Event," later in this chapter, if you would rather skip the morbid details for now.

Looking at How SkipLabels Works

If you're ready to look at some VBA code in detail, continue reading here. Be forewarned that the SkipLabels procedure (see Listing 8-1), which you're about to see in its entirety, isn't short. It probably looks more intimidating than need be. However, like all procedures, SkipLabels is just a series of small steps carried out in a specific order to achieve a goal; SkipLabels just has to go through more steps than most procedures.

Listing 8-1:   SkipLabels

```
Sub SkipLabels(ReportName As String, LabelsToSkip As Byte, _
    Optional PassedFilter As String)

    'Declare some variables.
    Dim MySQL As String
    Dim RecSource As String
    Dim FldNames As String
    Dim MyCounter As Byte
    Dim MyReport As Report

    'Turn off warning messages.
    DoCmd.SetWarnings False

    'Copy the original label report to LabelsTempReport
    DoCmd.CopyObject , "LabelsTempReport", acReport, ReportName

    'Open LabelsTempReport in Design view.
    DoCmd.OpenReport "LabelsTempReport", acViewDesign

    'Get name of report's underying table or query,
    'and store it here in the RecSource variable.
    RecSource = Reports!LabelsTempReport.RecordSource

    'Close LabelsTempReport
    DoCmd.Close acReport, "LabelsTempReport", acSaveNo

    'Declare an ADODB recordset named MyRecordSet
    Dim cnn1 As ADODB.Connection
    Dim MyRecordSet As New ADODB.Recordset
    Set cnn1 = CurrentProject.Connection
    MyRecordSet.ActiveConnection = cnn1
```

table or query to which the form or report is attached. However, VBA can get that information only if the report (or form) is open in Design view. In `SkipLabels`, this next statement opens `LabelsTempReport` in Design view:

```
'Open LabelsTempReport in Design view.
DoCmd.OpenReport "LabelsTempReport", acViewDesign
```

In the following lines of code, the first line stores in the variable named `RecSource` the name of the table or query from which the report gets its data. The second line then closes `LabelsTempReport` because there's no need for it to be open in Design view any more:

```
RecSource = Reports!LabelsTempReport.RecordSource

DoCmd.Close acReport, "LabelsTempReport", acSaveNo
```

Remember that from this point on in the code, the name `RecSource` refers to the name of the table or query in which data to be printed on labels is stored. The code can let that variable sit for now and move on to the task of creating `LabelsTempTable`, which is the table that `SkipLabels` uses to store blank records and data to be printed on labels.

Creating the recordset

`SkipLabels` uses a recordset (and some action queries) to do its job. The next lines in the procedure, as follows, create a recordset named `MyRecordSet`, which you see put to use shortly:

```
'Declare a recordset named MyRecordSet that gets its
'data from the current database's tables.
Dim cnn1 As ADODB.Connection
Dim MyRecordSet As New ADODB.Recordset
Set cnn1 = CurrentProject.Connection
MyRecordSet.ActiveConnection = cnn1
```

Creating LabelsTempTable from MyRecordSet

At this point in the code, an empty recordset named `MyRecordSet` is just waiting to get filled with some data. The following statement creates a SQL statement using whatever is stored in `RecSource` as the name of the table from which to get records:

```
MySQL = "SELECT * FROM [" & RecSource & "]"
```

```
'Load data from RecSource into MyRecordSet
MySQL = "SELECT * FROM [" & RecSource & "]"
MyRecordSet.Open MySQL, , adOpenDynamic, adLockOptimistic

'Grab field names and data types from Fields collection.
Dim MyField As ADODB.Field
For Each MyField In MyRecordSet.Fields
    'Convert AutoNumber fields (Type=3) to Longs
    'to avoid insertion problems later.
    If MyField.Type = 3 Then
        FldNames = FldNames & "CLng([" & RecSource & _
            "].[" & MyField.Name & "]) As " & MyField.Name & ","
    Else
        FldNames = FldNames & _
            "[" & RecSource & "].[" & MyField.Name & "],"
    End If
Next

'Remove trailing comma.
FldNames = Left(FldNames, Len(FldNames) - 1)

'Create an empty table with same structure as RecSource,
'but without any AutoNumber fields.
MySQL = "SELECT " & FldNames & _
    " INTO LabelsTempTable FROM [" & _
    RecSource & "] WHERE False"
MyRecordSet.Close

DoCmd.RunSQL MySQL

'Next we add blank records to empty LabelsTempTable.
MySQL = "SELECT * FROM LabelsTempTable"
MyRecordSet.Open MySQL, , adOpenStatic, adLockOptimistic
For MyCounter = 1 To LabelsToSkip
    MyRecordSet.AddNew
    MyRecordSet.Update
Next

'Now LabelsTempTable has enough empty records in it.
MyRecordSet.Close

'Build a SQL string to append all records from original
'recordsource (RecSource)into LabelsTempTable.
MySQL = "INSERT INTO LabelsTempTable"
MySQL = MySQL & " SELECT [" & RecSource & _
    "].* FROM [" & RecSource & "]"

'Tack on the PassedFilter condition, if it exists.
If Len(PassedFilter) > 1 Then
    MySQL = MySQL & " WHERE " & PassedFilter
End If
```

(continued)

Listing 8-1 *(continued)*

```
'Append the records
DoCmd.RunSQL MySQL

'LabelsTempTable is done now.
'Next we make LabelsTempTable the RecordSource for LabelsTempReport.
DoCmd.OpenReport "LabelsTempReport", acViewDesign, , , acWindowNormal
Set MyReport = Reports![LabelsTempReport]
MySQL = "SELECT * FROM LabelsTempTable"
MyReport.RecordSource = MySQL
DoCmd.Close acReport, "LabelsTempReport", acSaveYes

'Now we can finally print the labels.
DoCmd.OpenReport "LabelsTempReport", acViewPreview, , , acWindowNormal

'Note: As written, procedure just shows labels in Print Preview.
'To get it to actually print, change acPreview to acViewNormal
'in the statement above.

End Sub
```

Okay, that was intimidating. In the next few sections, we pick apart `SkipLabels` to see exactly what makes it tick. If you lost your appetite to get into the details of it all, you can still skip ahead to the section "Calling a Procedure from an Event," later in this chapter.

Passing data to SkipLabels

The first line of `SkipLabels` gives the procedure its name and sets it up to accept either two or three arguments from whatever programmer runs it. The first argument, `ReportName`, stores the name of the report to skip. The second argument stores the number of labels to skip as a number. The optional third parameter, if passed, is stored under the name `PassedFilter`:

```
Sub SkipLabels(ReportName As String, LabelsToSkip As Byte, _
    Optional PassedFilter As String)
```

For the sake of this example, say that an event procedure calls on `SkipLabels` by using this command:

```
Call SkipLabels ("My8462Labels",7)
```

Right away, the variable named `ReportName` gets the value `My8462Labels`, and `LabelsToSkip` gets the value `7`. The `PassedFilter` gets no value because it wasn't used in the calling command.

If a procedure calls `SkipLabels` by using all three parameters, like this:

```
Call SkipLabels ("My8462Labels",7,"[CustID]=123")
```

the variable named `PassedFilter` would store `[CustID]=123` as its value.

Declaring variables

The next task within `SkipLabels` is to create some variables for storing information as the code executes. Those statements are shown as follows. You see those variable names put to use later in the procedure:

```
'Declare some variables
Dim MySQL As String
Dim RecSource As String
Dim FldNames As String
Dim MyCounter As Byte
Dim MyReport As Report
```

The `SkipLabels` procedure executes some action queries (SQL statements) while doing its job. To prevent those queries from displaying warnings, the next line of code turns off the warning messages:

```
DoCmd.SetWarnings False
```

Copying the label report

To play it safe with original objects, `SkipLabels` works with copies of those objects. This next statement uses the `CopyObject` method of the `DoCmd` object to make a copy of the label report. Notice how it uses `ReportName`, passed to the procedure in an argument, to determine which report to copy:

```
DoCmd.CopyObject, "LabelsTempReport", acReport, ReportName
```

Referring to the earlier examples of calling `SkipLabels` with the syntax `Call SkipLabels ("My8462Labels",7)`, after the preceding line executes, the report format named `LabelsTempReport` would be an exact copy of the report named `My8462Labels`.

Getting a report's recordsource

To work with data from a report, `SkipLabels` needs to figure out where that report is getting its data. Every form and report has an exposed `.RecordSource` property that VBA can query to find out the name of the

```
'Load data from RecSource into MyRecordSet
MySQL = "SELECT * FROM [" & RecSource & "]"
MyRecordSet.Open MySQL, , adOpenDynamic, adLockOptimistic

'Grab field names and data types from Fields collection.
Dim MyField As ADODB.Field
For Each MyField In MyRecordSet.Fields
   'Convert AutoNumber fields (Type=3) to Longs
   'to avoid insertion problems later.
   If MyField.Type = 3 Then
      FldNames = FldNames & "CLng([" & RecSource & _
         "].[" & MyField.Name & "]) As " & MyField.Name & ","
   Else
      FldNames = FldNames & _
         "[" & RecSource & "].[" & MyField.Name & "],"
   End If
Next

'Remove trailing comma.
FldNames = Left(FldNames, Len(FldNames) - 1)

'Create an empty table with same structure as RecSource,
'but without any AutoNumber fields.
MySQL = "SELECT " & FldNames & _
   " INTO LabelsTempTable FROM [" & _
   RecSource & "] WHERE False"
MyRecordSet.Close

DoCmd.RunSQL MySQL

'Next we add blank records to empty LabelsTempTable.
MySQL = "SELECT * FROM LabelsTempTable"
MyRecordSet.Open MySQL, , adOpenStatic, adLockOptimistic
For MyCounter = 1 To LabelsToSkip
   MyRecordSet.AddNew
   MyRecordSet.Update
Next

'Now LabelsTempTable has enough empty records in it.
MyRecordSet.Close

'Build a SQL string to append all records from original
'recordsource (RecSource)into LabelsTempTable.
MySQL = "INSERT INTO LabelsTempTable"
MySQL = MySQL & " SELECT [" & RecSource & _
   "].* FROM [" & RecSource & "]"

'Tack on the PassedFilter condition, if it exists.
If Len(PassedFilter) > 1 Then
   MySQL = MySQL & " WHERE " & PassedFilter
End If
```

(continued)

Listing 8-1 *(continued)*

```
'Append the records
DoCmd.RunSQL MySQL

'LabelsTempTable is done now.
'Next we make LabelsTempTable the RecordSource for LabelsTempReport.
DoCmd.OpenReport "LabelsTempReport", acViewDesign, , , acWindowNormal
Set MyReport = Reports![LabelsTempReport]
MySQL = "SELECT * FROM LabelsTempTable"
MyReport.RecordSource = MySQL
DoCmd.Close acReport, "LabelsTempReport", acSaveYes

'Now we can finally print the labels.
DoCmd.OpenReport "LabelsTempReport", acViewPreview, , , acWindowNormal

'Note: As written, procedure just shows labels in Print Preview.
'To get it to actually print, change acPreview to acViewNormal
'in the statement above.

End Sub
```

Okay, that was intimidating. In the next few sections, we pick apart
SkipLabels to see exactly what makes it tick. If you lost your appetite to
get into the details of it all, you can still skip ahead to the section "Calling a
Procedure from an Event," later in this chapter.

Passing data to SkipLabels

The first line of SkipLabels gives the procedure its name and sets it up to
accept either two or three arguments from whatever programmer runs it. The
first argument, ReportName, stores the name of the report to skip. The
second argument stores the number of labels to skip as a number. The
optional third parameter, if passed, is stored under the name PassedFilter:

```
Sub SkipLabels(ReportName As String, LabelsToSkip As Byte, _
    Optional PassedFilter As String)
```

For the sake of this example, say that an event procedure calls on
SkipLabels by using this command:

```
Call SkipLabels ("My8462Labels",7)
```

Right away, the variable named ReportName gets the value My8462Labels,
and LabelsToSkip gets the value 7. The PassedFilter gets no value
because it wasn't used in the calling command.

If a procedure calls `SkipLabels` by using all three parameters, like this:

```
Call SkipLabels ("My8462Labels",7,"[CustID]=123")
```

the variable named `PassedFilter` would store `[CustID]=123` as its value.

Declaring variables

The next task within `SkipLabels` is to create some variables for storing information as the code executes. Those statements are shown as follows. You see those variable names put to use later in the procedure:

```
'Declare some variables
Dim MySQL As String
Dim RecSource As String
Dim FldNames As String
Dim MyCounter As Byte
Dim MyReport As Report
```

The `SkipLabels` procedure executes some action queries (SQL statements) while doing its job. To prevent those queries from displaying warnings, the next line of code turns off the warning messages:

```
DoCmd.SetWarnings False
```

Copying the label report

To play it safe with original objects, `SkipLabels` works with copies of those objects. This next statement uses the `CopyObject` method of the `DoCmd` object to make a copy of the label report. Notice how it uses `ReportName`, passed to the procedure in an argument, to determine which report to copy:

```
DoCmd.CopyObject, "LabelsTempReport", acReport, ReportName
```

Referring to the earlier examples of calling `SkipLabels` with the syntax `Call SkipLabels ("My8462Labels",7)`, after the preceding line executes, the report format named `LabelsTempReport` would be an exact copy of the report named `My8462Labels`.

Getting a report's recordsource

To work with data from a report, `SkipLabels` needs to figure out where that report is getting its data. Every form and report has an exposed `.RecordSource` property that VBA can query to find out the name of the table or query to which the form or report is attached. However, VBA can get that information only if the report (or form) is open in Design view. In SkipLabels, this next statement opens LabelsTempReport in Design view:

```
'Open LabelsTempReport in Design view.
DoCmd.OpenReport "LabelsTempReport", acViewDesign
```

In the following lines of code, the first line stores in the variable named RecSource the name of the table or query from which the report gets its data. The second line then closes LabelsTempReport because there's no need for it to be open in Design view any more:

```
RecSource = Reports!LabelsTempReport.RecordSource

DoCmd.Close acReport, "LabelsTempReport", acSaveNo
```

Remember that from this point on in the code, the name RecSource refers to the name of the table or query in which data to be printed on labels is stored. The code can let that variable sit for now and move on to the task of creating LabelsTempTable, which is the table that SkipLabels uses to store blank records and data to be printed on labels.

Creating the recordset

SkipLabels uses a recordset (and some action queries) to do its job. The next lines in the procedure, as follows, create a recordset named MyRecordSet, which you see put to use shortly:

```
'Declare a recordset named MyRecordSet that gets its
'data from the current database's tables.
Dim cnn1 As ADODB.Connection
Dim MyRecordSet As New ADODB.Recordset
Set cnn1 = CurrentProject.Connection
MyRecordSet.ActiveConnection = cnn1
```

Creating LabelsTempTable from MyRecordSet

At this point in the code, an empty recordset named MyRecordSet is just waiting to get filled with some data. The following statement creates a SQL statement using whatever is stored in RecSource as the name of the table from which to get records:

```
MySQL = "SELECT * FROM [" & RecSource & "]"
```

For the sake of example, say that the recordsource is a query named New Customers Qry. In that case, the MySQL variable would receive as its value the string

```
SELECT * FROM [New Customers Qry]
```

At this point in the procedure, MyRecordSet has the same fields as the original table. The code now needs to create a new table from that recordset, but there's a snag: If the current table contains any AutoNumber fields, you can't append blank records to the top of the table. So rather than create an exact clone of the original table, the procedure creates a semi-clone where any AutoNumber fields are converted to Long Integer fields. That way, you can append blank records to the final table.

To determine the name and data type of each field in the recordset, the following loop looks at each field in MyRecordSet's structure, particularly the .Name and .Type (data type) property of each field. When used in a recordset, the .Type property of a recordset returns a number indicating the data type of the field, as listed here:

AutoNumber	3
Text	202
Memo	203
Date/Time	7
Currency	6
Yes/No	11
OLE Object	205
Hyperlink	203
Byte	17
Integer	2
Long Integer	3
Single	4
Double	5

The next big step in the SkipLabels procedure involves creating a string of field names in the FldNames variable (declared earlier in the procedure as a string). To do this, the following code uses a For Each...Next loop to analyze the name (.Name property) and data type (.Type property) of each field in the recordset. If the field's data type is an AutoNumber field, the code uses the built-in CLng() (Convert to Long) function to convert it to a regular long integer:

```
Dim myField As ADODB.Field
For Each myField In myRecordSet.Fields
    'Convert AutoNumber fields (Type=3) to Longs
    'to avoid insertion problems later.
   If myField.Type = 3 Then
       FldNames = FldNames & "CLng([" & RecSource & _
          "].[" & myField.Name & "]) As " & myField.Name & ","
   Else
       FldNames = FldNames & _
          "[" & RecSource & "].[" & myField.Name & "],"
   End If
Next
FldNames = Left(FldNames, Len(FldNames) - 1) 'Remove trailing comma.
```

Suffice it to say that when the last statement is executed, the `FldNames` variable contains a list of field names organized in such a way that they can be used in a SQL statement to create a new table with a structure similar to the original recordsource table's (or query's) structure. For example, if the recordsource table contains an `AutoNumber` field named `CustID` and some text fields named `FirstName`, `LastName`, `Address1`, and so forth, `FldNames` ends up containing something like this (as one long line that's too wide for the margins here):

```
CLng([CustID]) As CustID, [FirstName], [LastName],
         [Company], [Address1], [Address2], [City],
         [StateProv], [ZIPPostalCode], [Country]
```

When executed as part of a SQL statement, the `CLng()` function converts the `AutoNumber CustID` field to a long integer, which makes it easier to append records to the top of the `LabelsTempTable`. The next line creates a SQL statement using field names from the recordset and the additional text needed to create a table:

```
mySQL = "SELECT " & FldNames & " INTO LabelsTempTable FROM
         [" & RecSource & "] WHERE False"
```

Recall that `RecSource` is the name of the table or query that contains the data to print on labels. If that table is named `Customers` and it has field names, as in the preceding example, `mySQL` ends up being a valid SQL statement, something like this:

```
SELECT CLng([CustID]) As CustID, [FirstName], [LastName],
         [Company], [Address1], [Address2], [City],
         [StateProv], [ZIPPostalCode], [LabelCountry]
         INTO LabelsTempTable FROM [Customers] WHERE
         False
```

The `WHERE False` part of the SQL statement prevents any records from being copied into the new `LabelsTemp` table. When executed, the following statements create `LabelsTempTable` as a new, empty table and then close the recordset (which was needed only to determine field names and data types from the original report's recordsource):

```
myRecordSet.Close

DoCmd.RunSQL mySQL
```

After the preceding statements execute, `LabelsTempTable` is an empty table that's nearly identical to the report's underlying table but with `AutoNumber` fields defined as `Long Integer` fields. The chunk of code creates a new recordset that matches the empty `LabelsTempTable` table. The `.AddNew` and `.Update` methods within the loop add one new, blank record to `LabelsTempTable`. Notice how those statements are in the `For...Next` loop that counts from 1 to `LabelsToSkip`. That `LabelsToSkip` variable contains the number of labels to be skipped over. The following code basically adds as many blank records to `LabelsTempTable` as are needed to skip over the appropriate number of labels:

```
'Next we add blank records to empty LabelsTempTable.
MySQL = "SELECT * FROM LabelsTempTable"
MyRecordSet.Open MySQL, , adOpenStatic, adLockOptimistic

For MyCounter = 1 To LabelsToSkip
    MyRecordSet.AddNew
    MyRecordSet.Update
Next

'Now LabelsTempTable has enough empty records in it.
MyRecordSet.Close
```

The next statements form a SQL statement to append all records from the original recordsource onto `LabelsTempTable`. For example, if the name of the original recordsource table is `Customers`, `mySQL` ends up being

```
INSERT INTO LabelsTempTable SELECT [Customers].* FROM
            [Customers]
```

That statement is basically an append query that adds all the records from the original table to `LabelsTempTable`. When the SQL statement executes, the records from the original table are appended onto `LabelsTempTable` beneath the blank records that are already in `LabelsTempTable`:

```
mySQL = "INSERT INTO LabelsTempTable"
mySQL = mySQL & " SELECT [" & RecSource & _
    "].* FROM [" & RecSource & "]"
DoCmd.RunSQL mySQL
```

After the preceding code runs, `LabelsTempReport` is an exact clone of the original label report. `LabelsTempTable` is a clone of all the records to be printed on the labels, with blank records on top, as shown in Figure 8-8.

The next statements open `LabelsTempReport` in Design view and set its recordsource to print all records from `LabelTempTable`. These statements accomplish this task by changing the `RecordSource` property of `LabelsTempReport` to a SQL statement that retrieves all records from `LabelsTempTable`:

```
DoCmd.OpenReport "LabelsTempReport", acViewDesign, , , acWindowNormal
Set myReport = Reports![LabelsTempReport]
mySQL = "SELECT * FROM LabelsTempTable"
myReport.RecordSource = mySQL
DoCmd.Close acReport, "LabelsTempReport", acSaveYes
```

At this moment, everything is ready to go. `LabelsTempReport` is bound to `LabelsTempTable`, which in turn contains all the necessary blank records on top followed by all the records that need to be printed. Now VBA just needs to print the report. As written, the code just displays the results in Print Preview, by using this statement:

```
'Now we can finally print the labels.
DoCmd.OpenReport "LabelsTempReport", acViewPreview, , , acWindowNormal
```

Using Print Preview is just a means of testing and debugging the code without wasting a lot of paper on trial runs. In a live working environment, you want the code to print the labels. That's simple to do: Just change the work `acViewPreview` to `acNormal` in that last statement:

```
DoCmd.OpenReport "LabelsTempReport", acViewNormal, , , acWindowNormal
```

`SkipLabels` is now done. The final two statements set the object variables named `cnn1` and `MyReport` (defined earlier in the procedure with `Set` statements) to `Nothing`. This is just a little housekeeping step before the procedure ends:

```
    'Free up the object variables.
    Set cnn1 = Nothing
    Set MyReport = Nothing
End Sub
```

By the time the `End Sub` statement is executed, the labels are printing (or getting ready to print), and `SkipLabels` is done. You can give the standard module any name you like and then close and save the module.

Calling a Procedure from an Event

At this stage of the game, your database contains a standard module that contains a Sub procedure named SkipLabels(). Because you haven't yet tied the SkipLabels procedure to any event, nothing is in the database yet to take advantage of SkipLabels().

Recall that earlier in this chapter, we show a form with a control named LabelsToSkip (it stores the number of labels to be skipped over) as well as a Cancel button and a Print button (refer to Figure 8-6). If the user clicks Cancel, you just want SkipLabelsForm to close without doing anything. If the user clicks the Print button, you want the form to call SkipLabels with the appropriate label report name and number of labels.

When you want an event procedure on a form to call a standard procedure, use the syntax

```
Call procedureName (arguments)
```

where *procedureName* is the name of the procedure to call, and *arguments* are values for whatever required arguments the procedure is expecting. SkipLabels() requires at least two arguments: the name of the labels report and the number of labels to skip. Here's how you could get the Print button in the SkipLabels form to call SkipLabels () when clicked:

1. **Open SkipLabelsForm (or whatever form you created) in Design view and click the button that will call SkipLabels.**

2. **On the Event tab of the Properties sheet, click the On Click event property for the Print button.**

3. **Click the Build button and choose Code Builder. You see the VBA Editor with the cursor inside the event procedure.**

4. **Type the following line into the procedure:**

   ```
   Call SkipLabels("[YourReportName]",
           [LabelsToSkip].Value)
   ```

   and substitute *YourReportName* with the name of the report in your database that prints labels.

   For example, if your database contains a report named Avery 8462 Labels, you type **Call SkipLabels("Avery 8462 Labels", [LabelsToSkip]. Value)**, as shown in the second procedure — PrintBttn_Click() in Figure 8-9.

Figure 8-9:
The `Print Bttn_ Click()` procedure called the `Skip Labels` Sub.

The first procedure in that figure — `CancelBttn_Click()` — in that class module just closes `SkipLabelsForm` without doing anything and is tied to the `On Click` event of the form's Cancel button.

The syntax for calling a custom VBA function from an `Event` procedure is `=functionName(arguments)`, which is clearly different from calling a `Sub` procedure with `Call procedureName (arguments)`. We talk more about custom functions in Chapter 11.

5. **Choose File⇨Save and Return to Microsoft Office Access from the VBA Editor's menu bar.**

The button's `On Click` event property shows `Event Procedure`, as usual. Now you can close and save the form and then reopen it in Form view to try it out.

You can do some fancier things with `SkipLabelsForm` in later chapters. For example, you can allow the user to choose any one of several label formats, or you can let the user specify a filter condition by using simple options on a form. For now, if you got this far, you did great. You created a `Sub` procedure named `SkipLabels()` that you can easily drop into just about any database you create.

Part IV
Applying VBA in the Real World

The 5th Wave   By Rich Tennant

"We're here to clean the code."

In this part . . .

Some of the programming techniques in these chapters are a bit trickier than techniques from previous chapters, but they're not just stupid pet tricks. They're useful tricks. What makes them tricky has more to do with the way you use VBA to trick Access into doing things it couldn't possibly do on its own. In the real world, people rarely write code that works perfectly right off the bat. Even experienced programmers have to spend some time testing and debugging their code. In this part, you also discover the many tools that VBA offers to help you with testing and debugging.

Chapter 9

Creating Your Own Dialog Boxes

. . . .

In This Chapter

▶ Asking questions, responding to answers

▶ Storing dialog box settings

▶ Creating custom dialog boxes

▶ Creating spin box controls

▶ Detecting a right-click

. . . .

*Y*ou see dialog boxes in Windows and other programs all the time. Each dialog box presents some options for you to choose from. The name *dialog box* stems from the fact that the user and the dialog box carry on a sort of conversation. The dialog box presents some options, and the user makes selections from those options and then clicks OK.

When you're creating a database, you might want to put your own dialog box (or other message) on-screen so that the user can make some choices. Creating dialog boxes in Access is easier than you might think because each dialog box is just an Access form with certain settings that make the form look and act more like a dialog box than a regular Access form.

In addition to displaying dialog boxes, your database can display small, custom messages on-screen. A message is a dialog box of sorts because it presents information or a question to the user and waits for the user to respond. And you don't even have to create an entire dialog box to display a small message on-screen: You can just use the VBA `MsgBox()` function instead.

In this chapter, we look at message boxes and dialog boxes, showing examples of programming each. We start with message boxes because those are the easiest to create.

Displaying and Responding to Messages

When you want your database to give the user a little feedback or have the user answer a simple Yes/No question, you can use a message box. The message box can be a simple feedback message with a single OK button, like the example shown at the left side of Figure 9-1. Or, the message box can ask a question and wait for an answer, as in the right side of Figure 9-1.

Figure 9-1:
Examples of
message
boxes.

There are two syntaxes for the `MsgBox` keyword. If you just want the message to show some text and an OK button, use the syntax

```
MsgBox "YourMessageHere"
```

where *YourMessageHere* is the text that you want the message box to display. For example, here's the complete VBA code to display the message on the left side of Figure 9-1:

```
MsgBox "Finished exporting records"
```

If you type that exact statement into the VBA Editor Immediate window and press Enter, you see the message box on-screen. When you click its OK button, the message box closes.

The preceding syntax, where you just follow the `MsgBox` statement with a message enclosed in quotation marks, works only when you don't specify buttons to display in the message box. The message box has only an OK button, and clicking that button closes the message box.

If you want your message box to ask a question and give the user some choices about how to respond, you have to use a different syntax, as discussed next.

Asking a question

If you want your message box to ask a question and show Yes/No buttons, you have to use the `MsgBox()` function with the following syntax:

```
Dim Variable As Integer
Variable = MsgBox("YourQuestion",buttons,["title"])
```

where

- ✔ *Variable* is a variable name of your choosing.
- ✔ *YourQuestion* is the text to be displayed in the box.
- ✔ *buttons* is a number or constant defining buttons to display and other message box properties, as discussed in the upcoming section "Designing a message box."
- ✔ *title* is an optional title that appears on the title bar of the message box.

For example, the following lines of code display the message box shown on the right side of Figure 9-1. When the user clicks a button, the variable named Answer stores a number indicating which button the user clicked.

```
Dim Answer As Integer
Answer = MsgBox("Did labels print OK?", vbQuestion + vbYesNo, "Question")
```

Whenever VBA displays a message box, it stops executing code in your procedure. In other words, any lines below the statement in the code are ignored until the user clicks a button in the message box. At that point, VBA can decide what to do based on which button the user clicked. Before we get to that topic, look in the next section at all the different ways you can control the appearance and behavior of a message box.

Designing a message box

You can use the *buttons* argument of the MsgBox keyword to define the exact appearance and behavior of your message box. Each possible value for the *buttons* argument can be expressed as either a constant or a number. You can add the constants or numbers together to combine properties.

For example, the constant vbYesNo (or number 4) tells MsgBox to display Yes and No buttons in the form. The constant vbQuestion (or number 32) tells MsgBox to display a question mark icon in the form. Combining the two arguments with a plus sign (+) in the MsgBox statement applies both properties. For example, using vbYesNo + vbQuestion together as the *buttons* argument in the following example displays the dialog box shown on the right side of Figure 9-1. There you can see the question mark icon and Yes/No buttons in the message box.

```
Answer = MsgBox("Did labels print OK?", vbQuestion + vbYesNo, "Question")
```

Whenever VBA encounters a MsgBox statement in code, it displays the message box on-screen and then waits for the user to respond to the box. Code beneath the MsgBox statement within the procedure isn't executed until the user responds to the message box.

Modal and pop-up messages

The *buttons* argument lets you define how the message box looks when it first opens and also how it behaves while it's open. By default, a message box is always *application modal*. That is, after the message box is on-screen, the user can't do anything else in Access until he or she replies to the message. With the *buttons* argument, you can make the message box *system modal,* which means that the user can't do anything in any other program until he responds to the message.

With the *buttons* argument, you can also make the message box a *pop-up.* As a pop-up, the message box always jumps to the top of the stack of whatever other windows happen to be open on-screen, therefore guaranteeing that the message box is visible to the user on-screen.

Message box default buttons

You can even define a default button for the message. The *default* button is the button that's automatically selected when the message box first opens. It's also the button that gets clicked if the user just presses the Enter key to close the message box. For example, the following statement displays a message box with Yes, No, and Cancel buttons with the third button (Cancel) already selected (highlighted) in the box:

```
Answer = MsgBox("Hello World", vbYesNoCancel + vbDefaultButton3)
```

Because the Cancel button is the default button in that example, if the user just presses the Enter key in response to the message, that's the same as the user clicking the Cancel button.

The complete set of MsgBox *buttons* argument settings are shown in Table 9-1. The first six settings (0 through 5) specify buttons to show in the message box. Those settings also specify which values the variable at the left side of the statement could get when the user clicks a button, as we discuss next.

Table 9-1	Constants and Numbers Used for the MsgBox *buttons* Argument		
Constant	*Number*	*Displays*	*Returns*
vbOKOnly	0	OK button	vbOK
vbOKCancel	1	OK, Cancel buttons	vbOK or vbCancel
vbAbortRetryIgnore	2	Abort, Retry, Ignore buttons	vbAbort, vbRetry, vbIgnore

Constant	Number	Displays	Returns
vbYesNoCancel	3	Yes, No, Cancel buttons	vbYes, vbNo, vbCancel
vbYesNo	4	Yes, No buttons	vbYes, vbNo
vbRetryCancel	5	Retry, Cancel buttons	vbRetry, vbCancel
vbCritical	16	Red X icon	
vbQuestion	32	Question icon	
vbExclamation	48	Exclamation icon	
vbInformation	64	Information icon	
vbDefaultButton1	0	First button as default	
vbDefaultButton2	256	Second button as default	
vbDefaultButton3	512	Third button as default	
vbDefaultButton4	768	Fourth button as default	
vbApplicationModal	0	Access objects suspended until user replies	
vbSystemModal	4096	All applications suspended until user replies	
vbMsgBoxHelpButton	16384	Help button in box	
VbMsgBoxSetForeground	65536	Message box as top window (pop-up)	
vbMsgBoxRight	524288	Text right-aligned in box	
vbMsgBoxRtlReading	1048576	Text from right to left for Hebrew or Arabic	

Adding the vbMsgBoxHelpButton argument displays a Help button in the message box. However, the button doesn't work unless you create custom Help files, and that's a large topic that's beyond the scope of this book. If you're interested in learning more, search the following site for **adding custom help access**:

```
http://msdn.microsoft.com/
```

Responding to a MsgBox button click

If your message box asks a question, you presumably want your VBA code to respond to whatever button the user clicked. That's fairly easy to do because when the user clicks a button, the variable to the left side of the MsgBox() function returns a value indicating which button the user clicked. Each button that you can show in a message box returns a unique value. For example, when the user clicks the Yes button, MsgBox() returns 6 (which also equals Access's built-in vbYes constant). If the user clicks the Cancel button, MsgBox returns 2 (which equals the vbCancel constant).

In your code, you can use either the constant or the number, but it's always easier to read the code later if you use the constant. Table 9-2 lists the value — expressed as both a constant and a number — that each message box button returns when clicked.

Table 9-2	Values Returned by Buttons	
If User Clicks	*MsgBox Returns (Constant)*	*MsgBox Returns (Integer)*
OK	vbOK	1
Yes	vbYes	6
No	vbNo	7
Cancel	vbCancel*	2
Abort	vbAbort	3
Retry	vbRetry	4
Ignore	vbIgnore	5

*MsgBox() *also returns* vbCancel (2) *if the user presses the Esc key or clicks the box's Close button.*

Code execution always stops at the line when a message box is on-screen. Thus, the next line of code in your procedure can make a decision based on the contents of the variable used at the start of the VBA MsgBox() statement.

For example, if the message box contains Yes and No buttons, you can use an
If statement to perform one set of steps if the user clicks Yes and another set
of steps if the user clicks No. Here's the basic idea:

```
Dim Answer As Integer
Answer = MsgBox("Click a button",vbYesNo,"Test")

'Make a decision based on button user clicked.
If Answer = vbYes Then
    'Code to execute if user clicked Yes goes here.
Else
    Code to execute if user clicked No goes here.
End If
```

Here's how the preceding code executes. The Dim statement creates a variable named Answer. The next statement displays a message box with Yes
and No buttons. Code execution stops there until the user clicks a button in
the message box. When the user clicks a button, the Answer variable
receives a value indicating which button the user clicked. In this example,
that value is either vbYes (6) or vbNo (7). Code execution then resumes normally at the next line in the procedure.

In the preceding example, the first executable line of code is an If...Then
statement that compares the value of the Answer variable with vbYes.
Then . . .

✔ If the value of Answer is vbYes, only the code between If and Else is
   executed; code between Else and End If is ignored.

✔ If the value of Answer value is not vbYes, code between If and Else is
   ignored, and only code between Else and End If executes.

Either way, code execution then resumes normally at the next statement after
the End If statement.

If you want to try it for yourself, you can type a little procedure like the
following example into any standard module:

```
Sub MsgTest2()'Show message with Yes and No Buttons
    Dim Answer As Integer
    Answer = MsgBox("Ready?", vbYesNo)

    If Answer = vbYes Then
        'Code to execute if user clicked Yes button.
        Debug.Print "You clicked Yes"
        Beep    'Sound a beep too.
    Else
        'Code to execute if user clicked No button.
        Debug.Print "You clicked No"
    End If
End Sub
```

After you type the entire procedure, you can just type its name, MsgTest2, into the Immediate window and try it. When you see the message box, click Yes. You hear a beep and see You clicked Yes in the Immediate window. Run the procedure a second time and click No, and you see You clicked No in the Immediate window.

You might have a situation where you want your code to do one thing if the user clicks Yes, do another thing if the user clicks No, and do something else if the user clicks Cancel or closes the dialog box without clicking a specific button. You can use a Select Case block of code to specify a different action for each of the three buttons' possibilities.

For example, when executed, the following Answer = MsgBox(...) statement displays a message box with Yes, No, and Cancel buttons. After the user clicks a button, the Select Case...End Select block takes one of three possible actions. If the user clicks the Yes button, only the code under Select Case vbYes executes. If the user clicks No, only the code under Select Case vbNo executes. If the user clicks the Cancel button or closes the message box by using the Close button or Esc key, only the code under Select Case vbCancel executes.

```
Dim Answer As Integer
Answer = MsgBox("Ready again?", vbYesNoCancel + _
        vbDefaultButton3)

Select Case Answer
    Case vbYes
          'Code to execute if user clicked Yes.
          Debug.Print "You clicked Yes"
    Case vbNo
          'Code to execute if user clicked No.
          Debug.Print "You clicked No"
    Case vbCancel
          'Code to execute if user cancelled.
          Debug.Print "You didn't click Yes or No."
End Select
```

For more information on If...Then...End If and Select Case...End Select, see Chapter 4.

Converting Forms to Dialog Boxes

Message boxes are fine when your code just needs to ask users a simple question, but sometimes you want to give them several options to choose from. You might want to use a variety of controls, such as check boxes and combo boxes, to present those options. (Read about this topic in the upcoming section "Creating Custom Combo Boxes.") When your code needs more than a simple answer to a single question, use a dialog box rather than a message box.

A dialog box (often called a *dialog,* for short) in an Access database is basically the same thing as a dialog box in Windows or any other program. It's a group of options from which the user can make choices. For example, if you right-click the Windows Start button and choose Properties, the Windows Taskbar and Start Menu Properties dialog box opens, giving you options for customizing your Windows desktop.

Storing dialog box settings

Although creating a dialog box is easy, you need to first think about how you want to deal with the settings that the user chooses. If you want your dialog box to remember settings from one session to the next, you need to store those settings in some sort of table. Otherwise, Access forgets all the user's settings each time the user closes the database.

The table that you create for storing dialog box settings needs only one record, with a field to store each dialog box setting that needs to be remembered. In this chapter, we show you how to create a fancy dialog box for the SkipLabels procedure you create in Chapter 8. We show you how to make the procedure remember which report the user last used for printing labels and how many labels the user skipped on each run. This makes it a little easier for the user to reuse settings in the dialog box.

For this example, create a tiny table that stores the name of the report as Text and the number of labels last skipped as Number. Figure 9-2 shows the structure of the table that we use here. You don't need to define a primary key in this table because the table never contains any more than one record. We named the table SettingsTable.

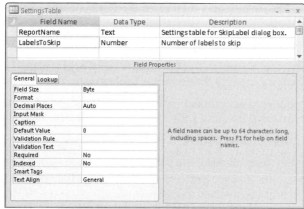

Figure 9-2:
Structure
of the
Settings
Table
table.

After you close and save the table, you need to open that table and type in the value of at least one field. That's because when you bind a dialog box to that table later, it works only if the table already contains one record. For example, Figure 9-3 shows one record that we typed into the `SettingsTable` table. The blank record beneath the filled record isn't an actual record in the table. That empty record appears only as a placeholder for any new record that you want to add to the table in Datasheet view.

Figure 9-3:
One table
record
stores
dialog box
settings.

You can see an example of using the `SettingsTable` values in a dialog box a little later in this chapter. For now, in the next section, you master how to create a dialog box in the first place.

Setting form properties

Creating a dialog box in Access is similar to creating any other form. You don't even need any VBA code to create the box. Rather, you just create a form and set its form properties so that the form looks and acts like a dialog box. Here's how:

1. **Click the Create tab, and then click the Form Design command in the Forms group.**

   This step creates a new, blank form in Design view.

2. **If the property sheet isn't visible, click the (Form Design Tools) Design tab and click Property Sheet in the Tools group, or press F4.**

3. **In the property sheet, make sure that Form is selected in the Selection Type drop-down list, and then click the All tab (see Figure 9-4).**

4. **Set the properties as indicated in Table 9-3.**

5. **Save the form by clicking the Save button on the Quick Access toolbar.**

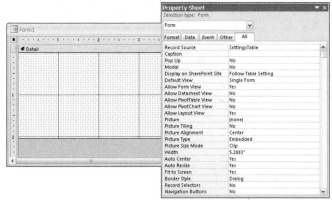

Figure 9-4:
Setting form
properties
for a
dialog box.

Table 9-3   Properties to Make a Form into a Dialog Box

Property	Setting	Reason
Record Source	SettingsTable	This is the table the form is bound to.
Default View	Single Form	Make it look like a dialog box.
Allow Form View	Yes	Make it look like a dialog box.
Allow Datasheet View	No	Dialog boxes have no such view.
Allow PivotTable View	No	Dialog boxes have no such view.
Allow PivotChart View	No	Dialog boxes have no such view.
Allow Layout View	No	User doesn't need to see this view.
Allow Edits	Yes	User needs to change data on the form.
Allow Deletions	No	Underlying table (if any) must contain only one record.
Allow Additions	No	Underlying table (if any) must contain only one record.

(continued)

Table 9-3 (continued)

Property	Setting	Reason
Allow Filters	No	Underlying table (if any) has only one record.
Data Entry	No	Underlying table (if any) must contain only one record.
Scroll Bars	Neither	Dialog boxes don't have scroll bars.
Record Selectors	No	Dialog boxes don't have record selectors.
Navigation Buttons	No	Dialog boxes don't have navigation buttons.
Dividing Lines	No	Dialog boxes don't need them.
Pop Up	Yes	Keep dialog box on top of other open windows.
Modal	Yes	Disable other open windows until user responds to dialog box.
Border Style	Dialog	Make it look like a dialog box border.
Control Box	Yes	Need to make Close button visible.
Min Max Buttons	None	Dialog box can't be minimized or maximized.
Close Button	Yes	Dialog boxes have a Close button, which acts like a Cancel button.
Cycle	Current Record	Only one record is in underlying settings table.

To color your dialog box, click the Detail section in Design view, click its Back Color property, and choose a color. For example, for a slightly off-white color, set the Back Color property of the Detail section to 16316664.

Adding controls to the dialog box

The form properties that you change to control the appearance and behavior of a form don't affect how you add controls to the form. You can still use all the standard techniques that you use in Access to create a form for scrolling through records. For example, to add a bound control to the form, click a control type in the Controls group on the (Form Design Tools) Design tab. Then drag the underlying field's name from the Field List to the form. To add an unbound control to the form, click a control type in the Toolbox and then click the form's Design grid.

If the Control Wizard opens after you drop a control on the form, you can step through the wizard as you normally would. If you're planning to attach custom code to the control later and don't want the wizard to create the control, just click the wizard's Cancel button. Then you can assign a name, a caption, and some events to the control by using the control's property sheet.

For example, the top half of Figure 9-5 shows in Design view a sample dialog box with four main controls: `ReportName`, `LabelsToSkip`, `CancelBttn`, and `PrintBttn`. In that example, the controls `ReportName` and `LabelsToSkip` are bound to fields in the `SettingsTable` described earlier in this section. Thus, the dialog box remembers the settings in those controls from one session to the next. The lower half of Figure 9-5 shows the same form open in Form view.

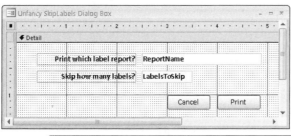

Figure 9-5:
Controls
on a form
(dialog box).

In the sample form shown in Figure 9-5, the CancelBttn and PrintBttn controls aren't bound to any table field. Instead, each just has some custom code tied to its On Click event. For example, the On Click event procedure for CancelBttn is DoCmd.Close acForm, Me.Name, acSaveNo, which closes the form without saving any changes or printing.

The On Click event procedure for PrintBttn can execute any VBA code or macro. For instance, to call the SkipLabels procedure described in Chapter 8, have that procedure execute the statement

```
Call SkipLabels ([ReportName].Value,[LabelsToSkip].Value)
```

Doing so prints whatever report name appears in the ReportName control, skipping the number of labels specified in the LabelsToSkip control. The procedure also closes the dialog box. The following code shows the On Click event procedure for both controls in the class module for the sample form:

```
Private Sub CancelBttn_Click()

    'Close the SkipLabels form without doing anything.
    DoCmd.Close acForm, Me.Name, acSaveNo

End Sub

Private Sub PrintBttn_Click()

    'Print the specified labels, skipping specified blanks.
    Call SkipLabels([ReportName].Value, [LabelsToSkip].Value)

    'Then close the SkipLabels form.
    DoCmd.Close acForm, Me.Name, acSaveNo

End Sub
```

We help you create a much fancier SkipLabels dialog box in the sections that follow. For now, you should be able to see how it works. The controls named ReportName and LabelsToSkip on the form serve as data to pass to the SkipLabels() Sub procedure. Clicking the Print button on the form calls the SkipLabels routine using the syntax

```
Call SkipLabels([ReportName].Value,[LabelsToSkip].Value)
```

When SkipLabels runs, it prints whatever report name appears in the ReportName control on the form and also skips however many labels are specified in the LabelsToSkip control on the form.

Creating Custom Combo Boxes

A *combo box* in Access is a control that acts as both a text box and a drop-down list of options. As you probably know, you can create two types of combo boxes in Access: those that get their values from a table or query and those that get their values from a simple value list that you type manually.

Suppose you have a database that contains a number of reports, as in the example shown in Figure 9-6. Ideally, you'd like to create a `SkipLabels` dialog box that provides a drop-down list of report names that the user can print labels on.

Figure 9-6: Sample reports in an Access database.

One way to do this is to add a `ComboBox` control to your `SkipLabels` form and simply type into the control's Value List the names of reports on which the user can print labels. For example, you might already have a `TextBox` control named `ReportName` on a form, and you want to change the text box to a combo box. Open the form in Design view, right-click the `ReportName` control, and choose Change To⇨Combo Box. The `ReportName` text box becomes a combo box (still named `ReportName`).

On the Data tab of the control's property sheet, set the Row Source Type to Value List and then set the Row Source property to the names of reports that you want to see in the drop-down list. ***Note:*** You need to spell each report name exactly as it's spelled in the database. Enclose each report name in quotation marks and also separate names with semicolons. To ensure that the user can choose only a report name from the list, set the Limit to List property to `Yes`.

Figure 9-7 shows an example where we converted the `TextBox` control named `ReportName` to a `ComboBox` control. On the Data tab of that control's property sheet, we set the Row Source Type to Value List and the Row Source to the list of report names, as shown here:

```
"Avery 5197 Labels";"Avery 8462 Labels";"Avery 8463 Labels";
            "Avery Name Tag Labels"
```

The lower-right section of Figure 9-7 shows the same combo box open in Form view. The drop-down list shows the report names in the `Value List` property of the control.

The drop-down list in the example shown in Figure 9-7 is *static:* It never changes. If you add, delete, or rename reports, those changes aren't automatically reflected in the drop-down list. To get the drop-down list to work correctly, open the form in Design view and manually change the `Value List` property to reflect current report names.

Selected control in Design view

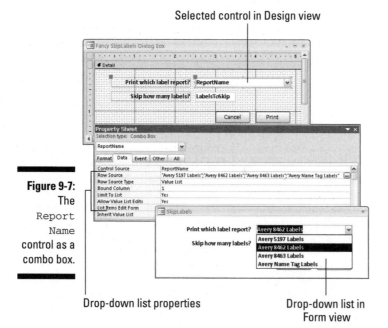

Figure 9-7:
The
Report
Name
control as a
combo box.

Drop-down list properties   Drop-down list in
                                    Form view

An easier approach is to make the drop-down list *dynamic* so that each time the form opens, VBA can build an accurate, up-to-date list of valid report names for the combo box. That way, the drop-down list always works, even if you add, change, or delete reports or drop the whole chunk of code into an entirely separate database.

The `CurrentProject.AllReports` collection in VBA contains the names of all reports in the current database. If you want the drop-down list to show the names of all reports each time the form opens, you need some sort of code that builds the combo box's Value List from those report names. You also need to attach that code to the form's `On Load` event, which is triggered each time the form opens and displays any data from its underlying table or query.

In this example, assume that the form is named and the control for which you want to build the Value List is named `ReportName`. The first step is to open `Fancy SkipLabels Form` in Design view and get to its property sheet. Choose Form from the property sheet's drop-down list so that you're setting properties for the form as a whole. Then click the Event tab, click the `On Load` event, click the Build button, click Code Builder, and then click OK. The VBA Editor opens with the cursor inside an event procedure named `Form_Load()`, like this:

```
Private Sub Form_Load()

End Sub
```

Any code that you place inside that procedure executes each time the form opens. In this case, you want that code to loop through the `AllReports` collection, building a string of report names separated by semicolons that you can use as the `ValueList` for the `ReportName` drop-down list. The following code creates that semicolon-delimited list of report names from all reports in the current database:

```
Private Sub Form_Load()
    'ValueList variable will store a string that can
    'be used as the Value List property for a combo box.
    Dim ValueList As String
    ValueList = ""

    'Loop through all report names.
    For Each AccessObject In CurrentProject.AllReports
        'Add current report name and semicolon to ValueList variable.
        ValueList = ValueList & Chr(34) & AccessObject.Name & Chr(34) & ";"
    Next

    'Now make ValueList the Value List for the ReportName combo box.
    Debug.Print ValueList
    ReportName.RowSource = ValueList
    ReportName.Requery
End Sub
```

Take a moment to see how this example works. The `For Each...Next` loop loops through each report in the database's `Reports` collection. For each report, the code adds a quotation mark (specified as `Chr(34)` in the code), the report name, another quotation mark, and a semicolon.

TIP

Every character on your keyboard has an ASCII number assigned to it. For example, a double quotation mark is character number 34. A single quotation mark is character number 39. Using Chr(34) in code tells VBA to insert a double quotation mark in place of Chr(34).

With each pass through the loop, the variable named ValueList gets another report name enclosed in quotation marks, followed by a semicolon. As written, the loop just adds every report name to the ValueList variable. So, referring back to the report names shown in Figure 9-6, by the time the loop has looked at every report name in the database, the ValueList variable contains this:

```
"Avery 8463 Labels";"Avery 8462 Labels";"Avery 5197
        Labels";"Customer Directory";"Avery Name Tag
        Labels";"Vendor Directory";"Invoices and
        Receipts Rpt";"Sales Tax Due
        Rpt";"LabelsTempReport";
```

The next lines change the ReportName control's RowSource property to the value of the ValueList variable:

```
ReportName.RowSource = ValueList
ReportName.Requery
```

The ReportName.Requery statement just makes sure that the form is aware of the change so that the combo box always shows the correct names. By the time the procedure has run, in this example, the ReportName combo box drop-down list would contain these options:

✔ Avery 8463 Labels

✔ Avery 8462 Labels

✔ Avery 5197 Labels

✔ Customer Directory

✔ Avery Name Tag Labels

✔ Vendor Directory

✔ Invoices and Receipts Rpt

✔ Sales Tax Due Rpt

✔ LabelsTempReport

There are a couple of little problems here. For one, not all these reports print mailing labels, so not all the report names are appropriate for the SkipLabels procedure. Also, LabelsTempReport isn't really a valid report name: It's just a temporary report name created by the SkipLabels procedure.

If you want to exclude `LabelsTempReport` from the drop-down list, you need to modify the code so that the name isn't added to the `ValueList` variable. The necessary lines to be added are shown here in boldface:

```
Dim ValueList As String
ValueList = ""
'Loop through all report names.
For Each AccessObject In CurrentProject.AllReports
    'Don't add LabelsTempReport to drop-down menu.
    If Not AccessObject.Name = "LabelsTempReport" Then
        'Add current report name and semicolon to ValueList variable.
        ValueList = ValueList & Chr(34) & AccessObject.Name & Chr(34) & ";"
    End If
Next

'Now make ValueList the Value List for the ReportName combo box.
ReportName.RowSource = ValueList
ReportName.Requery
```

By the time all the preceding code is executed, the `ValueList` property for the `ReportName` control contains all report names except `LabelsTempReport`, which got skipped over by the statement

```
If Not AccessObject.Name = "LabelsTempReport" Then
```

You can narrow the list of report names to just those reports that can print labels, but you need some means of being able to tell those reports apart from other ones. Suppose that we make this rule: Any report in this database that prints labels must have the word *labels* in its name. If we make that rule and stick to it, we can rewrite the preceding code so that only reports with the word *labels* in the name are added to `ValueList`, as shown in boldface here:

```
'ValueList variable will store a string that can
'be used as the Value List property for a combo box.
Dim ValueList As String
ValueList = ""

'Loop through all report names.
For Each AccessObject In CurrentProject.AllReports
    'Don't add LabelsTempReport to the Value List.
    If Not AccessObject.Name = "LabelsTempReport" Then
        'Only add report names that contain the word "labels".
        If InStr(AccessObject.Name, "Labels") > 1 Then
            'Add current report name and semicolon to ValueList variable.
            ValueList = ValueList & Chr(34) & _
            AccessObject.Name & Chr(34) & ";"
        End If
    End If
Next
```

```
'Now make ValueList the Value List for the ReportName combo box.
ReportName.RowSource = ValueList
ReportName.Requery
```

Excluding `LabelsTempReport` and any other reports that don't have the word *labels* in their names creates the following string in the `ValueList` variable and ultimately in the `ValueList` property of the `ReportName` combo box. Hence, the `ValueList` string ends up containing

```
"Avery 8463 Labels";"Avery 8462 Labels";"Avery 5197 Labels";
          "Avery Name Tag Labels";
```

which means that the drop-down list for the `ReportName` combo box ends up containing these options:

- ✔ Avery 8463 Labels
- ✔ Avery 8462 Labels
- ✔ Avery 5197 Labels
- ✔ Avery Name Tag Labels

Listing 9-1 shows the complete procedure with the ability to build the list of report names from only those reports that have the word *labels* in their name, excluding the report named `LabelsTempTable`.

Listing 9-1:   Building a List of Report Names

```
Private Sub Form_Load()
    'ValueList variable will store a string that can
    'be used as the Value List property for a combo box
    Dim ValueList As String
    ValueList = ""

    'Loop through all report names.
    For Each AccessObject In CurrentProject.AllReports
        'Don't add LabelsTempReport to the ValueList.
        If Not AccessObject.Name = "LabelsTempReport" Then
            'Only add report names that contain the word "labels".
            If InStr(AccessObject.Name, "Labels") > 1 Then
                'Add current report name and semicolon to ValueList variable.
                ValueList = ValueList & Chr(34) & _
                Access Object.Name & Chr(34) & ";"
            End If
        End If
    Next

    'Now make ValueList the Value List for the ReportName combo box.
    ReportName.RowSource = ValueList
    ReportName.Requery
End Sub
```

The main point to glean from this example, though, is that the drop-down list for a combo box need not be set in concrete. With VBA, you can customize the drop-down list as needed by changing the control's .RowSource property. In this example, the code to build the ReportName drop-down list is executed each time Fancy SkipLabels Form opens. Hence, if any reports have been added, renamed, or deleted since the last time the form opened, the drop-down list still accurately reflects the names of all reports in the current database that contain the word *labels*.

If you import Fancy SkipLabels Form into an existing database, the drop-down list automatically displays all report names that contain the word *labels* (excluding LabelsTempReport) in that database. Of course, if that other database didn't follow the rule of including the word *labels* in all label reports, the procedure as it stands wouldn't work. you would need to either rename reports in that database to follow the rule (which could be disastrous for any existing macro or code that refers to existing report names) or make copies of all existing label reports and rename the copies to include the word *labels*.

If you already have some other means of uniquely identifying label reports in your database, you can change the rule in the code accordingly. For example, if all the label reports contain the word *Avery*, you can change the inner If...End If block to exclude report names that don't contain the word *Avery*, as shown here:

```
'Only add report names that contain the name "Avery".
If InStr(AccessObject.Name, "Avery") > 1 Then
    'Add report name and semicolon to ValueList variable.
    ValueList = ValueList & Chr(34) & _
    AccessObject.Name & Chr(34) & ";"
End If
```

The Form_Load() procedure executes as soon as you open the form. To fully test the form after creating or changing the Form_OnLoad() event procedure, close and save the form first. Then open it in Form view from the Navigation pane.

Creating a Spin Box Control

Many Windows dialog boxes offer a *spin box* control, which lets you change a number without typing. Oddly enough, there's no spin box control in the Controls group to let you create such a control on your Access forms. If you want to add a spin box control to an Access form, you have to fudge it. Writing the code for the spin buttons is easy; creating the little buttons is the real challenge.

We've used numerous techniques to create the spin buttons. We've imported ActiveX controls, used command buttons with special characters, like up or down arrows, and even used transparent-background GIFs to put a tiny arrow on each command button. Because the spin buttons are so tiny, though, getting the command button to look right is difficult.

We finally just gave in and drew each button as a tiny graphical image. (It really doesn't matter whether you use a command button or a picture for the spin button because buttons and pictures both have On Click event properties to which you can tie code.) Figure 9-8 shows buttons that we drew for this example magnified 800 percent in Paint. The lower half of that figure shows the buttons in place on a form. To get the button images onto the form, we just used the Image control in the Controls group on the (Form Design Tools) Design tab.

Figure 9-8:
Spin button
images in
a program
(top) and on
a form
(bottom).

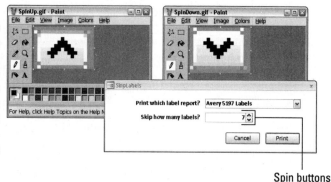

Spin buttons

Regardless of whether you use command buttons or pictures to get spin buttons onto a form, getting them to work is the same. You can name each button or image as you would any other control (via the Name property on the All tab of the property sheet). We named our two image controls SpinUpBttn and SpinDownBttn.

After you have the controls on the form in Design view, click the Spin Up image control, click Events in the property sheet, click the On Click event property, click the Code button, and then choose Code Builder. The VBA Editor opens with the cursor already in a procedure named SpinUpBttn_Click() (assuming that you named your Spin Up button SpinUpBttn). In our example, we want each click of the Spin Up button to increase the value in the LabelsToSkip control by 1.

Use an If...Then...End If statement to put an upper limit on how high the value can go. We chose 80 as an upper limit (because we doubt that many label sheets offer more than 80 labels per page), but you can set your upper limit to any value you want. The following code increases the value in the LabelsToSkip control each time a user clicks the form's SpinUpBttn control:

```
Private Sub SpinUpBttn_Click()
    'Increase LabelsToSkip by 1 to a maximum of 80.
    If Me!LabelsToSkip.Value < 80 Then
        Me!LabelsToSkip.value = Me.LabelsToSkip.Value + 1
    End If
End Sub
```

After writing the code for the SpinUpBttn and returning to your form in Design view, click the SpinDownBttn control on your form. Again, get to that control's On Click event property in the property sheet and write a routine like the one that follows. In that example, we put a lower limit of 0 (zero) on the value in the LabelsToSkip control:

```
Private Sub SpinDownBttn_Click()
    'Decrease LabelsToSkip by 1 to a minimum of 0.
    If Me!LabelsToSkip.Value > 0 Then
        Me!LabelsToSkip.value = Me.LabelsToSkip.Value - 1
    End If
End Sub
```

The following code shows both procedures in place in the class module for our Fancy SkipLabels dialog box example. Again, the biggest trick to getting spin buttons on a form is getting buttons that are small enough to fit next to the control. After you have a command button or picture in place, you can program its On Click event procedure to increase or decrease the value in a numeric field by 1 with each click.

```
Private Sub SpinDownBttn_Click()
    'Decrease LabelsToSkip by 1 to a minimum of 0.
    'If Me!LabelsToSkip.Value > 0 Then
        Me!LabelsToSkip.Value = Me.LabelsToSkipValue - 1
    End If
End Sub

Private Sub SpinUpBttn_Click()
    'Increase LabelsToSkip by 1 to a maximum of 80.
    If Me!LabelsToSkip.Value < 80 Then
        Me!LabelsToSkip.Value = Me.LabelsToSkip.Value + 1
    End If
End Sub
```

Detecting a Right-Click

You might have noticed that just about every control has an `On Click` event to which you can tie code. The `On Click` event occurs only when the user points to the item and then presses and releases the left mouse button. There's no `On Right-Click` event that you can use to detect whether the user right-clicks an item.

If you want to write different code for different types of clicks, you have to use the `On MouseDown` event. When you click an object's `On MouseDown` event in the property sheet and choose the Code Builder, the procedure that's created looks something like this (where *objectName* is the name of the object to which you're tying the code):

```
Private Sub objectName_MouseDown _
   (Button As Integer, Shift As Integer, _
   X As Single, Y As Single)

End Sub
```

The arguments that get passed automatically to the procedure are listed as follows:

- ✔ *Button*: Returns a number or constant indicating which mouse button the user pressed.

  - Left mouse button: `Button` argument contains `acLeftButton`.

  - Middle mouse button (or mouse wheel): `Button` contains `acMiddleButton`.

  - Right mouse button: `Button` contains `acRightButton`.

- ✔ *Shift*: Returns a constant indicating whether the user held down the Shift, Alt, or Ctrl key while pressing the mouse button. Possible values for Shift include

  - `acShiftMask`: The Shift key was held down.

  - `acCtrlMask`: The Ctrl key was held down.

  - `acAltMask`: The Alt key was held down.

- ✔ *X*: Returns a number indicating the horizontal position of the mouse pointer.

- ✔ *Y*: Returns a number indicating the vertical position of the mouse pointer.

In your procedure, you can use `If...Then...End If` statements to write different code for different mouse activities. For example, Listing 9-2 shows the basic skeletal structure that responds differently to a left, middle, or right mouse click.

Listing 9-2:   Skeletal Structure of Code to Distinguish between Left and Right Mouse Clicks

```
Private Sub ObjectName_MouseDown(Button As Integer, _
   Shift As Integer, X As Single, Y As Single)

   'Code for left mouse button.
   If Button = acLeftButton Then
      'Code to execute for left button goes here.
      MsgBox "You pressed the Left mouse button"
   End If

   'Code for right mouse button.
   If Button = acRightButton Then
      'Code to execute for left button goes here.
      MsgBox "You pressed the Right mouse button"
   End If

   'Code for middle mouse button.
   If Button = acMiddleButton Then
      'Code to execute for middle button goes here.
      MsgBox "You pressed the Middle mouse button"
   End If

End Sub
```

As it stands, the sample procedure just provides a little message on-screen indicating which mouse button you pressed. In your actual code, you replace the `MsgBox` statements with the VBA code that you want to execute after the left, middle, or right mouse click.

In the next chapter, we dig deeper into the whole topic of creating custom drop-down lists by using VBA code. The techniques that you can see there apply to any form that you create, whether that form is a dialog box or just a regular Access form for scrolling through table records.

Chapter 10

Customizing Combo Boxes and List Boxes

In This Chapter

▶ Programming combo boxes and list boxes

▶ Linking lists

▶ Updating one form's control from another form

▶ Discovering cool combo box tricks

*T*yping information into forms takes time, and typing always means the possibility of making typographical errors. Whenever you can eliminate typing by giving the user something to click, you're making your data entry quicker and more accurate.

Combo boxes and list boxes are both good tools for giving the user options to choose from when typing would otherwise be necessary. A *combo box* is basically a text box with a drop-down arrow on the right, as in the left side of Figure 10-1. The options available to the user — also shown on the left side of Figure 10-1 — aren't visible until she clicks the drop-down arrow. The user can either type in the text box or choose an option from the drop-down list.

The right side of Figure 10-1 shows an example of a list box. Like a combo box, the list box shows a list of options, but it has no hidden drop-down list: The list (or at least some portion of it) is plainly visible. Also, with a list box, there's no place to type text. The user has to choose an option from the list by clicking it. The selected option is highlighted in the control.

Because both combo and list boxes display a list of values on-screen, they have many similar properties. For example, every combo box and list box has a Row Source property that defines where the list of options comes from. When you use the Control Wizards to create a combo or list box, the wizard sets the Row Source property according to how you answer its questions. In forms Design view, you can set the Row Source property via the property sheet. From VBA, you can change the Row Source property by using the .RowSource keyword.

Combo box

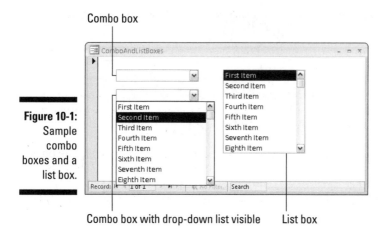

Figure 10-1:
Sample
combo
boxes and a
list box.

Combo box with drop-down list visible   List box

Programming Combo and List Boxes

When working with combo and list boxes through VBA, you often want to start with just a simple *unbound control* (one that's not attached to any field in the form's underlying table or query) and then let VBA control the properties.

To add an unbound `ComboBox` or a `ListBox` control to a form, first make sure that the form is open in Design view. Then click the (Form Design Tools) Design tab to see the Controls group (see Figure 10-2). To prevent the Control Wizards from helping you create the control, click the Use Control Wizards command so that it's no longer highlighted. Then follow these steps:

Figure 10-2:
List box and
combo box
buttons in
the Controls
group.

Combo box

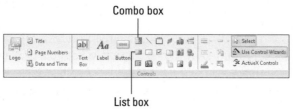

List box

1. **Click the (Form Design Tools) Design tab on the Ribbon, and then in the Controls group, click either the Combo Box or List Box tool, depending on which one you want to create.**

   If it's hard to tell one button from the other in the Controls group, just hover the mouse pointer over any button in the Controls group to see its name appear in a ScreenTip.

2. **In the form, click where you want the left edge of the control to appear.**

3. **If the wizard appears and you don't want to use it, click the Cancel button in the wizard.**

After the combo box or list box is on your form, you can view its properties in the property sheet. As always, if the property sheet isn't already open, you can press F4 or right-click the control and choose Properties.

Like all controls, combo boxes and list boxes have lots of properties. The ones that you're most likely to refer to from VBA are summarized in the following list. The first name (in bold) is the property name as it appears in the property sheet; the following name in parentheses is the name of the property as written in VBA:

- **Name** (.Name): Defines the name of the control.

- **Row Source Type** (.RowSourceType): Specifies where the list gets its data: from records in a Table/Query, from a simple Value List typed into the Row Source property, or from a Field List of field names from a table or query.

- **Row Source** (.RowSource): Depending on the Row Source Type, this can be a SQL statement that gets data from a table or query, a typed list of options, or the name of a table or query.

- **Default Value** (.DefaultValue): The item that's automatically selected when you're adding a new record.

- **List Rows** (.ListRows): (Combo box only) The number of items to shown in the drop-down list.

- **List Width** (.ListWidth): (Combo box only) The width of the drop-down list. If it's set to Auto, the drop-down list width is equal in width to the ComboBox control.

- **Limit To List** (.LimitToList): (Combo box only) If Yes, the user's entry in the combo box must match an item in its drop-down list. Otherwise, whatever the user typed is rejected as an invalid entry.

- **Value** (.Value): (VBA only) The value contained within the control.

To name a control on a form, first click the control to select it. Then click the All tab in the property sheet. Set the Name property at the top of the All tab to whatever you want to name your control.

In addition to the properties from the property sheet, VBA has an ItemData(*x*) property (where *x* is a number) that lets you refer to each item in the list by its position in the list. The first item is always zero (0), so the first item in the list can be referred to as ItemData(0), the next item as ItemData(1), and then ItemData(2) down to the end of the list.

A list box doesn't have a `List Rows` or `List Width` property because there's no drop-down list in a list box. The width and height of the `ListBox` control, as a whole, determine the width and length of the list. There's no `Limit To List` property for a list box because there's no optional text box in which the user could type a value. With a list box, the user is always required to choose an option in the list.

Combo boxes and list boxes are both examples of list controls (in that they show some sort of list to the user). After the preceding quick peek at some commonly used properties of those controls, read on to take a look at how you work those puppies.

In the form's Design view, you can easily change a text box to a combo box or to a list box or whatever. Just right-click the control that you want to change and then choose Change To⇨*xx* (the type of control you want).

Listing field names

If you want a list box or combo box to list the names of fields in a table or query, set the control's `Row Source Type` property to `Field List` and set its `Row Source` property to the name of the table or query that contains the fields whose names you want to list.

For example, Figure 10-3 shows a `ComboBox` control named `FldNamesCombo` on a form. As you can see in the property sheet, its Row Source Type is set to `Field List`, and its Row Source is set to `Customers`. The names in the control's drop-down list (CustID, FirstName, LastName, and so forth) are field names from a table named `Customers`.

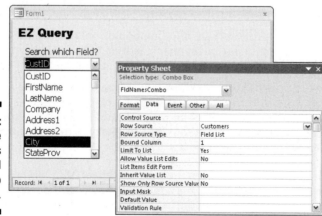

Figure 10-3: Row Source properties for a Field List combo box.

From a VBA standpoint, if you want the FldNamesCombo control to show field names from a different table or query in response to some event, change the control's .RowSource property to the name of the table or query from which you want the control to get field names. For example, this statement sets the Row Source property of the control named FldNamesCombo to a table named Products (so the control shows field names from the Products table):

```
Me!FldNamesCombo.RowSource = "Products"
```

The Me! in these examples refers to the form to which the control is attached and works only from a class module. From a standard module, Me! would have to be replaced with the full identifier for the open form — for example:

```
Forms![EzQueryFrm]![FldNamesCombo].RowSource = "Products"
```

if the control is on an open form named EZQueryFrm.

In your code, you can take extra steps to make sure that the control's Row Source Type is set correctly to Field List before putting in the new table name. After the field receives its new list, you can use the statement

```
Me!FldNamesCombo.Value = Me!FldNamesCombo.ItemData(0)
```

to set the selected option in a combo box to the first item in the drop-down list. Here's all the code together to change the drop-down list:

```
'Make sure the control's Row Source Type is Field List.
Me!FldNamesCombo.RowSourceType = "Field List"

'Change the Row Source table to Products table.
Me!FldNamesCombo.RowSource = "Products"

'Set combo box value to first item in drop-down list.
Me!FldNamesCombo.Value = Me!FldNamesCombo.ItemData(0)
```

Using the keyword Me! in the preceding examples assumes that the code is in the class module for whatever form the FldNamesCombo control is on. To change the FldNamesCombo properties from a standard module or another form's class module, include the complete identifier for the open form. For example, if the FldNamesCombo control is on a form named EZQueryFrm, the complete identifier for the form is Forms![EzQueryFrm]! rather than Me!. The complete identifier to the FldNamesCombo control is Forms![EzQueryFrm]![FldNamesCombo].

In code, you can spell out the complete identifier in each line of code, like this:

```
'Make sure the control's Row Source Type is Field List.
Forms![EzQueryFrm]![FldNamesCombo].RowSourceType = "Field List"

'Change the Row Source table to Products table.
Forms![EzQueryFrm]![FldNamesCombo].RowSource = "Products"

'Set combo box value to first item in drop-down list.
Forms![EzQueryFrm]![FldNamesCombo].Value _
    = Forms![EzQueryFrm]![FldNamesCombo].ItemData(0)
```

To avoid typing `Forms![EzQueryFrm]![FldNamesCombo]` repeatedly in your code, define a `Control` object variable that refers to the control through a shorter name:

```
'Make short name MyControl refer to
'Forms![EZQueryFrm]![FldNamesCombo]
Dim MyControl As Control
Set MyControl = Forms![EZQueryFrm]![FldNamesCombo]

'Make sure the control's Row Source Type is Field List.
MyControl.RowSourceType = "Field List"

'Change the Row Source table to Products table.
MyControl.RowSource = " Products"

'Set combo box value to first item in drop-down list.
MyControl.Value = MyControl.ItemData(0)
```

For example, the first line of the preceding code (`Dim MyControl As Control`) defines a new, empty `Control` object variable named `MyControl`. The second line

```
Set MyControl = Forms![EzQueryFrm]![FldNamesCombo]
```

makes the short name `MyControl` refer specifically to the control named `FldNamesCombo` on the form named `EZQueryFrm`. The last two lines are the same as the last two lines in this example except that they use the shorter name `MyControl` to refer to `Forms![EzQueryFrm]![FldNamesCombo]` (which makes the code a little easier to read).

The main point here though is that if you have a combo box or list box on a form, you can programmatically change the contents of the list (or drop-down list) to show the field names from any table or query in the database. Now turn your attention to the second type of list — one that gets its values from a Value List.

Listing text options

A combo box or list box can get its values from a simple string called a Value List. The string just contains each item in the list separated by semicolons. If the items in the list are all text, you should enclose each item in quotation marks.

For example, Figure 10-4 shows a combo box (named `OpsCombo`) added to a form. You can see the items in the open combo box: =, `Like`, <, >, and so forth. You can also see the properties for the control. Notice that the Row Source Type is Value List, and the Row Source is a bunch of little chunks of text enclosed in quotation marks and separated by semicolons. On the form, each little chunk of text is shown as an option on the control's drop-down list.

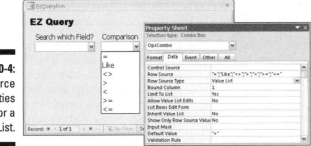

Figure 10-4:
Row Source
properties
for a
Value List.

The Row Source for the `OpsCombo` control is

```
"=";"Like";"<>";">";"<";">=";"<="
```

which is why the drop-down list displays the various comparison operators. You can programmatically change the contents of a Value List combo or list by using the `RowSource` property. The new Row Source value must follow the rules of syntax, though, with each item separated by a semicolon and each string enclosed in quotation marks.

In code, you can represent a quotation mark as `Chr(34)` (the 34th ASCII character). That's generally easier than trying to add quotation marks by enclosing them in single quotation marks, like ' " ', which doesn't always work and is difficult to read. For example, Listing 10-1 declares a string variable named `NewValList` and then adds some text, quotation marks, and semicolons to that string.

Listing 10-1:   Filling a Combo Box Value List Property

```
'Create a string variable named NewValList
Dim NewValList As String

'Build NewValList string in chunks.
NewValList = Chr(34) & "First Item" & Chr(34) & ";"
NewValList = NewValList & Chr(34) & "Second Item" & Chr(34) & ";"
NewValList = NewValList & Chr(34) & "Third Item" & Chr(34) & ";"
NewValList = NewValList & Chr(34) & "Fourth Item" & Chr(34)
'At this point, NewValList contains...
'"First Item";"Second Item";"Third Item";"Fourth Item"

'Make new string the Row Source for value list named OpsCombo
Me!OpsCombo.RowSourceType = "Value List"
Me!OpsCombo.RowSource = NewValList
'Set selection to first item in drop-down list.
Me.OpsCombo.Value = Me.OpsCombo.ItemData(0)
```

When you create a list box or combo box with its Row Source Type set to Value List, you can leave the Row Source property empty. When the form first opens, the list is also empty, which means that the user can't select anything. However, you can write some code that fills the list and then attach it to the form's On Load event. This allows you to create dynamic, flexible lists that adapt themselves to the current database. We look at some examples in the sections that follow.

Making a list of table and query names

Sometimes you might want a combo box or list box to display a list of all the tables, or all the queries, or both. There isn't a simple property setting that lets you do that. You need to programmatically fill the list with names as soon as the form opens. Whenever you want code to execute as soon as a form opens, attach that code to the form's On Load event.

For example, Figure 10-5 shows an empty control named TblQryCombo. Its Row Source Type is set to Value List, but its Row Source property is empty. So without any code, when the form opens, TblQryCombo displays nothing.

Suppose now that when the form opens, you want it to display a list of all table names in the current database. You can write some code that loops through the AllTables collection and adds the name of each table to a string. Then use that string as the Row Source for the control.

Note this catch, though. The AllTables collection includes hidden system tables that Access uses behind the scenes. Because the names of those system tables normally don't appear in the Navigation pane, you should exclude them from the drop-down list as well.

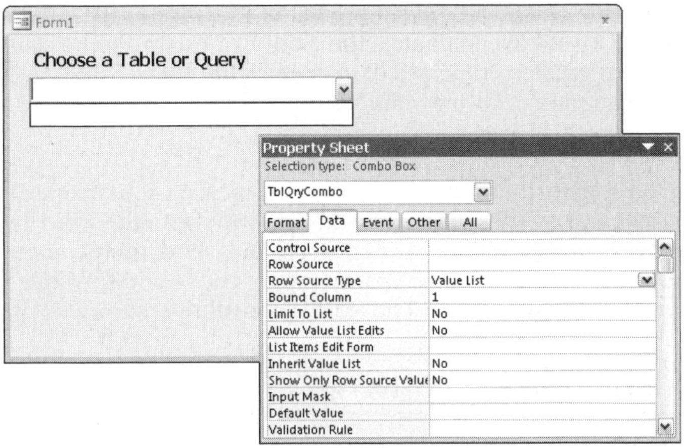

Figure 10-5:
Sample
empty
combo box
named
`TblQry`
`Combo`.

Luckily, all the system tables have names that start with the letters `MSys`. To eliminate those table names from the drop-down list, you can use an `If...Else...End If` block to skip over any name that starts with `MSys`. The complete code to fill `TblQryCombo` with a list of table names as soon as the form opens is shown in Listing 10-2. Each comment refers to the line or lines that follow the comment.

Listing 10-2:   Creating a Combo Box of Table Names

```
Private Sub Form_Load()
    'Declare an empty string to store a value list.
    Dim TblNames As String
    TblNames = ""

    'Loop through AllTables connection, add each table's name to TblNames
    'variable, each enclosed in quotation marks and followed by a semicolon.
    Dim tbl As AccessObject
    For Each tbl In CurrentData.AllTables
        'Exclude system tables, whose names all start with Msys.
        If Not Left(tbl.Name, 4) = "Msys" Then
            TblNames = TblNames & Chr(34) & tbl.Name & Chr(34) & ";"
        End If
    Next tbl

    'TblNames string now has all table names (except system tables).
    'Make it the Row Source for the TblQryCombo control.
    Me!TblQryCombo.RowSourceType = "Value List"
    Me!TblQryCombo.RowSource = TblNames

    'Show first item as selected item in control.
    Me!TblQryCombo.Value = Me!TblQryCombo.ItemData(0)
    'Make sure user can only select a valid name.
    Me!TblQryCombo.LimitToList = True
End Sub
```

If you want the combo box to show a list of all queries rather than all tables, you basically just have to change the word `AllTables` to `AllQueries` so that the loop gathers up names of queries rather than tables. Also, there are no system queries, so you wouldn't need the `If...Then...End If` block to exclude names that begin with `MSys`.

Taking it a step further, suppose that you want the list to display the names of all tables and queries in the current database, with the word `Table:` in front of table names and the word `Query:` in front of query names. You need two loops in the form's `On Load` procedure: one to add the table names and one to add the query names. The entire procedure is shown in Listing 10-3.

Listing 10-3: Creating a Combo Box of Table and Query Names

```
Private Sub Form_Load()
    'Declare an empty string to store a value list.
    Dim TblNames As String
    TblNames = ""

    'To keep lines below short, we'll store the quotation mark
    'as a variable named QM, and just refer to it by
    'name (QM) in code that follows.
    Dim QM As String
    QM = Chr(34)

    'Loop through AllTables connection, add each table's
    'name to TblNames variable, each enclosed in quotation
    'marks and followed by a semicolon.
    Dim tbl As AccessObject
    For Each tbl In CurrentData.AllTables
        'Exclude MSys table names from list.
        If Not Left(tbl.Name, 4) = "MSys" Then
            TblNames = TblNames & QM & "Table: " & tbl.Name & QM & ";"
        End If
    Next tbl

    'Next we loop through the AllQueries collection and add their names.
    Dim qry As AccessObject
    For Each qry In CurrentData.AllQueries
        TblNames = TblNames & QM & "Query: " & qry.Name & QM & ";"
    Next qry

    'TblNames string now has all table and query names.
    'Make it the Row Source for the TblQryCombo control.
    Me!TblQryCombo.RowSourceType = "Value List"
    Me!TblQryCombo.RowSource = TblNames

    'Show first item as selected item in control.
    Me!TblQryCombo.Value = Me!TblQryCombo.ItemData(0)
    'Make sure user can only select a valid name.
    Me!TblQryCombo.LimitToList = True
End Sub
```

Referring to the empty `TblQryCombo` control shown at the start of this section — and assuming that the code in Listing 10-3 is tied to that form's `On Load` event — by the time the form is visible to the user, the control will contain the names of all tables and queries in the current database, as in the example shown in Figure 10-6.

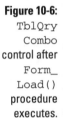

Figure 10-6: `TblQry Combo` control after `Form_ Load()` procedure executes.

Making a list of form or report names

You can use a similar technique to Listing 10-2 to make a drop-down list display the names of all forms or all reports in the current database. For example, Figure 10-7 shows an empty `ComboBox` control named `ObjCombo` (for lack of a better name).

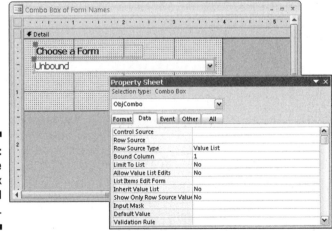

Figure 10-7: Sample combo box named `ObjCombo`.

To fill the `ObjCombo` with a list of all form names in the current database, tie the form's `On Load` event to a procedure that creates a value list of form names, as we do in Listing 10-4.

Listing 10-4: Filling a Combo Box with Form Names

```
Private Sub Form_Load()
    'Define string variable to store new Value List.
    Dim NewValList As String
    NewValList = ""

    'Loop through collection and add each object name
    'with quotation marks and semicolons to NewValList.
    Dim obj As AccessObject
    For Each obj In CurrentProject.AllForms
        NewValList = NewValList & Chr(34) & obj.Name & Chr(34) & ";"
    Next obj

    'Now NewValList contains all object names in proper format.
    'Make that string the Row Source for objCombo control.
    Me!ObjCombo.RowSourceType = "Value List"
    Me!ObjCombo.RowSource = NewValList

    'Set option to first item in list.
    Me!ObjCombo.Value = Me!ObjCombo.ItemData(0)
End Sub
```

If you want that combo box to list all reports rather than all forms in the current database, change the code to loop through the `AllReports` collection rather than the `AllForms` collection. That just involves changing the collection name in the `For Each...Next` loop code block, as shown in boldface:

```
    'Loop through collection and add each object name
    'with quotation marks and semicolons to NewValList.
    Dim obj As AccessObject
    For Each obj In CurrentProject.AllReports
        NewValList = NewValList & Chr(34) & obj.Name & Chr(34) & ";"
    Next obj
```

The basic idea is still the same in all these examples. When the form opens, the form's `On Load` event occurs, which then triggers the code in the `Form_Load()` procedure, which in turn creates a valid, up-to-date list of object names to show in the list box or combo box.

Listing Table/Query field values

The third type of combo box or list box that you can create gets its values from a field (or fields) in a table or query. The Row Source Type for such a list is Table/Query, and the Row Source is generally a SQL statement that specifies which fields and values to show in the list. Back up a moment and take a look at the bigger picture.

Suppose that you want to create a drop-down list that shows an alphabetized list of all unique company names from a table. By *unique,* we mean that if a given company name appears multiple times in the table, it still appears only once in the drop-down list (or list box). To create such a query in the query's Design view, you add the field name to the Query By Example (QBE) grid and also choose Ascending as the sort order. To prevent empty records from showing up in the query results, set a criterion to Is Not Null, as in the example shown in Figure 10-8.

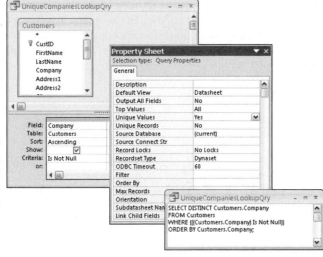

Figure 10-8: Sample unique values query for a text field.

To see the SQL view of a query on your own screen, as shown on the bottom of Figure 10-8, right-click the query's title bar and choose SQL View. For more information, see Chapter 7.

To ensure that only unique addresses appear, you then need to double-click the gray area at the top of the query to open the Query property sheet. In the Query property sheet, set the Unique Values property to Yes, as in the example shown in Figure 10-8.

We also managed to sneak the SQL view of the same query into Figure 10-8. Like any SQL statement, it describes in words what the query will do when it's opened. In this case, those words are

```
SELECT DISTINCT Customers.Company
FROM Customers
WHERE (((Customers.Company) Is Not Null))
ORDER BY Customers.Company;
```

The SQL statement says the same thing that the items in the QBE grid say, which is "Select unique Company names from the `Customers` table, excluding blanks (nulls), and put them in alphabetical order."

The `Unique Values` property eliminates duplicate values within a single field. If a query contains multiple fields and you want only records with identical values in every field to be considered a duplicate, set the `Unique Records` property to Yes (or `True`). The SQL keyword for Unique Values is `DISTINCT`, and the SQL keyword for Unique Records is `DISTINCTROW`.

The SQL statement would work as the `Row Source` property for a `ListBox` or `ComboBox` control. In VBA, however, you'd probably prefer to use the following slightly different syntax, partly because you can omit all the parentheses and partly because the table name in front of the field name (for example, `Customer.Company`) is required only when the query involves two or more tables with identical field names. In the following syntax, *tableName* is the name of a table in the current database, and *fieldName* is the name of any field within that table:

```
SELECT DISTINCT [fieldName]
FROM [tableName]
WHERE [fieldName] Is Not Null
ORDER BY [fieldName]
```

For example, Figure 10-9 shows a `ComboBox` control named `SearchVal` with its drop-down list already visible. That drop-down list contains an alphabetized list of company names from a table named `Customers` because the control's Row Source Type is set to Table/Query, and its `Row Source` property is set to the following SQL statement (shown as one lengthy line within the property):

```
SELECT DISTINCT [Company] FROM Customers WHERE [Company] Is Not Null ORDER BY
            [Company];
```

Now, suppose that you want to programmatically change the `SearchVal` combo box so that it shows all unique zip codes from the `Customers` table. This example assumes that the `Customers` table stores zip codes in a field named `ZipCode`. But the idea is to create a new SQL statement that refers to the `ZipCode` field rather than to the `Company` field, as follows. Then use that new SQL statement as the `Row Source` property for the `SearchVal` control:

```
'Create a string named MySql, and put a SQL statement in
            it.
Dim MySQL As String
MySQL = "SELECT DISTINCT [ZipCode] FROM [Customers]"
MySQL = MySQL & " WHERE [ZipCode] Is Not Null"
MySQL = MySQL & " ORDER BY [ZipCode]"

'Now MySQL contains a valid SQL statement. Use that SQL
```

```
'statement as the Row Source for the SearchVal control.
Me!SearchVal.RowSource = MySQL

'Make the first menu option the selected item in list.
Me!SearchVal.Value = Me.SearchVal.ItemData(0)
```

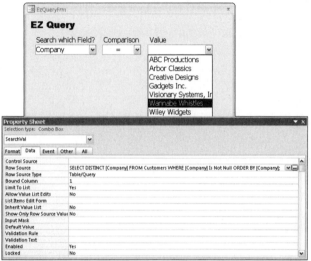

Figure 10-9:
`Search`
`Val` is a
ComboBox
control.

Even though the SQL statement is built in chunks in the code (just to make the lines short enough to fit inside these margins), the SQL statement that's created and stored in the `MySQL` variable is one long line of text composed of all the chunks. By the time the last `MySQL = MySQL & . . .` statement has executed, the `MySQL` variable contains

```
SELECT DISTINCT [ZipCode] FROM [Customers] WHERE [ZipCode]
        Is Not Null ORDER BY [ZipCode]
```

In the procedure, the statement `Me!SearchVal.RowSource = MySQL` puts the complete SQL statement into the `Row Source` property of the control. When the user clicks the drop-down button, the control shows all unique zip codes from the `Customers` table, as in Figure 10-10.

The bottom line here is that programmatically, you can do anything you want with a `ListBox` or `ComboBox` control. Like with anything you do through VBA, controlling when a combo box gets changed is a matter of choosing an appropriate event. Often the triggering event is a change to some other control on the form or even a different form. In this way, you can control what appears in a combo or list box based on the contents of some other control, which brings us to linking lists.

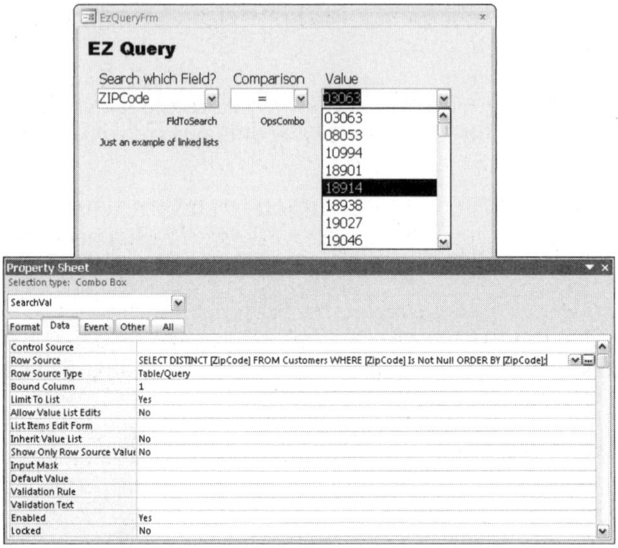

Figure 10-10:
Result of
changing
a combo
box's Row
Source
property.

Linking Lists

One of the many reasons for programming ListBox and ComboBox controls
is to create *linked lists,* where the options in one control depend on what's
selected in another control. As an example, Figure 10-11 shows a form named
Fancy SkipLabels Dialog Box that contains three dynamic combo boxes
named LabelRpt, FldToSearch, and ValueToFind. Because the fourth
combo box (not pointed out) is *static,* its drop-down list never changes.

LabelRpt

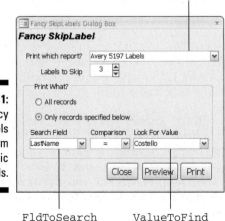

Figure 10-11:
Fancy
SkipLabels
form
dynamic
controls.

FldToSearch   ValueToFind

The names of the dynamic controls and the relationships between the control are summarized here:

- ✔ `LabelRpt`: This `ComboBox` lists names of all reports in the current database that contain the word *label*. It needs to be filled once — the moment when the form opens.

- ✔ `FldToSearch`: This `ComboBox` lists the names of fields from the selected report's underlying table or query. The list needs to be updated each time the user chooses a report to print from the `LabelRpt` control.

- ✔ `ValueToFind`: This displays a list of all unique values in the field selected in the `FldToSearch` combo box. Each time the user chooses a field to search on, this combo box needs to be changed to list values from the selected field.

You can envision the relationships between the combo boxes as *dependencies,* in the sense that the exact items in a combo box depend on what's selected and available at the moment. For example, what appears in the `FldToSearch` combo box depends on what report is selected at the moment in `LabelRpt`. Similarly, what appears in the `ValueToFind` combo box depends on what field name is selected in the `FldToSearch` control. As is always the case, just writing the code to make these controls always show the "right stuff" is only part of the problem. You also have to control exactly *when* that code runs. Look at some examples of that first, which we follow with some of the code.

To make life simpler, we encapsulated the code that updates each combo box as its own little procedure. The fancy programming term *encapsulation* translates to something along the lines of *Save yourself from having to deal with this problem more than once.* For example, if we create a procedure named `UpdateFldToSeachCombo()` and make its job to ensure that the `FldToSearch` control is up-to-date, we don't have to worry about when the code gets executed. We can just tie the statement `UpdateFldToSeachCombo` to any event on any control in the form when we want that event to update the `FldToSearch` control.

That's sort of a programming strategy. To encapsulate the code needed to update each of the three dynamic controls shown in Figure 10-11, we wrote three separate procedures and named each one so that it describes what it does. The names of those procedures are

- ✔ `Sub UpdateLabelRptCombo()`: This procedure updates the list of reports in the `LabelRpt` combo box on the form to accurately reflect label reports in the current database.

- ✔ `Sub UpdateFldToSearchCombo()`: This procedure ensures that the `FldToSrch` combo box accurately reflects the names of fields in the selected report's recordsource. It allows the user to choose a field name on which to create a filter.

✔ Sub UpdateValueToFindCombo(): As its name suggests, this procedure ensures that the unique values displayed in the ValueToFind combo box accurately reflect the contents of the field specified in the FldToSearch control.

The advantage of creating these procedures is that we could just concentrate on getting each one to work (at all) without worrying about *when* the procedure will do its thing. In our code, when we want to tie the procedure to a particular event, the triggered procedure need only call the appropriate Sub procedure to get its job done. Again, we look at each procedure in a moment. Just focus on the *when* for now.

Running code when a form opens

If you want a procedure to execute as soon as a form opens and any data from the form's underlying table or query has been loaded into the form, tie a procedure to the forms On Load event. The name of that procedure, in every form, is Form_Load(). The Form_Load() procedure for the sample form shown in Figure 10-11 looks something like this:

```
Private Sub Form_Load()
    Call UpdateLabelRptCombo
    Call UpdateFldToSearchCombo
    Call UpdateValueToFindCombo
End Sub
```

In the form's Design view, make sure that the property sheet shows the word Form in the drop-down list. Double-clicking the gray area behind the form's Design grid or the gray box where the rulers meet instantly displays Form properties in the property sheet.

The basic logic of the Form_Load() procedure is straightforward: It simply updates each of the three ComboBox controls in the order that they need to be updated. When the form opens, each ComboBox control has actual, reasonable data in its drop-down list.

Suppose that the form is open and the user chooses a report name from the LabelRpt drop-down list. When that happens, the two controls beneath LabelRpt need to have their drop-down lists updated. First the FieldToSearch drop-down list needs to be updated to reflect field names from the selected report's recordsource (underlying table or query). Then, after that control gets a new value, the ValueToFind drop-down list needs to be updated to reflect legitimate values for the selected field name. To make that happen, a change to the LabelRpt control needs to run two of the update procedures. Here's the AfterUpdate event procedure for the LabelsRpt control:

```
Private Sub LabelRpt_AfterUpdate()
    Call UpdateFldToSearchCombo
    Call UpdateValueToFindCombo
End Sub
```

The preceding procedure says, "After the user chooses a different report to print, update the FldToSearch and ValueToFind combo boxes on this form."

Running code when the user makes a choice

To make a procedure execute after the user chooses an option from a combo or list box, tie the procedure to the control's After Update event property. For example, when the user chooses a different field to search on from the Search Field option on the Fancy SkipLabels form (the FldToSearch control), the Look For Value drop-down list needs to be updated to show unique values from that field. To make sure that the ValueToList control gets updated whenever the user chooses a different field to search, we added the following procedure to the form's class module:

```
Private Sub FldToSearch_AfterUpdate()
    Call UpdateValueToFindCombo
End Sub
```

The preceding class procedure says, "After the user chooses a different field to search on, update the Value to Find combo box to list unique values from the specified field."

Getting fancy SkipLabels

You can download the Fancy SkipLabels Dialog Box form and all its code from www. dummies.com/go/access2007vbaprog. You won't find any standard modules in that database. All the code for Fancy SkipLabels Dialog Box are in the form's class module. If you look at that code, you see more than just what's shown in this chapter. (That's because much of the code there isn't relevant to this chapter's topic.)

To use Fancy SkipLabels Dialog Box in your own database, you first need to create at least one report for printing labels and also make sure to save that report with the word *label* in its name so that SkipLabels finds the report. Then you need to import Label SettingsTable and Fancy SkipLabels Dialog Box Form from the downloaded database into your own database. The Web site provides more information.

Getting back to the encapsulation strategy, you can see that it wouldn't be too tough to make other events on other controls update any dynamic list on the form. Just click the control, click its After Update event property, and add the code needed to call the appropriate procedures in the event procedure.

The various preceding called procedures all follow the examples presented earlier in this chapter. For example, the LabelRpt control, which displays a drop-down list of reports with the word *label* in their names, gets its information from the AllReports collection (see Listing 10-5):

Listing 10-5:   Updating a Combo Box of Report Names

```
'** UpdateLabelRptCombo() updates the LabelRpt control.
Private Sub UpdateLabelRptCombo()
    'ValListVar variable will store a string that can
    'be used as the Value List property for a combo box.
    Dim ValListVar As String
    ValListVar = ""

    'Get names of label reports from AllReports collection,
    'and assemble into a valid Value List for a Combo Box.
    Dim rpt As AccessObject
    For Each rpt In CurrentProject.AllReports
        'Don't add LabelsTempReport to the ValListVar.
        If Not rpt.Name = "LabelsTempReport" Then
            'Only add report names that contain the word "label".
            If InStr(rpt.Name, "Labels") > 1 Then
                'Add label report names to ValListVar with Double Quotes.
                ValListVar = ValListVar & Chr(34) & rpt.Name & Chr(34) & ";"
            End If
        End If
    Next

    'ValListVar now contains valid report names, so next
    'lines make it the Row Source property for LabelRpt.
    Me!LabelRpt.RowSourceType = "Value List"
    Me!LabelRpt.RowSource = ValListVar
    Me!LabelRpt.Requery
End Sub
```

The UpdateFldToSearchCombo procedure updates the drop-down list in the FldToSearch control. The code gets the name of the label report to print from the LabelRpt control on the form (referred to as Me!LabelRpt.Value in the code). It then (invisibly) opens that report in Design view and copies its Record Source property (which is the name of the report's underlying table or query) into its own variable named LabelRecSource. After that, the rest of the code sets the control's Row Source Type to Field List and the Row Source to the name that's stored in that LabelRecSource variable. Listing 10-6 shows the whole procedure with comments to help explain each step.

Listing 10-6: Updating a Combo Box with Field Names

```
'** UpdateFldToSearchCombo() updates the FldToSearch Combo Box.
Private Sub UpdateFldToSearchCombo()

    'Open specified report in Design view.
    DoCmd.OpenReport Me!LabelRpt.Value, acViewDesign, , , acHidden

    'Copy its recordsource name to LabelRecSource variable.
    Dim LabelRecSource As String
    'Placeholder for record source.
    LabelRecSource = Reports(Reports.Count - 1).RecordSource

    'Close the report (only needed to grab record source).
    DoCmd.Close acReport, Me!LabelRpt.Value, acSaveNo

    'Set FldToSearch Combo Box Row Source properties.
    Me!FldToSearch.RowSourceType = "Field List"
    Me!FldToSearch.RowSource = LabelRecSource
    Me!FldToSearch.Requery

End Sub
```

The last dynamic control on the form, `ValueToFind`, gets updated by a `Sub` procedure named `UpdateValueToFindCombo`. This procedure updates the list of unique values in the control's drop-down list to accurately reflect unique values in whatever field the user specified in the `FldToSearch` control. The Row Source Type for the control needs to be Table/Query, and the Row Source has to be a valid SQL statement that specifies what to display. The code in Listing 10-7 builds a valid `SELECT DISTINCT...` query for whatever field's name is selected in the `FldToSearch` control (`Me!FldToSearch.Value` in VBA). Listing 10-7 holds the whole procedure with comments.

Listing 10-7: Updating a Combo Box from a Table

```
Private Sub UpdateValueToFindCombo()
    'Build a SQL statement to pull unique values
    'from whatever field name is selected in form.
    '(If FldToSearch is empty, do nothing)
    If Not IsNull(Me!FldToSearch.Value) Then
        Dim MySQL As String
        MySQL = "SELECT DISTINCT [" & FldToSearch.Value & "]"
        MySQL = MySQL & " FROM [" & LabelRecSource & "]"
        MySQL = MySQL & " WHERE [" & FldToSearch.Value & "] Is Not Null"
        MySQL = MySQL & " ORDER BY [" & FldToSearch.Value & "]"

        'Now that we have the right SQL statement, make it the
        'Row Source for the ValueToFind control.
        Me!ValueToFind.RowSourceType = "Table/Query"
        Me!ValueToFind.RowSource = MySQL
        Me!ValueToFind.Requery
    End If
End Sub
```

In case you're wondering about the `If Not IsNull(!FldToSearch.Value) Then...End If` statements, we originally wrote the procedure without those. At first, the procedure seemed to work fine when tested. But then we discovered that if the `FldToSearch.control` is null (empty) when `UpdateValueTo FindCombo` is called, the procedure crashes and yelps out an error message. To ward off that irritant, we make execution of the code dependent on the `FldToSearch` control's not being null. In other words, the procedure executes only if a field name is selected in the `FldToSearch` control. Otherwise, the procedure does nothing to prevent the error from occurring.

From a programming perspective, the main thing to remember is that every `ListBox` and `ComboBox` control that you create exposes many properties to VBA. Two of those properties, Row Source Type and Row Source, give you strong programmatic control over the choices presented by those controls.

Linking Lists across Forms

Working with list controls (such as `ListBox` and `ComboBox` controls) isn't always a matter of controlling the Row Source Type and Row Source properties of the control. In some cases, it's just getting the darn control to show what's in the underlying table or query — or worse yet, getting it to accept a value that should be acceptable to the control, but isn't. These types of problems happen a lot when two or more forms are involved in the scenario.

We suppose that a typical example is a user who is trying to type in a new order, perhaps coming in over the phone. The user might be sitting there looking only at the `Orders` form shown on the left side of Figure 10-12. To start typing an order, she can choose an existing customer from the `CustID` combo box (labeled "Customer:") on the `Orders` form, or she can click the New Customer button (`NewCustBttn`) to enter name and address info for a new customer.

Disclaimer: All the names and e-mail addresses shown in these figures are fictional, and any resemblance to real people or e-mail addresses is purely coincidental.

If your user clicks the New Customer button, the `NewCust` form (also shown in Figure 10-12) opens at a blank record, ready to type in a new customer's info. Then the user types in the info and clicks the Done - Fill Order button (named `DoneBttn`). At that point, the `NewCust` form closes, and the user is returned to the `Orders` form. That moment — when the `NewCust` form closes and the focus returns to the `Orders` form — is where most troubles begin. The problem has to do with *when* a combo box or list box gets its data from an underlying table or query, which (in general) is only once — when the form opens.

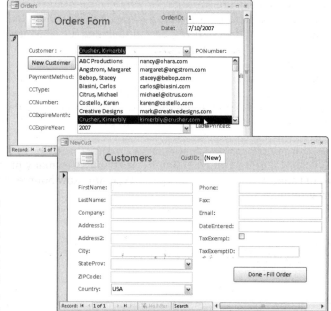

Figure 10-12:
Sample
open
Orders and
NewCust
forms.

Updating a combo box or a list box

A typical combo box or list box gets the values that it shows in its list only once, right after the form opens. For example, the CustID control in the Orders form pictured earlier gets its list of customers from a field in a table named Customers. It gets that list when the Orders form opens. When a user adds a new record to the Customers table via the NewCust form, the Orders table knows nothing of the new record. The drop-down list in the CustID control just continues to show the same names it did before the NewCust form added a new record to the Customers table.

The solution to the problem is the Requery method, which every list box and combo box control exposes to VBA. As its name implies, the Requery method forces a list box to update its list or a combo box to update its drop-down list immediately. The syntax for using the method is

```
controlName.Requery
```

where controlName is the name of the combo box or list box that needs updating. When you need to update a control on a form (other than the one in which the code is running), you need a complete identifier at the start of the name, specifying the name of the form on which the control resides. For example, the following line updates the CustID control in the Orders form from code that's in the class module for the NewCust form (or any other form):

```
Forms![Orders]![CustID].Requery
```

The preceding statement says "Update the control named CustID on the open form named Orders."

Go back to the sample Orders and NewCust forms shown in Figure 10-12. First, clarify that the Orders form there is bound to a table named Orders. The CustID control on the Orders form is bound to the CustID control in the Orders table, which is a Long Integer. The CustID control on the NewCust form is bound to the CustID control in the Customers table, where it's defined as an AutoNumber field and Primary key (ensuring that every new customer automatically gets a unique, unchangeable CustID value the moment a new record is added). Figure 10-13 shows the structures of the Orders and Customers tables.

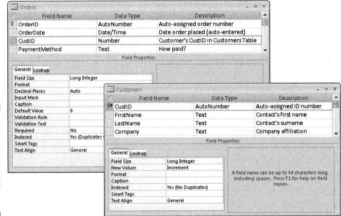

Figure 10-13:
Tables
underlying
Orders and
NewCust
forms.

When you look at the CustID combo box in Figure 10-12, it doesn't look like it's bound to an Integer field in a table because the control displays text. However, the actual value in that CustID control is an integer; the integer is just hidden from view. Read more on that in the upcoming section "Using hidden values in combo and list boxes."

Suppose that you have a form like the Orders form that has a button to add a new record through some other form. The first thing you need to do is get the button to open the appropriate form pointing at a new, blank record. Tackle that problem first.

Opening a form to enter a new record

Suppose that you have the `Orders` form open in Design view and you need to get that New Customer button to open the `NewCust` form poised to accept a new record. You can do that with a macro, or you can assign the following procedure to the New Customer button's (`NewCustBttn`) `On Click` event property:

```
Private Sub NewCustBttn_Click()
    'Open NewCust form at new, blank record (asFormAdd).
    DoCmd.OpenForm "NewCust", acNormal, , , acFormAdd
End Sub
```

That's it for the `Orders` form's role in all of this, so you close and save that form. When the user clicks the New Customer button on the `Orders` form (in Form view), the `NewCust` form opens. Presumably, the user then types in the new customer's information, clicks the Done button, and returns to the `Orders` form. That's where the `CustID` control on the `Orders` form gets out of sync.

When the `NewCust` form closes and saves the new record, the `CustID` control on the `Orders` form doesn't know about the new record. Hence, its drop-down list is out of sync. Somehow you have to get the `NewCust` form to tell the `Orders` form, "Hey, update your `CustID` control" before the form closes.

To solve the problem, write some code that updates the `CustID` control on the `Orders` form every time the `NewCust` form adds a new record to the `Customers` table. As it turns out, anytime a form adds a new record to its underlying table or query, that form's `After Insert` event occurs. Thus, a guaranteed way to ensure that the `Orders` form's `CustID` combo box is up-to-date is to requery that control every time the `NewCust` form's `After Insert` event occurs.

To make that happen, do the following:

1. **First make sure to open the NewCust form (not the Orders form) in Design view.**

2. **Make sure Form is selected in the property sheet (so that you're setting Form properties).**

3. **Click the Event tab in the property sheet.**

4. **Click the Build button next to the After Insert event property.**

5. **Choose Code Builder.**

6. **Click OK.**

7. **Type the VBA statement needed to requery the control on the Orders form:**

    ```
    Forms![Orders]![CustID].Requery
    ```

The entire `Form_AfterInsert` procedure in the NewCust form's class module looks like this:

```
Private Sub Form_AfterInsert()
    'Update CustID combo on open Orders form.
    Forms![Orders]![CustID].Requery
End Sub
```

The problem is now solved because every time the user adds a customer to the `Customers` table from the `NewCust` form, the `CustID` control on the `Orders` form is automatically requeried to include that new record. You could leave it at that. However, in solving that problem, you created a new problem, as described next.

Seeing whether a form is open

VBA can requery a control only on a form that's open. If a form is closed, you have no way to (and no reason to) requery any of its controls because any list controls on the form are created (and hence up-to-date) the moment the form opens. If VBA code tries to requery a control on a form that's closed, the procedure crashes, and an error message appears on-screen. Not good.

To get around the problem of the `Form_AfterInsert()` procedure crashing when the `Orders` form isn't open, put the statement that updates the control inside an `If...End If` block. Make the condition of the `If` statement `CurrentProject.AllForms("FormName").IsLoaded` in your code but substitute *FormName* with the name of the form that needs to be open. For example, the following modified `Form_AfterInsert()` procedure requeries the `Orders` form's `CustID` control only if the `Orders` form is open when the procedure executes:

```
Private Sub Form_AfterInsert()
    'If the Orders form is open (loaded...)
    If CurrentProject.AllForms("Orders").IsLoaded Then
        '...update CustID combo on open Orders form.
        Forms![Orders]![CustID].Requery
    End If
End Sub
```

If the `Orders` form is closed when the preceding procedure is executed, the procedure does absolutely nothing. That's good because as we mention, there's no need to requery a control on a closed form.

Getting forms in sync

Requerying the CustID control on the Orders form keeps the combo box's drop-down list up-to-date with the current contents of the Customers table at all times. However, it doesn't change the value that's displayed in that control. In other words, requerying a ComboBox control fixes the combo box's hidden drop-down list, but it doesn't change which option on that menu is now selected and visible in the control. You can always add some code to take care of that.

A perfect example is when the user adds a new customer via the NewCust form and returns to the Orders form. Ideally, you want the Orders form to already show a new, blank order form with the new customer already chosen as the one placing the order. From a VBA perspective, when the user closes the NewCust form, it makes sense to add a new, blank record to the Orders form and set the CustID control on the Orders form to the new customer's CustID value. In other words, when the user clicks the Done - Fill Order button, you want VBA to

✔ Copy the new customer's CustID to a variable for holding

✔ Close the NewCust form, saving the new customer's record

✔ Make sure you're at new, blank record in Orders form

✔ Copy the new customer's CustID into Orders form's CustID control

✔ On the Orders form, put the cursor in whatever control the user is most likely to resume typing the order

Making those steps happen whenever someone clicks the DoneBttn button in the NewCust form requires the procedure in Listing 10-8 in the NewCust form's class module.

Listing 10-8:   Updating a Control on a Separate Form

```
Private Sub DoneBttn_Click()

   'Do these steps only if Orders form is open.
   If CurrentProject.AllForms("Orders").IsLoaded Then

      'Copy the new customer's CustID to a variable.
      Dim NewCustID As Long
      NewCustID = Me!CustID.Value

      'Close the NewCust form.
      DoCmd.Close acForm, "NewCust"

      'Make sure were at new, blank record in Orders form
```

(continued)

Listing 10-8 *(continued)*

```
        DoCmd.GoToRecord acDataForm, "Orders", acNewRec

        'Copy new CustID into Orders form's CustID control
        Forms![Orders]!CustID.Value = NewCustID

        'Move cursor to PaymentMethod control in Orders
            form.
        Forms![Orders]![PaymentMethod].SetFocus

    End If

End Sub
```

You might notice that none of the statements in the preceding procedure requeries the CustID control on the Orders form. That's because you already wrote a Form_AfterInsert() procedure to ensure that anytime any record gets added to Customers via the NewCust form, code immediately updates the CustID control on the Orders form. When VBA executes the statement DoCmd.Close acForm, "NewCust", it saves the current record (because when you close a form, the current record is saved automatically). Right after the form inserts the new record into the Customers table, the Form_AfterInsert() procedure runs, updating the CustID combo box on the Orders form.

In other words, by the time execution reaches the first statement under the DoCmd.Close acForm, "NewCust" statement, the Form_AfterInsert() event has already occurred and updated the CustID control on the Orders form to include the new customer's record.

More Combo Box Tricks

In this section, we show you a few more combo box tricks, starting with an explanation of why what you *see* in a combo box isn't always what you *get* in VBA. For example, the CustID control on the Orders form shown in Figure 10-12 is bound to a Long Integer field in its underlying table, yet its combo box shows a bunch of names and addresses. How can that be?

Using hidden values in combo and list boxes

A combo box or list box can show any data from a table or query even though the control contains some simple value like a Long Integer. The long integer, which is usually a primary key value, can be hidden in the control as the control's actual value while some more meaningful (to humans) text is shown to the user. This disappearing-value act works thanks to multicolumn lists and the `Bound Column` property. Here, in a nutshell, is how it works:

- ✔ Whatever is in the first visible column of the list is what *shows* (visibly) in the control.

- ✔ Whatever value is defined as the Bound Column is the value that's actually *stored* in the control, although it might not be visible to the user.

For example, to create the drop-down list of customer names and e-mail addresses shown back in the `Orders` form (refer to Figure 10-12), we first created a query based on the `Customers` table. In that query, we used some fancy expressions to display the name and e-mail address of each customer in the list. The first column in the query, as shown in Figure 10-14, contains the calculated field (which is too wide to show completely in the figure):

```
SortName: IIf(IsNull([LastName]),[Company],[LastName] & ", " & [FirstName])
```

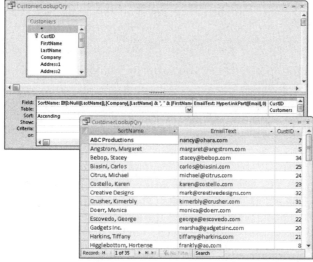

Figure 10-14: The Customer Lookup Qry query in Design and Datasheet views.

The preceding expression says, "If the Last Name field in this record is null (empty), just show the company name. Otherwise, show the person's `LastName` followed by a comma and a space and then the `FirstName`."

The second column in the query contains the calculated field:

```
EmailText: HyperLinkPart([EmailAddress],0)
```

In this example, EmailAddress refers to a Hyperlink field in the underlying Customers table. Hyperlink fields can look weird in drop-down lists. The HyperLinkPart() function there isolates just the display portion of the field. That basically ensures that the e-mail address looks like an e-mail address in the query results.

The third column in the CustomerLookupQry represents the CustID control from the Customers table, which is defined as an AutoNumber field in the table's design. The lower-right window in Figure 10-14 is the same CustomerLookupQry in Datasheet view. Notice how the names are presented in the first column; the e-mail address in the second column; and the CustID value — a Long Integer — in the third column. Later, when you use that query as the drop-down list for a combo box, you can make that third column the Bound Column while still showing the fancy SortName value in the control.

If you create, close, and save a query like CustomerLookupQry, you might want to use that query's columns as a drop-down list for a combo box that allows the user to choose a customer by name or e-mail address. To get started, you need a form open in Design view. Optionally, you can turn on the Control Wizards by clicking the Use Control Wizards button in the Controls group on the (Form Design Tools) Design tab.

Next, create the combo box as you normally would. For example, to create the CustID combo box on the Orders form, you click the Combo Box tool in the Controls group and then drag the CustID control from the Orders table's Field List onto the form. (Dragging the CustID control to the form after you click the Combo Box tool binds the new combo box to the CustID control.)

When the Combo Box Wizard starts, just follow its instructions to design the combo box. For example, tell it to get its values from the CustomerLookupQry described earlier. When it asks which fields from that query to display, choose all three field names. When you get to the wizard page where you set column widths, you initially see all the columns from the query, as in the top-left side of Figure 10-15. To hide the CustID number from the user, narrow its column to the point that it's not visible. Set the widths of the other two columns to whatever fits best, as in the lower-right portion of that same figure.

The next page of the wizard asks which field from the query should be stored in the ComboBox control. In this case, you choose CustID because you want to store the selected customer's CustID value (not the name or e-mail address) in the CustID field of the Orders form. The last wizard page asks which field should store that value; choose CustID. We clicked Next, and the last wizard page asked for a label. We typed **Customers** and then clicked Finish.

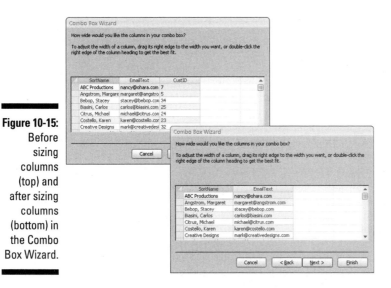

Figure 10-15:
Before
sizing
columns
(top) and
after sizing
columns
(bottom) in
the Combo
Box Wizard.

The `ComboBox` control is now on the form. Figure 10-16 shows the results with the combo box drop-down list visible. You can also see the property sheet there, and that's where you can see what's really going on. For example, the `Column Count` property shows that the drop-down list contains three columns. The column widths are 1.5", 2.5", and 0", which makes the third column invisible (zero inches wide). The `Bound Column` property (3) tells you that whatever is in that third column is what gets stored in the `CustID` control that the drop-down list is attached to.

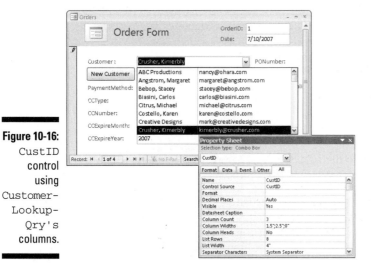

Figure 10-16:
`CustID`
control
using
`Customer-`
`Lookup-`
`Qry's`
columns.

Because a combo box always *shows* whatever is in the first visible column of the drop-down list, only the selected person's name appears in the combo box after the user makes a selection because that SortName control is the first visible column in the CustomerLookupQry query. The only purpose of the e-mail column in that query is to act as a tiebreaker. For example, if two customers happen to have the same first and last names, the user can tell which is which by the e-mail address.

The most important thing to glean from all this is that what you see in a ComboBox control isn't always what Access and VBA see. What's *stored* in the combo box is whatever is defined as the combo box's Bound Column property. What you *see* in the control is whatever is in the first visible column of the drop-down list.

If you add an unbound text box control to your form that contains an expression like =*fieldname*.Value as its control source (where *fieldname* is the name of a ComboBox or ListBox control), that control shows you the true value of the *fieldname* control as opposed to what *appears* in the control.

Giving users a quick find

You can use a combo box as a tool for allowing a user to quickly find a specific record in a table. For example, you might have a form that allows a user to find and edit customers. At the top of that form, you can provide a drop-down list, perhaps named *Quick Find,* as in Figure 10-17. When the user chooses a name from the drop-down list, the form instantly displays that customer's record. (We also point out some of the properties for the QuickFind control in that figure.) You can assign those properties when you use the Control Wizards to create the initial combo box.

Figure 10-17:
A Quick-Find control offers fast customer name lookup.

Look at an example of creating a `QuickFind` control. Like with any combo or list box, you can begin by creating a query that defines the columns to be displayed in the list. For this example, you can use the `CustomerLookupQry` shown a little earlier in this chapter as the drop-down list for a combo box named `QuickFind`. Here are the basic steps for creating such a control:

1. **In the Access Navigation pane, right-click the name of the form to which you want to add a Quick Find capability, and then choose Design View.**

2. **If you want to use the Combo Box Wizard to create the initial control, make sure that the Use Control Wizards button in the Controls group is highlighted. Then click the Combo Box tool and click where you want to place the control on your form.**

   The Combo Box Wizard opens.

3. **On the first wizard page, select the I Want the Combo Box to Look Up the Values in a Table or Query option button and then click Next.**

4. **On the second wizard page, choose the Queries option button and then select the query that contains the values to be displayed in the drop-down list. Then click Next.**

   In our example, we clicked Queries and then CustomerLookupQry.

5. **On the third wizard page, click the >> button to add all the fields from your query to the drop-down list; then click Next.**

6. **(Optional) You can choose a sort order on the fourth wizard page. If your query already has all the records in order, you can just ignore that page and click Next.**

7. **On the fifth wizard page, size your columns; then click Next.**

   As shown in Figure 10-15, earlier in this chapter, you can hide any column by narrowing it to the point where it's invisible.

8. **The sixth wizard page asks which value from the query the combo box should store. Click whichever field name would provide the most accurate search; then click Next.**

   In our example, `CustID` is unique to each customer, so we specify the `CustID` field.

9. **On the seventh wizard page, select the Remember the Value for Later Use option button and then click Next.**

   Because you aren't storing the value in a field, this step creates an unbound combo box.

10. **On the last wizard page, type a label for the control and then click Finish.**

    We gave our combo box the label Quick Find.

That takes care of creating the initial unbound combo box. To get it to act as a Quick Find procedure, you need to write some VBA code. First, we suggest that you go to the All tab of the property sheet and change the Name property to something more meaningful — for example, QuickFind rather than Combo01 or whatever Access named the control. Then click the Event tab in the property sheet and click the After Update event property. You're taken to the VBA Editor with the cursor in a procedure named *control*_AfterUpdate() where *control* is the name of your unbound ComboBox control.

The basic skeleton structure needed for a Quick Find procedure looks like this:

```
Private Sub controlName_AfterUpdate()
    'Clone the form's table/query into a recordset.
    Dim MyRecSet As Object
    Set MyRecSet = Me.Recordset.Clone

    'Find first matching record in the recordset.
    MyRecSet.FindFirst "[fieldName] = " & Me![controlName]

    'Set the form's record to found record.
    Me.Bookmark = MyRecSet.Bookmark
End Sub
```

where *controlName* is the name of the unbound combo box, and *fieldName* is the name of the field being searched in the form's underlying table or query. In our example, the QuickFind control contains a long integer value that matches the CustID value of the customer you're searching for. (Both values are long integers.) The code for the QuickFind control, which searched the CustID control in the Customers table, looks like this:

```
Private Sub QuickFind_AfterUpdate()
    'Clone the form's table/query into a recordset.
    Dim MyRecSet As Object
    Set MyRecSet = Me.Recordset.Clone

    'Find first matching record in the recordset.
    MyRecSet.FindFirst "[CustID] = " & Me![QuickFind]

    'Set the form's record to found record.
    Me.Bookmark = MyRecSet.Bookmark
End Sub
```

Like all procedures, this one is a series of steps. Starting at the first line, the name of the procedure defines when it runs. In this case, the procedure runs after a user chooses a customer from the QuickFind control's drop-down list:

```
Private Sub QuickFind_AfterUpdate()
```

The following lines provide for a speedy search without any activity on the screen by using an invisible recordset to do the search behind the scenes. The `Dim` statement declares a general object named `MyRecSet`. The `Set` statement makes `MyRecSet` into a recordset that's an exact clone of the table or query underlying the current form:

```
'Clone the form's table/query into a recordset.
Dim MyRecSet As Object
Set MyRecSet = Me.Recordset.Clone
```

With a simple clone recordset like this, you can use the `FindFirst` method to quickly locate a specific value in a single field. You can't do any sort of fancy SQL `WHERE` clause — only a simple _fieldname = value_ type expression is allowed, which is all you need when searching in the primary key field.

The next statement in the procedure uses the `FindFirst` method to locate `CustID` value in the recordset that matches whatever value is stored in the `QuickFind` control:

```
MyRecSet.FindFirst "[CustID] = " & Me![QuickFind]
```

It takes less than an eyeblink's time for the preceding statement to search the `CustID` field in the recordset. After the record is found, the recordset's `Bookmark` property contains a value that indicates that record's position in the recordset. To get the form to show the record that was found in the recordset, the next statement sets the form's underlying table or query `Bookmark` property equal to the `Bookmark` property of the recordset:

```
Me.Bookmark = MyRecSet.Bookmark
```

The job is done after the form is displaying the requested record, so the `End Sub` statement marks the end of the procedure:

```
End Sub
```

After the procedure is written, you can close the VBA Editor, as usual, save the form, and try out the new control in Form view. The lookup should work when you open the form and choose a customer from the `QuickFind` combo box.

Avoiding retyping common entries

Here's another situation where a dynamic combo box can be very helpful in data entry. Suppose that you have a table like `Customers` that includes a City field, and as it turns out, most of your customers are from a few nearby cities. Thus, you find yourself typing the same city name over and over again as you enter customers' data.

As an alternative to typing the same city name repeatedly, you can make the City field on the form a *self-referential* combo box that automatically lists every unique city name that has ever been typed into the form. For example, the first time you type **Los Angeles** as the city entry, that name gets added to the City field's drop-down list. In the future, when it's time to type Los Angeles into another record, you can just choose that name from the drop-down list rather than retype it again.

To get started, you need a drop-down list of unique city names. You can use a query to design the initial drop-down list. For example, Figure 10-18 shows a query named `UniqueCitiesQry` that lists, in alphabetical order, every unique city name in a field named City. Setting the `Unique Values` property in the query's property sheet to `Yes` provides the unique city names.

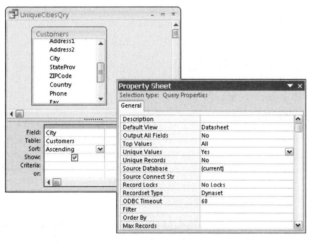

Figure 10-18:
`Unique Cities Qry` lists unique city names from the City field.

In the query, switch to Datasheet view to make sure the query shows each city name only once, and then close and save the query. You can then use the query as the Row Source for any combo box or list box that's bound to the City field. For example, on any form that will display the City field from the `Customers` table, you can create a unique value's combo box by following these steps:

1. **In the Controls group, make sure the Use Control Wizards button is highlighted, and then click the Combo Box tool.**

2. **Drag the City field from the Field List onto your form.**

   The Combo Box Wizard opens.

3. On the first wizard page, select the I Want the Combo Box to Look Up the Values in a Table or Query option button and then click Next.

4. On the second wizard page, choose the Queries option button and then choose the query that shows the unique values (UniqueCitiesQry in our example). Then click Next.

5. On the third wizard page, click the >> button to add the field to the Selected Fields column; then click Next.

6. On the fourth wizard page, you can just click Next rather than a sort order (because the query has already defined a sort order).

7. On the fifth wizard page, adjust your column width (if necessary), and then click Next.

8. On the sixth wizard page, select the Store That Value in This Field option button and the name of the field to which the combo box is attached; then click Next.

   Most likely, the correct options are already selected for you because you already dragged the bound field's name to the form in Step 2.

9. Type in a label for the control (City in our example) and then click Finish.

That's it. When you switch to Form view, the City drop-down list should display the name of each unique city that's in the Customers table. It might seem like you're done, but there's just one small problem: As you add and edit records in the Customers table, the drop-down list in the City field cannot keep up at first because the City field's drop-down list doesn't automatically requery with each change.

The problem is easily solved with a single line of code that requeries the City control every time a record is updated in the Customers table. To requery a control with each update, follow these steps:

1. In the form's Design view, double-click the gray area behind the Design grid to get to the Form properties in the property sheet.

2. In the property sheet, click the Event tab and choose the After Update event property.

3. Click the Build button next to the After Update event property and choose Code Builder.

   You're taken to a procedure named Form_AfterUpdate(), which runs every time the current form updates a record in its underlying table.

   4. Within the procedure, type Me!*fieldName*.Requery **where** *fieldName* **is the name of the control that contains the self-referential combo box.**

   In our example, it's

   ```
   Me![City].Requery
   ```

   5. Choose File⇨Close and Return to Microsoft Office Access.

   6. Close and save your form.

In the future, whenever you add or change records in the Customers table through the form, you can either type a new city name or choose an existing city name from the City drop-down list. If you type a new city name, that name is added to the drop-down list of existing field names automatically, thanks to the little, one-line VBA procedure.

Chapter 11

Creating Your Own Functions

· ·

· ·

A s you might already know, Access has lots of built-in functions that you can use in creating expressions. When you use the Expression Builder in Access to create an expression, you can view a list of all the built-in functions and also choose any function that you want to incorporate into the expression you're writing.

First, you need to get to a place where one might actually write an expression. For example, if you're designing a table and decide to set a Default Value for a field, as soon as you click the Default Value field property, a Build button appears. Clicking that Build button opens the Expression Builder. If you set the Default Value to =Date(), =Date() is an expression that uses the built-in Date() function to return the computer's date.

You can also use expressions to create calculated fields. For example, in Chapter 10, you can read how the CustomerLookupQry query uses expressions to create fields named SortName and EmailText. You can also use expressions to create calculated controls on forms, where the control's Control Source property contains an expression that does some math or returns some value based on other data in the same form.

The Role of Functions in VBA

All the functions that are available to you in Access are also available to you in VBA. In VBA, you use the same function syntax that you use in Access. In Access, the Expression Builder is a good tool for finding out which functions are available as well as how to use them. To open the Expression Builder, open a form in Design view, click a text box control, click a property that can accept an expression (like `Control Source` or `Default Value`), and then click the Build button in that property.

After you're in the Expression Builder, click the plus sign (+) next to functions and then click Built-In Functions. If you then select <All> from the top of the middle column, the right column lists all the built-in functions in alphabetical order, as in Figure 11-1. Optionally, you can click a category name in the middle column to limit the third column's list to just the functions in that category.

When you click the name of a specific function in the third column, the syntax for using that function appears in the lower-left corner of the Expression Builder. For example, the `Abs` function is selected in Figure 11-1, so the window shows `Abs (number)`. That just tells you that the `Abs` function expects a single number to be passed to it. For more information about the selected function, click the Help button in the Expression Builder.

Before you go trying to create your own custom functions, we recommend knowing which functions are already available to you as built-in functions. You don't need to reinvent the wheel by creating a custom function that duplicates a built-in function.

Build button

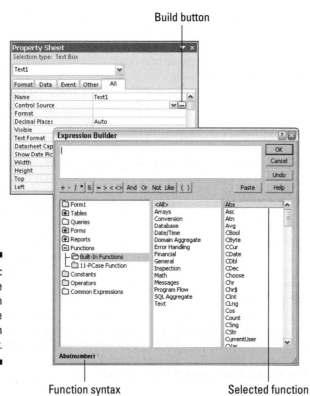

Figure 11-1:
Click the
Build button
to open the
Expression
Builder.

Function syntax   Selected function

Every function returns some value. For example, the `Date()` function returns the current date. You can see this for yourself right in the VBA Editor Immediate window. For example, if you type this line

```
? Date()
```

into the Immediate window and press Enter, the Immediate window shows the value returned by the `Date` function, which is the current date.

We suppose we should point out that sometimes in VBA, you can often omit any empty parentheses that follow a function name. In fact, the VBA Editor might even remove the parentheses for you, and the statement will still work after the VBA Editor removes the parentheses. For example, if you enter **? Date** in the Immediate window, you get the same result if you enter **? Date( )**. However, if the parentheses aren't empty, you should definitely include both the opening and closing parentheses in your code.

Look at another example. The `Sqr()` function accepts a single number as an argument and returns the square root of that number. For example, if you type the line

```
? Sqr(81)
```

into the VBA Editor Immediate window, you get back 9, which is the square root of 81.

It often helps to imagine that the word *of* follows a function's name. For example, think of `?  Sqr(81)` in the Immediate window as "What is the square root of 81?"

Creating Your Own Functions

In VBA, you can create your own, custom functions to add to those that are built into Access. As a rule, put all custom functions in a standard module rather than in a class module because putting a custom function in a standard module makes the function available to all the objects in the current database. In other words, any function that you create in a standard module can be used just as though it were a built-in function throughout the current database.

Work through the whole process, starting with a simple example of a custom function that calculates and returns the sales tax for any numeric value that's passed to it. You can put the function in any standard module — it doesn't really matter which. For this case, just start with a new, empty standard module.

1. In the Access database, click the Create tab.

2. **In the Other group, select Module from the drop-down list on the far right side of the Ribbon.**

   You're taken to the VBA Editor with a brand-new, almost empty module to work with.

   All modules have the words `Option Compare Database` at the top already, so that's why we say that the module is *almost empty*. That first declaration, `Option Compare Database`, just tells the module that any comparisons using operators like = or > should be performed using the same rules as the rest of the current database. There's no need to change that line.

3. **Choose Insert⇨Procedure from the VBA Editor menu bar.**

   The Add Procedure dialog box opens, asking for the name, type, and scope of the procedure.

   The name must start with a letter and cannot contain any blank spaces. For this example, you can name the function `SalesTax`.

4. **Choose Function as the type (because you're creating a custom function) and Public as the scope (so that all other objects within the database can use the function).**

5. **Click OK in the Add Procedure dialog box.**

   The module contains the first and last lines of the procedure:

   ```
   Public Function SalesTax()

   End Function
   ```

Passing data to a function

In most cases, you want your function to accept one or more values that you pass to it as data for the function to operate on. For example, the `Sqr()` function accepts a single argument, which must be a number. To define the arguments that your custom function accepts, use the following syntax, inside the parentheses that follow the function name:

```
name As Type
```

where *name* is just some name that you make up to use as a placeholder for the incoming value, and *Type* is a valid data type. For example, you might want the custom `SalesTax()` function to accept a single numeric value as an argument. You need to make up a name for that, so just call it `AnyNum`. You also have to define that incoming value as some sort of number. Most likely, the passed value is a `Currency` value anyway, so you can modify the custom `SalesTax()` function as follows to accept a single number as an argument:

```
Public Function SalesTax(AnyNum As Currency)

End Function
```

What the first line really means is "Expect some number to be here when called. Refer to that number as `AnyNum` and treat it as a `Currency` number."

A function can accept any number of arguments. If you want a function to accept multiple arguments, give each argument a name and data type by using the same preceding syntax. Separate each definition with a comma. The `SalesTax()` function needs to accept only one argument, so don't modify that one. However, just as a general example, if you want a function to accept two arguments, you define each as in this example:

```
Public Function funcName(AnyNum As Currency, AnyText As String)

End Function
```

Returning a value from a function

A function can also return a value — that is, only *one* value because a function can't return multiple values. To make your function return a value, you just add

```
As Type
```

where `Type` is a valid data type, to the end of the first statement, outside the closing parenthesis of the function name. You specify only the data type of the returned value — don't give it a name. For example, you might want the `SalesTax()` function to return a single value that's a `Currency` number. In that case, modify the `SalesTax()` function this way:

```
Public Function SalesTax(AnyNum As Currency) As Currency

End Function
```

The custom function doesn't return its value until all the code in the procedure has been executed. To define the value returned by the function, use the syntax

```
functionName = value
```

where `functionName` is the same as the name of the function itself, without the parentheses, and `value` is the value that you want the function to return (although the value can be an expression that calculates a return value).

Suppose you want to be able to pass to the SalesTax() function some Currency value, like $100.00 or $65.45 or whatever, and have it return the sales tax for that amount. To pick a number out of a hat, the sales tax rate is 6.75 percent. The following SalesTax() function performs the appropriate calculation (by multiplying the number that's passed to it by 0.0675) and then returns the results of that calculation:

```
Public Function SalesTax(AnyNum As Currency) As Currency
    'Multiply passed value by 6.75% (0.0675) and
    'return the result of that calculation.
    SalesTax = AnyNum * 0.0675
End Function
```

Testing a custom function

You might remember, earlier in this chapter, when we said that a public custom function in a standard module can be used anywhere that a built-in function can be used. After you type in the SalesTax() function, you can see that for yourself by testing it the same way that you test a built-in function. For example, if you type the following line into the Immediate window

```
? SalesTax(100)
```

and then press Enter, you get

```
6.75
```

because the sales tax on $100.00 is $6.75. If you type

```
? SalesTax(14.99)
```

and press Enter, you get 1.0118 because the sales tax on $14.99 is about $1.02.

In case you're wondering why all the numbers aren't automatically rounded off, it's because the Immediate window always displays its results as sort of a plain number. In real life, you don't create a function just to use it in the Immediate window. More likely, you use the custom function in queries, forms, reports, or macros.

Suppose you create the preceding SalesTax() function and then choose File⇨Close and Return to Microsoft Office Access from the VBA Editor menu bar. Next, you want to create a query that lists the unit price and sales tax for all the records in a table. Because you can use a custom function just like you use a built-in one, you can set up the query as shown in the Query Design portion of Figure 11-2, where the Unit Price column refers to a field in the Order Details table, and Tax is a calculated field that uses the custom SalesTax() function.

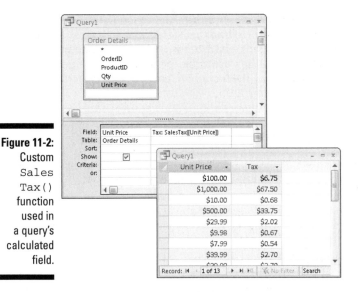

Figure 11-2:
Custom
`Sales`
`Tax()`
function
used in
a query's
calculated
field.

The lower half of Figure 11-2 shows the results of the query in Datasheet view. The Unit Price column displays the unit price from each record in the underlying table. The Tax column shows the sales tax amount for each unit price.

The query in Figure 11-2 is just an example, of course. You can use the custom `SalesTax()` function anywhere that you could use a built-in function, such as in the `Control Source` property of a calculated control or wherever you would use a built-in function in a VBA statement.

A Proper Case Function

Take a look now at a somewhat larger custom function that does more than a simple match calculation. Suppose you have a table filled with names and addresses, but for whatever reason, all the text is in uppercase (or lowercase) letters. For example, maybe the table has a Name field containing names like JOE SMITH or joe Smith. You want to tidy that up, but you certainly don't want to go in and edit all the data manually.

Technically, you could just use the built-in `StrConv(`*string*`, vbProperCase)` function to solve this problem. For example, `StrConv("JOE SMITH", vbProperCase)` returns Joe Smith. Problem solved — except that `StrConv()` doesn't take into consideration little quirks like the uppercase *D* in McDonald. `StrConv("MCDONALD", vbProperCase)` returns Mcdonald. Likewise, `StrConv("p.o. box 123", vbProperCase)` returns P.o. Box 123, which doesn't look quite right because the *O* should be uppercase.

To get around that, you can create your own, custom function that takes any string as its argument and then returns that string with initial caps (the first letter of each word is capitalized), just like the StrConv() function does. But your custom function can then use some If...End If statements to correct any little problems, like the Mcdonald and P.o. Box examples.

You don't really have to type any of the functions shown in this book into your own database. You can download them from www.dummies.com/go/access2007vbaprog and just import them into a database.

You might want to use this function to fix several fields in several tables, so you want the function to be public, like any built-in function. For starters, you need to open or create a standard module. Think up a name for your function (we call this one PCase()) and create an appropriate function. In this case, you need to pass a string (which we refer to as AnyText) to the function. The return value for the function is also a string (whatever text was passed is converted to initial caps). Listing 11-1 shows the function in its entirety. We take a look at how it works in a moment.

Listing 11-1: Sample PCase() Custom Function

```
'The PCase() function accepts any string, and returns
'a string with words converted to initial caps (proper case).
Public Function PCase(AnyText As String) As String
    'Create a string variable, then store AnyText in that variable already
    'converted to proper case using the built-in StrConv() function
    Dim FixedText As String
    FixedText = StrConv(AnyText, vbProperCase)

    'Now, take care of StrConv() shortcomings

    'If first two letters are "Mc", cap third letter.
    If Left(FixedText, 2) = "Mc" Then
        FixedText = Left(FixedText, 2) & _
            UCase(Mid(FixedText, 3, 1)) & Mid(FixedText, 4)
    End If

    'If first three letters are "Mac", cap fourth letter.
    If Left(FixedText, 3) = "Mac" Then
        FixedText = Left(FixedText, 3) & _
            UCase(Mid(FixedText, 4, 1, )) & Mid(FixedText, 5)
    End If

    'If first four characters are P.o. then cap the "O".
    If Left(FixedText, 4) = "P.o." Then
        FixedText = "P.O." & Mid(FixedText, 5)
    End If

    'Now return the modified string.
    PCase = FixedText
End Function
```

Looking at how PCase () works

Before we talk about using the PCase() function, take a moment to see how it works. PCase() uses several built-in Access functions — StrConv(), Left(), UCase(), and Mid() — to work with chunks of text in the passed string. For the sake of example, see what happens when PCase() gets called with something like PCase("MACDONALD").

When PCase() is called in this example, AnyText becomes a string variable that contains the text MACDONALD. The AnyText argument is defined as a string in the Function() statement itself, as shown here:

```
Public Function PCase(AnyText As String) As String
```

The next two statements declare a new string variable named FixedText, which acts as a placeholder for text being operated on by the function. The Dim statement just declares the variable as a string. The second statement stores a copy of AnyText, already converted to the proper case by using the StrConv() method:

```
Dim FixedText As String
FixedText = StrConv(AnyText, vbProperCase)
```

In VBA, you can use constants (like vbProperCase) rather than numbers (like 3) in built-in functions. For a list of other available constants for the StrConv() function and how to use them, highlight the word StrConv in the code and then press F1 to open the Help feature for that function.

Back in the example of calling the function, by the time the two preceding statements have been executed, the FixedText variable contains Macdonald. That's close to what you need, but the function isn't done working yet.

The next statements say, "If the first two letters of FixedText are *Mc,* leave the first two characters of FixedText unchanged, followed by changing the third letter to uppercase, followed by all the rest unchanged."

```
'If first two letters are "Mc", cap third letter.
If Left(FixedText, 2) = "Mc" Then
    FixedText = Left(FixedText, 2) & _
        UCase(Mid(FixedText, 3, 1)) & Mid(FixedText, 4)
End If
```

Because FixedText at this moment contains *Macdonald,* this block of code is ignored because its first two letters are *ma,* not *mc.* By the time the preceding statements execute (in this example), FixedText still contains Macdonald. Nothing has changed there.

The following block of code says, "If the first three characters are *mac,* change FixedText to the first three letters of itself, followed by the fourth letter in uppercase, and then leave the rest of the string unchanged."

```
'If first three letters are "Mac", cap fourth letter.
If Left(FixedText, 3) = "Mac" Then
    FixedText = Left(FixedText, 3) & _
        UCase(Mid(FixedText, 4, 1)) & Mid(FixedText, 5)
End If
```

In the current example, FixedText contains Macdonald when code execution reaches the If statement. And the first three letters of FixedText are indeed *mac;* thus, the code inside the If...End If block executes. In doing so, it changes FixedText to its own first three letters unchanged *(Mac),* plus the fourth letter in uppercase *(D),* plus the rest of the string, unchanged *(onald).* By the time execution gets past the End If statement in this example, FixedText contains *MacDonald.*

The following block of code does basically the same thing as the two preceding blocks: It looks to see whether the first four letters of the string are *P.o.* — and if so, changes those first four letters to *P.O.* Of course, the first four letters of *MacDonald* aren't *P.O.,* so that whole block of code is skipped over.

These final statements assign the current contents of the FixedText variable (MacDonald, now) to the function name sans parentheses (PCase). The End Function statement then ends the function and returns the contents of PCase (MacDonald) to the code (or object) that called the function:

```
    PCase = FixedText
End Function
```

If you type **? PCase("macdonald")** into the Immediate window, it returns MacDonald. If you type **? PCase("P.O. BOX 123")** into the Immediate window, you get P.O. Box 123. If you type **? PCase("HELLO WORLD")** into the Immediate window, you get Hello World. The StrConv() function inside PCase() still does its thing. The If...End If statement just makes minor corrections for *Mc, Mac,* and *P.O..*

Using the PCase () function

Like with any custom function, you can use PCase() wherever you would use a built-in function. Look at an example where you have a large table of names and addresses and everything is in uppercase, as in Figure 11-3. For the sake of example, call this table UglyCustomers (which isn't an insult to the customers — just the way their names are typed in!).

Figure 11-3: Sample problem table in all uppercase.

Now that you have a `PCase()` function that can convert text to the proper case — without messing up the Mc's, Mac's and P.O.'s — you can use that function in an update query to convert all the text fields to the proper case.

Test your function on a *copy* of your original table first. That way, if you make any mistakes that mess up the data, only the copy of the table gets ruined.

To create an update query to do the job, close the VBA Editor to get back to Access. Then create a new query that uses the problem table as its source. Next, in the (Query Tools) Design tab, choose Update from the Query Type group to convert the query to an update query. The Query By Example (QBE) grid gains an Update To column, in which you can add an expression that defines the new value for a field. Thus, you can add any Text field that needs converting to the QBE grid, and then you can use the expression `=PCase([fieldname])` (where *fieldname* is the same name as the field at the top of the column) to convert that field to the proper case.

Figure 11-4 shows an example in which we're fixing the `FirstName`, `LastName`, `Company`, `Address`, and `City` fields. Notice that the Update To row for the `FirstName` field is `PCase([FirstName])`. The Update To row for the `LastName` field is `PCase([LastName])`, and so forth. In other words, when the query runs, you want it to change the contents of that field, in every record, to the proper case.

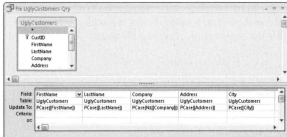

Figure 11-4: Query to fix uppercase problems in a table.

The query shown in Figure 11-4 wouldn't work in a database that doesn't contain the PCase() function. It works only in a database that has the PCase() function defined in one of its standard modules.

Because the query shown in Figure 11-4 is an action query, you need to run the query before it can do anything. Follow these steps:

1. **Click the Run button in the Results group of the (Query Tools) Design tab.**

   You get the standard warning message (You are about to update x rows . . .).

2. **Click Yes and wait a second. Then just close and save the query.**

3. **Back in the Navigation pane, click Tables, and then click the table that you changed.**

   If all went well, the fields are in the proper case. Figure 11-5 shows the result of running the sample query on the UglyCustomers table.

Figure 11-5: Convert text fields by using the custom PCase() function.

CustID	FirstName	LastName	Company	Address	City
1	Tori	Pines	Arbor Classics	345 Pacific Coast Hwy	Escondido
2	Marilou	Midcalf		500, 999-6th Street Sw	Edmonton
3	Wilma	Wannabe	Wannabe Whistles	1121 River Road, Suite 23	Cornball
4	Frankly	Unctuous		734 N. Rainbow Dr.	Staten Island
5	Margaret	Angstrom		P.O. Box 1295	Daneville
6	Margie	McDonald		1370 Washington Lane	Buckingham
8	Hortense	Higglebottom	Abc Productions	P.O. Box 1014	Escondido
9	Penny	MacDougal		P.O. Box 10	New Hope
10	Matilda	Starbuck		323 Shire Lane	Skeedadle
11	Scott And Natc	Schumack		228 Hollywood Drive	Hollywood
12	Linda	Peterson		823 Paseo Cancun	Redmond
13	Ino	Yasha		1788 Port Carlo Circle	Framington
15	Dominic	McFerrin		45 Albany Road	Maritime
16	Rosemary	Stickler		1205 Huntingdon Ct.	Willow Grove
17	Edmund	Kane		615 Levick Street	Pine Valley

Record: 1 of 33

As you can see, the names and addresses in the fixed UglyCustomers table look a lot better than those in the original table. And the Mc and Mac last names — as well as the P.O. Box entries — look okay, too. Still, not everything is perfect. For example, Abc Productions probably should be ABC Productions. However, it would be pretty tough to write a function that deals with every conceivable exception to the standard use of uppercase letters in proper nouns. You might have to polish some fields manually, but editing a few of them is a heck of a lot easier than retyping them all!

A Function to Print Check Amounts

Suppose you want to use Access to print checks from a table of payable amounts. You have your printer and your preprinted checks, and maybe you already created a report format to print the checks. What about the part of the check where you're supposed to write out the dollar amount, such as "One Hundred Thirty-Five and 49/100"? How can you get that part of the check printed? No built-in function is capable of doing that for you. And heaven knows you don't want to type all those words!

The solution is a custom function, like `NumWord()`, that takes as its argument any number and returns that number translated to words. For example, typing **? NumWord(1234.56)** returns `One Thousand Two Hundred Thirty-Four and 56/100`. Because the `NumWord()` function is fairly lengthy, download it from `www.dummies.com/go/access2007vbaprog` rather than try to type it in yourself. Just in case, Listing 11-2 holds the whole kit and caboodle, which you can place in any standard module in any database.

Listing 11-2:   Custom NumWord() Function

```
'NumWord() converts a number to its words.
'For example, NumWord(999.99) returns
'Nine Hundred Ninety-Nine and 99/100.
Public Function NumWord(AmountPassed As Currency) As
          String

    'Declare some general working variables.
    Dim English As String, strNum As String
    Dim Chunk As String, Pennies As String
    Dim Hundreds As Integer, Tens As Integer
    Dim Ones As Integer, StartVal As Integer
    Dim LoopCount As Integer, TensDone As Boolean

    'Make array of number words called EngNum.
    Dim EngNum(90) As String
    EngNum(0) = ""
    EngNum(1) = "One"
    EngNum(2) = "Two"
    EngNum(3) = "Three"
    EngNum(4) = "Four"
    EngNum(5) = "Five"
    EngNum(6) = "Six"
    EngNum(7) = "Seven"
    EngNum(8) = "Eight"
    EngNum(9) = "Nine"
    EngNum(10) = "Ten"
```

(continued)

Listing 11-2: *(continued)*

```
EngNum(11) = "Eleven"
EngNum(12) = "Twelve"
EngNum(13) = "Thirteen"
EngNum(14) = "Fourteen"
EngNum(15) = "Fifteen"
EngNum(16) = "Sixteen"
EngNum(17) = "Seventeen"
EngNum(18) = "Eighteen"
EngNum(19) = "Nineteen"
EngNum(20) = "Twenty"
EngNum(30) = "Thirty"
EngNum(40) = "Forty"
EngNum(50) = "Fifty"
EngNum(60) = "Sixty"
EngNum(70) = "Seventy"
EngNum(80) = "Eighty"
EngNum(90) = "Ninety"

'** If Zero or Null passed, just return "VOID".
If Nz(AmountPassed) = 0 Then
    NumWord = "VOID"
    Exit Function
End If

'** strNum is the passed number converted to a string.
strNum = Format(AmountPassed, "000000000.00")

'Pennies variable contains last two digits of strNum
Pennies = Mid(strNum, 11, 2)

'Prep other variables for storage.
English = ""
LoopCount = 1
StartVal = 1

'** Now do each 3-digit section of number.
Do While LoopCount <= 3
    Chunk = Mid(strNum, StartVal, 3) '3-digit chunk.
    Hundreds = Val(Mid(Chunk, 1, 1)) 'Hundreds portion.
    Tens = Val(Mid(Chunk, 2, 2)) 'Tens portion.
    Ones = Val(Mid(Chunk, 3, 1)) 'Ones portion.

    '** Do the hundreds portion of 3-digit number.
    If Val(Chunk) > 99 Then
        English = English & EngNum(Hundreds) & " Hundred
        "
    End If
```

```
        '** Do the tens & ones portion of 3-digit number.
        TensDone = False
        '** Is it less than 10?
        If Tens < 10 Then
            English = English & " " & EngNum(Ones)
            TensDone = True
        End If

        '** Is it a teen?
        If (Tens >= 11 And Tens <= 19) Then
            English = English & EngNum(Tens)
            TensDone = True
        End If

        '** Is it evenly divisible by 10?
        If (Tens / 10) = Int(Tens / 10) Then
            English = English & EngNum(Tens)
            TensDone = True
        End If

        '** Or is it none of the above?
        If Not TensDone Then
            English = English & EngNum((Int(Tens / 10)) * 10)
            English = English & "-" & EngNum(Ones)
        End If

        '** Add the word "Million" if necessary.
        If AmountPassed > 999999.99 And LoopCount = 1 Then
            English = English & " Million "
        End If

        '** Add the word "Thousand" if necessary.
        If AmountPassed > 999.99 And LoopCount = 2 Then
            English = English & " Thousand "
        End If

        '** Do pass through next three digits.
            LoopCount = LoopCount + 1
            StartVal = StartVal + 3
    Loop

    '** Done: Return English with Pennies/100 tacked on.
    NumWord = Trim(English) & " and " & Pennies & "/100"

End Function
```

That function is too long to show in the Code window (and too boring to discuss in any detail right now). Just assume that you already stuck the entire NumWord() procedure into a standard module in your database and now you want to use the procedure to print checks.

Using the NumWord function

For the sake of example, assume that you already put `NumWord()` into a standard module in your database. You already have a table that contains data to be printed on checks. Just to give this whole example some context, suppose that you have a table with field names and data types similar to those shown in the sample `Payables` table in Figure 11-6. The top-left side of the figure shows the table's structure, and the bottom-right side of the figure shows some sample data in the table.

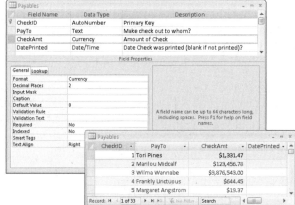

Figure 11-6: Sample field names and data types for printing checks.

Next, you need to create a report format for printing on the checks. When you get to the part of the report where the check amount needs to be printed, just add a calculated control that prints the `NumWord` of the numeric check amount. For example, in the `PrintChecks` report shown in Figure 11-7, you can see where we placed various controls to line up with blanks on each check (even though we don't really have a preprinted check here to show you). Presumably, all the other info the check needs is already printed on the check.

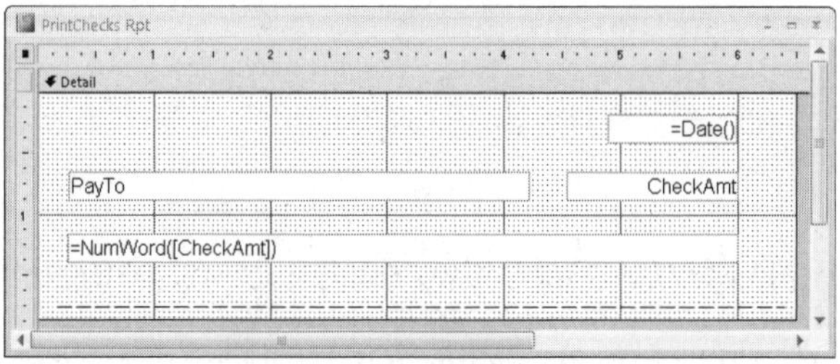

Figure 11-7: Sample report format for printing checks.

In the report format shown in Figure 11-7, the PayTo and CheckAmt fields come straight from the underlying Payables table. The check date and check amount in words are both calculated controls. The calculated control for printing the check date has as its Control Source property the expression =Date(), which prints the current date on the check. The calculated control for printing the check amount in words contains this expression as its Control Source property:

```
=NumWord([CheckAmt])
```

There, the field name CheckAmt refers to the field named CheckAmt, which contains the check amount expressed as a number. Once again, the example illustrates how after you add a custom function to a standard module, you can use that function anywhere that you would use a built-in function. For example, the check date is printed by using the built-in Date() function, and the check amount (in words) is printed by the custom NumWord() function.

Figure 11-8 shows a print preview for the report in Figure 11-7 (with some dashed lines artificially thrown in to make it easier to see where each check begins and ends). As mentioned, we assume that any other information that needs to be printed on the check is already on the checks.

Figure 11-8: Print preview of a sample check-printing report.

Looking at how NumWord () works

NumWord() is a fairly lengthy procedure mainly because the rules for converting numbers to words, in English, are a little complicated. But like any procedure, NumWord() is just a series of small decisions and steps needed to get the job done.

The first line of the procedure, as follows, defines the name of the procedure, NumWord(), and declares that it will accept a number Currency value (number) as an argument. Whatever number gets passed to the argument is referred to as AmountPassed in the rest of the procedure. The As String part at the end declares that NumWord() returns a string (text) to whatever called the function:

```
Public Function NumWord(AmountPassed As Currency) As
           String
```

The next lines declare some variables used for temporary storage by the procedure. Because there are lots of things to keep track of in this procedure, you need quite a few variables to store bits of information. In the following Dim statements, we're just declaring the names and data types of the variables. You can see how to put them to use later in the procedure:

```
'Declare some general working variables.
   Dim English As String, strNum As String
   Dim Chunk As String, Pennies As String
   Dim Hundreds As Integer, Tens As Integer
   Dim Ones As Integer, StartVal As Integer
   Dim LoopCount As Integer, TensDone As Boolean
```

Next, the statement Dim EngNum(90) As String declares any array of variables, all containing text. The variables created by the statement are named EngNum(0), EngNum(1), EngNum(2), and so forth, up to EngNum(90). The Dim statement, as always, just sets aside space for those 90 variables. The variables don't contain any data at first:

```
Dim EngNum(90) As String
```

The next statements assign text to some of the variables that the Dim statement just declared. You don't need all 90 variables here — just enough of them to cover every possible unique number word. For example, you need *ninety* as a unique word, but you don't need *ninety-one* as a unique word because it can be built from two words: *ninety* and *one*.

The subscript for each variable matches the word that the variable contains. For example, EngNum(1) contains "One", EngNum(11) contains "Eleven", EngNum(70) contains "Seventy", and so forth. In a sense, you already solved part of the problem just by having the array subscript match the word that you need:

```
EngNum(0)  = ""
EngNum(1)  = "One"
EngNum(2)  = "Two"
EngNum(3)  = "Three"
EngNum(4)  = "Four"
EngNum(5)  = "Five"
EngNum(6)  = "Six"
EngNum(7)  = "Seven"
EngNum(8)  = "Eight"
EngNum(9)  = "Nine"
EngNum(10) = "Ten"
EngNum(11) = "Eleven"
EngNum(12) = "Twelve"
EngNum(13) = "Thirteen"
EngNum(14) = "Fourteen"
EngNum(15) = "Fifteen"
EngNum(16) = "Sixteen"
EngNum(17) = "Seventeen"
EngNum(18) = "Eighteen"
EngNum(19) = "Nineteen"
EngNum(20) = "Twenty"
EngNum(30) = "Thirty"
EngNum(40) = "Forty"
EngNum(50) = "Fifty"
EngNum(60) = "Sixty"
EngNum(70) = "Seventy"
EngNum(80) = "Eighty"
EngNum(90) = "Ninety"
```

For the lowdown on arrays, see Chapter 4.

With all the needed variables declared, the procedure can get to work on translating whatever number was passed to it. The first `If...End If` block takes care of the problem of a zero or null value being passed to the function. The built-in `Nz()` (null-to-zero) converts a null value to a zero. Thus, the `If` statement `Nz(AmountPassed) = 0 Then` really says, "If the amount that's passed to me to work on is zero (or a null), then do the following lines up to `End If`. Otherwise, ignore those statements."

What happens if `AmountPassed` is a zero or null? The statement `NumWord = "VOID"` makes the return value for the function into the word `VOID`, and the `Exit Function` statement tells VBA to just bail out of the procedure now without doing anything else:

```
'** If Zero or Null passed, just return "VOID".
If Nz(AmountPassed) = 0 Then
   NumWord = "VOID"
   Exit Function
End If
```

Assuming that the amount passed to `NumWord()` is not a zero or null, execution then picks up at the following statement. This one is a little tricky. It uses the built-in `Format` function to make a string named `strNum` that exactly matches the amount passed. However, this string has exactly nine zeroes to the left of the decimal point and also two to the right. Suppose `NumWord` gets called with `NumWord(7609511.98)`. By the time the following statement executes, the `AmountPassed` variable (a number) contains `7609511.98`, and `strNum` contains (as a string) `007609511.98`. Having those leading zeroes in place makes it easier to make decisions about how to handle the number later in the procedure:

```
'** strNum is the passed number converted to a string.
strNum = Format(AmountPassed, "000000000.00")
```

Getting back to the `NumWord(7609511.98)` call, after the preceding statement executes, you have two copies of the amount that's passed to work with: the original `AmountPassed` (a number) and `strNum`, which is basically that same number with a fixed amount of leading zeroes:

```
AmountPassed = 7609511.98
strNum = "007609511.98"
```

Next, the following statement grabs the last two digits from `StrNum` and stores that value in a variable named `Pennies`:

```
'Pennies variable contains last two digits of strNum
Pennies = Mid(strNum, 11, 2)
```

In this example, where we're using 7609511.98 as the number that's passed, the variable named `Pennies` contains the following line after the preceding statement executes:

```
Pennies = "98"
```

Now you need to get some starting values in some variables for the code to follow. The variable named `English` (which will eventually contain the entire number word) starts off as a zero-length string (`""`). `LoopCount` and `StartVal` each get values of 1. You can see how to use those variables in the code that follows the line `'Prep other variables for storage`.

```
'Prep other variables for storage.
English = ""
LoopCount = 1
StartVal = 1
```

Next, start a loop that repeats until the `LoopCount` variable is greater than 3. Within that tool, the first thing you do is peel off chunks of the `strNum` variable and assign them to integer variables:

```
'** Now do each 3-digit section of number.
Do While LoopCount <= 3
    Chunk = Mid(strNum, StartVal, 3) '3-digit chunk
    Hundreds = Val(Mid(Chunk, 1, 1)) 'Hundreds portion
    Tens = Val(Mid(Chunk, 2, 2)) 'Tens portion
    Ones = Val(Mid(Chunk, 3, 1)) 'Ones portion
```

Getting back to the initial `strNum` number, `007609511.98`, by the time the preceding statements execute, the following variables contain the corresponding values:

```
Chunk = "007"
Hundreds = 0
Tens = 7
Ones = 7
```

The next statement says, "If the value of chunk (007, right now) is greater than 99, add `EngNum(Hundreds)` plus the word *hundred* to the string." In the current example, where `Chunk` is not greater than 99, nothing happens in this `If...End If` block:

```
'** Do the hundreds portion of 3-digit number
If Val(Chunk) > 99 Then
    English = English & EngNum(Hundreds) & " Hundred "
End If
```

The next statements set the `Boolean` variable `TensDone` to `False`. Then the next statement says, "If the `Tens` portion is less than 10, add a blank space and `EngNum(Ones)` to the `English` variable, and change `TensDone` to `True`."

```
'** Do the tens & ones portion of 3-digit number
TensDone = False
'** Is it less than 10?
If Tens < 10 Then
    English = English & " " & EngNum(Ones)
    TensDone = True
End If
```

In this case, where `Tens` contains 7, the statement is true. By the time the preceding statements have executed (given the sample number), the following variables have the corresponding values:

```
English = " Seven"
TensDone = True
```

The next `If...End If` statement deals with numbers in the range of 11–19. It says, "If the `Tens` number is between 11 and 19, add `EngNum(Tens)` to `English` and set `TensDone` to `True`." In this example, `Tens` is 7, which is not between 11 and 19, so this `If` block is skipped over. The contents and `English` and `TensDone` haven't changed:

```
'** Is it a teen?
If (Tens >= 11 And Tens <= 19) Then
    English = English & EngNum(Tens)
    TensDone = True
End If
```

The next block deals with `Tens` values that are evenly divisible by 10, such as 10, 20, 30, and so forth, up to 90. In this case, where `Tens` contains 7 (which is not evenly divisible by 10), nothing happens, so the `English` and `TensDone` variables hang on to their current values:

```
'** Is it evenly divisible by 10?
If (Tens / 10) = Int(Tens / 10) Then
    English = English & EngNum(Tens)
    TensDone = True
End If
```

The next `If` block kicks in only if the `Tens` portion of the number is still unresolved: that is, only if `TensDone` is still `False`. In this case, where `TensDone` got set to `True` already, the whole `If...End If` block is once again skipped over:

```
'** Or is it none of the above?
If Not TensDone Then
    English = English & EngNum((Int(Tens / 10)) * 10)
    English = English & "-" & EngNum(Ones)
End If
```

Next, look at adding the word *million* to the word. The `If` statement says, "If the amount that's passed is greater than 999,999.99 and the `LoopCount` variable equals one, add the word Million to `English`."

```
'** Add the word "Million" if necessary
If AmountPassed > 999999.99 And LoopCount = 1 Then
    English = English & " Million "
End If
```

Using the running example, the number that's passed is greater than 999,999.99, and right now `LoopCount` equals 1. By the time the preceding `If` statement executes, the `English` variable has had the word `Million` tacked onto it, like this:

```
English = "Seven Million"
```

The next statement says that if the amount that's passed is greater than 999.99 and `LoopCount` equals 2, tack on the word *Thousand*. In the running example, where `LoopCount` now equals 1, this whole block of code is skipped over:

```
'** Add the word "Thousand" if necessary
If AmountPassed > 999.99 And LoopCount = 2 Then
    English = English & " Thousand "
End If
```

The next statements increase the value of the `LoopCount` variable by 1 and increase the value of the `StartVal` variable by 3; then the `Loop` statement sends execution back up to the `Do While LoopCount <= 3` statement for the next pass through the loop.

Converting the rest of the number involves more of the same. The next pass through the loop just has to work with the next three-digit chunk of `strNum`. In this example, where `strNum` contains `007609511.98`, the next three digits after 007 are 609. By the time `Chunk`, `Hundreds`, `Tens`, and `Ones` have received their new values near the top of the loop, those variables contain these values:

```
Chunk = 609
Hundreds = 6
Tens = 9
Ones = 9
```

Looking through just the `If...End If` statements that prove true for this second pass through the loop, the statement `Val(Chunk) > 99` is true this time. Thus, the statement `English = English & EngNum(Hundreds) & " Hundred "` executes, adding `EngNum(6)` plus the word "Hundred" to EngNum. By the time that statement has executed, the `English` variable has a new value:

```
English = "Seven Million Six Hundred"
```

The statement `If Tens < 10 Then` is also `True` on this second pass through the loop, so the statement `English = English & " " & EngNum(Ones)` adds a space and `EngNum(9)` to the `English` variable:

```
English = "Seven Million Six Hundred Nine"
```

No other `If` statement proves `True` here until `If AmountPassed > 999.99 And LoopCount = 2 Then` executes. Because it's true that `AmountPassed` is greater than 999.99 and `LoopCount = 2` right now, the statement `English = English & " Thousand "` executes, and the `English` variable contains this line:

```
English = "Seven Million Six Hundred Nine Thousand"
```

Now you're at the bottom of the loop again, where `LoopCount` gets increased by `1` and `StartVal` gets increased by `3`. By the time the `Loop` statement sends control back up to the `Do While` statement, those variables contain these values:

```
LoopCount = 3
StartVal = 9
```

At the top of the loop, the `Chunk`, `Hundreds`, `Tens`, and `Ones` variables all get new values, as follows, by peeling off the last three digits to the left of the decimal point:

```
Chunk = "511"
Hundreds = 5
Tens = 11
Ones = 1
```

Once again, execution goes through all the statements, but only certain `If...End If` statements prove true. For example, the first `True` statement, `If Val(Chunk) > 99`, executes the statement `English = English & EngNum(5) & " Hundred "`. By the time that `If...End If` block has executed, the `English` variable contains this line:

```
English = "Seven Million Six Hundred Nine Thousand Five Hundred"
```

Going through the procedures that follow, the next `If` statement to prove `True` is `If (Tens >= 11 And Tens <= 19) Then`. So the statement `English = English & EngNum(11)` executes, making the `English` variable contain this line:

```
English = "Seven Million Six Hundred Nine Thousand Five Hundred Eleven"
```

No other `If...End If` statements execute. At the bottom of the loop where `LoopCount = LoopCount + 1`, the value of `LoopCount` increases to 4. The `Do While` loop repeats only while `LoopCount` is less than 4, so execution falls through the `Loop` statement, executing the statement `NumWord = Trim(English) & " and " & Pennies & "/100"`. At that moment, `NumWord` (which is also the name of the function) gets `" and "`, the `Pennies` variable's value, and `"/100"` tacked on. The procedure then ends with an `End Function` statement. The value returned after calling `NumWord(7609511.98)` is

```
Seven Million Six Hundred Nine Thousand Five Hundred Eleven and 98/100
```

which, happily, is exactly right.

The procedure is designed to translate any number in the range of 0–999,999,999.99 where `NumWord(999,999,999.99)` returns

```
Nine Hundred Ninety-Nine Million Nine Hundred Ninety-Nine
       Thousand Nine Hundred Ninety-Nine and 99/100
```

If that's not big enough for you (because you print checks for a billion dollars or more), you could probably talk us into personally modifying the procedure to accommodate your needs.

You can download the `NumWord()` custom function from `www.dummies.com/go/access2007vbaprog`.

To get away from the nitty-gritty details of how a complex procedure like `NumWord()` works, the most important concepts to remember are that you can create your own custom function in Access. To make the function freely available to all other objects in your database, you just have to put the custom function in a standard module. After you do that, you can treat your custom function as though it were any built-in function.

We admit that we got into some fairly intense code in this last example. If you're thinking that we just made up that procedure in our heads and jotted it down so that it worked the first time, you're way off base. Programming rarely works that way. It's all a matter of breaking down a large problem into small pieces. Then you attack one piece of the problem at a time, and get each little piece to work before moving on to the next one.

Along the way, you generally run into a whole lot of error messages because it's tough to write code that works right off the bat. You really need to create, test, and debug every little piece of code as you go along. Chapter 12 describes *debugging* strategies for building your code so that it always works and never crashes.

Chapter 12

Testing and Debugging Your Code

· ·

In This Chapter

▶ Identifying types of errors (bugs)

▶ Eradicating compile errors

▶ Coping with logical errors

▶ Trapping and fixing runtime errors

· ·

*W*riting code is nothing like writing in English. When you write in English, you can make all kinds of spelling and grammatical mistakes, and the reader can still get your meaning because a human reader has a brain that can figure out what you mean just by the context of the message you send.

Unfortunately, writing code for a computer to read doesn't work that way. Computers don't have brains and can't figure out anything. When it comes to writing code, every letter of every word that you type has to be exactly right. Punctuation marks such as commas, periods, and blank spaces are critical and must be typed exactly as specified in the statement's syntax chart. If you have one small typographical error, the statement doesn't work.

Because it's nearly impossible to type every statement correctly every time, every program will have some *bugs* (errors) in it that need to be corrected. Diagnosing and fixing these errors, called *debugging,* is something that beginning and seasoned programmers alike spend quite a bit of time doing. In fact, debugging is so commonplace that the VBA Editor offers several debugging tools designed strictly for finding and fixing those bugs.

Before we get to specific debugging tools and techniques, though, we think it helps to understand a little bit about what's going on behind the scenes as you're pounding away at the keyboard and trying to write some code that does something other than throw up error messages.

Understanding Compilation and Runtime

How a machine (like your computer) works and how your brain works are two entirely different concepts. All machines are basically as dumb as rocks because they're just machines. Your computer is nothing more than a mindless machine that can pump a few billion instructions per second through a little toenail-size chip. No thought or thinking or awareness is involved in any of that. It's all just electrons zooming around at the speed of light in a controlled manner inside a small area.

Each of those zooming electron creates a little friction as it travels, like when you rub the palms of your hands together really fast. That friction is what causes your computer to heat up.

Programmers often refer to how a machine processes information as *low-level*. For example, by the time information gets to the processor in your computer, that information is nothing more than a string of ones and zeroes, something like this:

```
0010101001100010101011010100001110101011010101101010101010101011
0101000111110101011000111110101010101110000010101011000110011100 01
1111010011000110001100111110000011101010111000111001101011011
```

In ProgrammerSpeak, you refer to the preceding lines as *low-level machine language* or *machine code*.

Human brains don't process information as ones and zeroes. Human brains process and communicate information by using higher-level concepts, like words, sentences, and paragraphs (not to mention pictures, sound, and video). Although you could write code by using just the 1 and 0 characters on your keyboard, it would be neither easy nor quick — thus the invention of high-level programming languages.

A *high-level programming language* is one that uses words and sentences, rather than ones and zeroes, to control the computer. For example, VBA is a high-level language. When you want VBA to do something — like open a form named `MyForm` — you don't have to type a bunch of ones and zeroes. Instead, you can type a sentence that looks more like words, like this:

```
DoCmd.OpenForm "MyForm"
```

The code that you type into the VBA Editor is often referred to as *source code*. Every line of source code that you type needs to be *compiled* (translated) into a lower-level language that the computer can process. To keep you from writing a whole lot of code that makes no sense to the computer (which makes for extremely difficult debugging), the VBA Editor quickly compiles each line of code you type the moment you finish typing that line.

Note that the VBA Editor doesn't *run* (or *execute*) each line the moment you type it. Rather, it just compiles each line to make sure that when you do run the code, each statement in that code will work. When you type a line of code that VBA can't translate to lower-level machine code, the VBA Editor gives you a Compile error message, like the example shown in Figure 12-1, to let you know that there's a problem with that line.

Figure 12-1: Sample compile error caused by a mistyped statement.

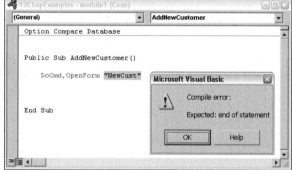

The real problem with the statement in Figure 12-1 is the comma (,) between DoCmd and OpenForm. That comma should be a period.

Programmers refer to the brief instant when your code is converted to a lower-level language as *compilation* or *compile time*. At compilation, the source code gets converted to the lower-level language that the computer needs in order to do what the code tells it to do. Later, when you run the code, the lower-level compiled code is what gets executed. The moment when the code is executed is *runtime*. Figure 12-2 illustrates the basic idea.

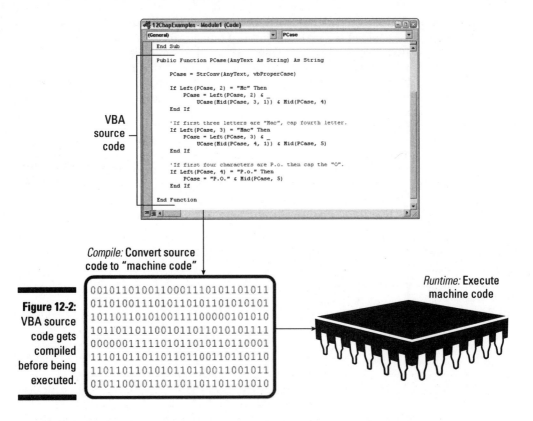

VBA source code

Compile: Convert source code to "machine code"

Runtime: Execute machine code

Figure 12-2:
VBA source code gets compiled before being executed.

```
0010110100110001110101101011
0110100111010110101101010101
1011011010100111100000101010
1011011011001011011010101111
0000001111101011010110110001
1110101101011011001101101 10
1101101101010110110011001011
0101100101011011011011011010
```

Considering Types of Program Errors

Errors in code can happen at any time in the create-compile-execute sequence. Programmers generally categorize the types of errors that they have to deal with in three ways:

- **Compile errors:** Any problem that prevents the VBA Editor from translating a line of source code to something executable generates a compile error, like the example shown in Figure 12-1. Such errors are usually syntax errors, which means that you didn't obey the rules of syntax for that statement when typing the code.

- **Logical errors:** If your code runs without generating an error message but fails to do what you expected it to do, that's a logical error. In other words, the code can and does run, but the logic of the procedure isn't the right logic for achieving the desired result.

- **Runtime errors:** The code compiles, but when you run the code, it doesn't work. Instead, it pops a runtime error message on-screen, perhaps looking something like the example shown in Figure 12-3.

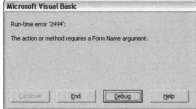

Figure 12-3:
Sample
runtime
error
message.

In the following sections, we look at the tools and techniques for dealing with each type of error, starting with the ubiquitous compile error, which rears its ugly head quite often.

Conquering Compile Errors

Common error messages that you face are the compile errors that happen in the VBA Editor Code window. Every time you type a complete VBA statement and then move the cursor to some other line in the procedure, VBA quickly compiles that line of code. It doesn't *run* the code — it just compiles the one line to make sure that it runs when you run the procedure.

When you're first learning to program, compile errors might seem incessant and unstoppable. That's only because you're not yet familiar enough with the VBA language to write valid statements. And perhaps you haven't yet accepted the fact that when it comes to writing code, guessing *never* works. Either you know how to use a particular statement or you don't. You really have to know how to use all the help that's available to you — and use it well.

For more information on the various types of help available to you in the VBA Editor, read about understanding syntax in Chapter 3 and objects and collections in Chapter 5.

Compile error messages are rarely specific about what the problem is. For example, Figure 12-4 shows an `Expected:  =` message, triggered by the `MsgBox` statement shown in the code. The error message tells you that the compiler was expecting to find an equal sign (=) in that statement, but it doesn't tell you where the equal sign belongs. (If it knew, it wouldn't have to show the message. It could just put in the equal sign for you.)

Clicking the Help button in the error message box rarely helps much. In this case, you would just get a brief description of the problem and a few examples. However, the examples aren't necessarily relevant to the code that you're writing now: They're just general examples.

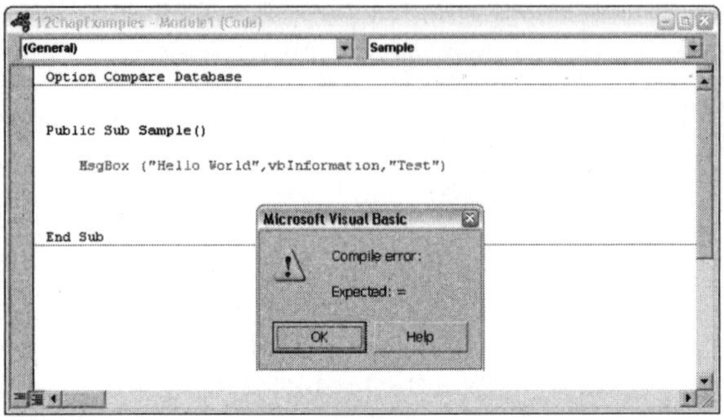

Figure 12-4:
Sample
compile
error.

The only real solution is to find out the correct syntax for the MsgBox keyword. As it turns out, there are two syntactical forms of MsgBox. The first form, which you can use to just show a simple message with an OK button, is

```
MsgBox prompt
```

where *prompt* is the message to display in the box (either as literal text enclosed in quotation marks or the name of a variable that contains text).

The second form allows you to retrieve a value while using multiple arguments, such as the title, buttons, and icon to show. Using MsgBox in that manner requires the following syntax (note the parentheses):

```
variable = MsgBox(prompt[,buttons][,title][,helpfile,context])
```

Here's where you get a clue to the whereabouts of the missing equal sign. Because the MsgBox statement in the code uses parentheses, we have to use *variable* = at the left side of MsgBox(), with parentheses around its arguments. The value returned by MsgBox() is a number indicating which button the user clicked, so the variable accepting that value should be declared as an integer. Thus the correction to the problem code in Figure 12-4 is this bit of corrected code:

```
Public Sub Sample()
    Dim Answer As Integer
    Answer = MsgBox("Hello World", vbInformation, "Test")
End Sub
```

The main point here is that the error message Expected: = really didn't tell you how to solve the problem. The only real solution to the problem was to find out how to use the MsgBox() statement and to see some examples of its use in Help. That's typical of compile error messages: They might give you a vague hint of what the problem might be, but they neither solve the problem for you nor even tell you how to solve it.

Take a look at some more common (and usually unhelpful) compile error messages and the solutions to the problems they found.

Expected: expression

The `Expected: expression` compile error means that while trying to compile the line, things went haywire because the compiler was expecting to find an expression but found nothing. This error usually happens if you leave one or more dangling commas at the end of a statement.

For example, the `MsgBox` statement in Figure 12-5 generated the compile error shown in the figure. If you look closely, you might also notice that the closing parenthesis in the code is highlighted. The compile error is trying to help out by highlighting the place where it ran into the problem.

Figure 12-5:
Sample
Expected:
expres-
sion
compile
error.

The problem with the line of code is that last comma, just to the left of the closing parenthesis. You use a comma only when you're about to type another expression into the list of arguments. In other words, while compiling that line of code, the compiler saw that last comma and expected to find an expression after that comma, but instead found a closing parenthesis.

One solution to the problem is to get rid of that last comma:

```
Answer = MsgBox("Hello World", vbInformation)
```

Or, you can leave the comma but add the argument that belongs in that spot. For example, in the `MsgBox` statement, the third argument is the title to show in the message box. To make that title read as `Test`, just go ahead and make that word the third argument (after the last comma):

```
Answer = MsgBox("Hello World", vbInformation,"Test")
```

Expected: end of statement

The `Expected: end of statement` message is another common (and rarely helpful) compile error. Once again, all the message is telling you is that you have some sort of syntactical error in the statement. In Figure 12-6, the string literal `"MyForm"` at the end of the statement is highlighted, but it tells only you that the compiler got lost at that point.

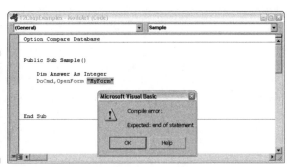

Figure 12-6:
Expected:
end of
statement
compile
error.

The real problem with the statement shown in Figure 12-6 is the comma between `DoCmd` and `OpenForm`. The correct syntax for using the `DoCmd` object is

```
DoCmd.method...
```

where a period — not a comma — appears between the first two words. The fix for the problem is to replace that comma with a period:

```
DoCmd.OpenForm "MyForm"
```

Expected: list separator or)

The `Expected: list separator or )` error message tells you that the compiler was expecting to find either a *list separator* (such as the comma that separates arguments in a function) or a closing parenthesis in the statement. In most cases, it highlights where the problem began. For example, the following statement, when compiled, generates an `Expected: list separator or )` error message with the word `World` highlighted:

```
Answer = MsgBox(Hello World, vbInformation, "Test")
```

The problem with the preceding line is that the words `Hello World` are supposed to be a string literal enclosed in quotation marks, but we forgot the quotation marks. The blank space between the words `Hello` and `World` has sent the compiler into a tizzy because it was expecting something else there. To correct the problem, put the quotation marks around the string literal:

```
Answer = MsgBox("Hello World", vbInformation,"Test")
```

With the quotation marks in place, the compiler can see that the entire string of text "Hello World" is the first argument, vbInformation is the second argument, and "Test" is the third argument.

Sometimes the Expected: list separator or) error message points out a missing parenthesis in a statement. For example, the following statement generates such an error message when compiled:

```
PCase = "Mc" & UCase(Mid(PCase, 3, 1) & Mid(PCase, 4)
```

It's rarely easy to see where a parenthesis needs to be added to a statement, especially if the statement contains lots of them. One fact is always true, though: Any statement that uses open parentheses must also use an equal number of closed parentheses.

Here's a little trick that programmers use to see whether they have the right number of parentheses. You start with the number 0 in mind. Then you read from left to right. Each time you encounter an open parenthesis, add 1 to that 0. Each time you come to a closed parenthesis, subtract 1 from that number. By the time you get to the end of the line, you should be back to 0. If you end up at any other number, you have a problem.

As an example, Figure 12-7 shows the preceding troublesome line after counting open and closed parentheses. After you add 1 for each open parenthesis and subtract 1 for each closing parenthesis, you end up with 1. That number shows that you either have one too many open parentheses or you're lacking one closed parenthesis.

Needless to say, you can't just stick an extra closing parenthesis into the statement at random. Rather, you need to understand the syntax rules of the various functions used in the expression. The example in Figure 12-7 uses two functions named UCase() and Mid(). Each function needs its own, complete pair of parentheses.

Figure 12-7:
Counting
open and
closed
parentheses
in a
statement.

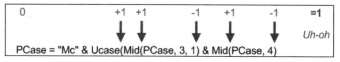

The Mid(PCase, 4) function at the end of the statement is fine because the Mid() function requires exactly one open and one closed parenthesis. The larger Mid() function, Mid(PCase, 3, 1), is also okay because it has one open and one closed parenthesis.

The problem occurs with the UCase() function. That larger Mid(PCase, 3, 1) function is the argument for the UCase() function, and there's no closing parenthesis for UCase(). That needs to be added right after the closing parenthesis for Mid(). Each of the Mid() functions also has a pair of open and closed parentheses. If you count the parentheses in the modified statement shown in Figure 12-8, the count ends up at 0, which is exactly what you want.

Figure 12-8:
Equal number of open and closed parentheses.

Regardless of which compile error message you get, you have to fix the problem before you can even run the procedure. Don't expect the compile error message to pinpoint the solution for you. The message in a compile error is often too vague and too general for that. In most cases, your only recourse is to look up the correct syntax in Help (or through the Object Browser) and apply it to whatever you're trying to accomplish.

Dealing with Logical Errors

Even if your code compiles and runs without generating an error message, the code isn't necessarily perfect. It can also contain logical errors. Unlike a compile error, which is an error in syntax or a typographical error, a logical error is an error in your thinking (logic). The computer always does exactly what the code tells it to do, even if you tell it to do the wrong thing.

Suppose that you intend to write a line of code to open some form, but you accidentally write the code to close the form. When you run the code, the computer (of course) closes — not opens — the form. The computer would never look at your code and think, "Hmmmm. I bet she meant to open a form here, so I'll do that instead." Computers just don't work that way. The computer always does *exactly* what the code tells it to do.

Pinpointing logical errors in your code is often difficult mainly because when you run a procedure, everything happens in less time than it takes to blink your eyes. Often it helps to take a look at what's going on behind the scenes while the code is running. The VBA Editor provides a few tools that allow you to see what's going on behind the scenes.

Checking on variables with Debug.Print

In earlier chapters, you can see examples of using the VBA Editor Immediate window to test procedures and try out expressions. For example, typing a simple expression like **? 1+1** (What is one plus one?) results in 2, which is the sum of one plus one. Typing the expression **? CurrentProject.AllForms.Count** displays the number of forms in the current database.

You can also force your code to display information in the Immediate window. However, in code, you use a `Debug.Print` expression rather than a **?** expression to make the code print to the Immediate window. This is an easy way to watch what's happening to variables behind the scenes while your code is running.

The real beauty of `Debug.Print` is that it allows you to write a little code, test it to see what's going on, and make sure that all is well before writing more code. For example, in Chapter 11, we show you an example of a function named `PCase()` that can convert any text to proper noun case (the first letter of each word in uppercase).

When you look at a completed procedure like that, you might think that the programmer just typed it like typing a note, and the thing just ran perfectly right off the bat. That's not even close to how programmers really work. A programmer knows that every line of code is just one step in the overall procedure. For the procedure as a whole to work, make sure that each individual piece is doing exactly what you think it's doing.

To write the `PCase()` function, we started out by just writing this bit of code:

```
Public Function PCase(anyText) As String
   PCase = StrConv(anyText, vbProperCase)
   Debug.Print "PCase = " & PCase
End Function
```

That was the entire function, at first. To test it, we typed **? PCase("MARVIN DODoskY")** into the Immediate window and pressed Enter. When we did, the `Debug.Print` statement in the code displayed the following line in the Immediate window:

```
PCase = Marvin Dodosky
```

To test it again, we typed **? PCase("123 OAK TREE LANE")** into the Immediate window and got back `PCase = 123 Oak Tree Lane`. At this point, we knew that the basic problem — converting the first letter of each word to uppercase and making all other letters lowercase — was solved.

Granted, having the procedure show a small result like that in the Immediate window is of no value to a potential user of the function. But the result showed us — the *programmers* — that after the statement `PCase = StrConv(anyText, vbProperCase)` executes, the `PCase` variable contains the passed text with the first letter of each word capitalized. At that point, we knew that the basic problem of capitalizing the first letter of each word was solved, so we could then move on to writing code to solve the next problem.

We decided to tackle the *Mc* problem next. First, we had to figure out how to tell the procedure that if the first two letters are *mc*, change `PCase` so that the first and third letters are uppercase. We already knew that we could use the `Mid()` function to grab any portion of any string and that we could use the `UCase()` function to convert any letter to uppercase.

So we typed out the `If...Else...End If` block of code to handle any string that starts with the letters *Mc* and moved the `Debug.Print "PCase = " & PCase` statement below that, as shown here:

```
Public Function PCase(anyText) As String
    PCase = StrConv(anyText, vbProperCase)

    If Left(PCase, 2) = "Mc" Then
        PCase = "Mc" & UCase(Mid(PCase, 3, 1)) & Mid(PCase,
            3)
    End If

    Debug.Print "PCase = " & PCase

End Function
```

To test our progress, we typed? **PCase("MCDONALD")** into the Immediate window and pressed Enter. The Immediate window showed `PCase = McDdonald`. Oops — that should have been McDonald — not McDdonald (with three *d*'s rather than two). This is a logical error in the sense that the code ran without generating any error messages. The problem lies in the logic of how we handled the problem.

After studying the code more closely, we realized that the last `Mid` statement — `& Mid(PCase,3)` — was wrong: It should have been `Mid(PCase,4)`. So we changed the code, as shown here:

```
Public Function PCase(anyText) As String
    PCase = StrConv(anyText, vbProperCase)

    If Left(PCase, 2) = "Mc" Then
```

```
      PCase = "Mc" & UCase(Mid(PCase, 3, 1)) & Mid(PCase,
         4)
   End If

   Debug.Print "PCase = " & PCase

End Function
```

Once again, we tested the procedure by entering **? PCase("MCDONALD")** into the Immediate window. We got back

```
PCase = McDonald
```

in the Immediate window. Now we knew that the *Mc* problem was solved. On to the next problem — dealing with the *Mac* last names. From there on out, it was more of the same. We wrote a little code, tested our progress, and fixed any problems that we discovered. By making sure that each piece of the puzzle worked at each step in the process, we could finally create a custom function that did what we wanted it to.

The much larger NumWord() procedure from Chapter 11 was harder to write, of course. Again, it was all a matter of doing a little at a time, testing our progress, fixing all compile and logical errors, and then moving on to the next problem. Basically, we started out by declaring variables, setting up the array, and typing the first statement, followed by a couple of Debug.Print statements. Here's the basic idea: To save space, we put an ellipsis (. . .) in place of most of the array element definitions:

```
Function NumWord(AmountPassed As Currency) As String
   'Declare all variables and arrays.
   Dim English As String, strNum As String
   Dim Chunk As String, Pennies As String
   Dim Hundreds As Integer, Tens As Integer
   Dim Ones As Integer, LoopCount As Integer
   Dim StartVal As Integer, TensDone As Boolean
   Dim EngNum(90) As String
   EngNum(0) = ""
   EngNum(1) = "One"
   EngNum(2) = "Two"
   EngNum(3) = "Three"
      '...
   EngNum(80) = "Eighty"
   EngNum(90) = "Ninety"

   strNum = Format(AmountPassed, "000000000.00")
   'strNum is original number converted to string

   Debug.Print "AmountPassed = " & AmountPassed
   Debug.Print "strNum = " & strNum

End Function
```

To test our progress at this point, we typed **? NumWord(1234.56)** into the Immediate window and then pressed Enter. The Immediate window returned this result:

```
AmountPassed = 1234.56
strNum = 000001234.56
```

We could then see what we really had to work with before writing more code. Also, we knew that because `strNum` is a string, we could use the built-in `Mid()` function to isolate portions of the string and still use `AmountPassed` to check for other things, like how large of a number was being translated to English.

Knowing that we had `AmountPassed` and `strNum` to work with, we then wrote a little more code for the procedure, tested the code, and worked out any kinks until all was well to that point. And so it goes: You write a little code, maybe use the Help system to work out any compile errors, test the code, fix any errors in logic, and then move on to the next bit of code.

If we had tried to just type the whole procedure in one fell swoop before testing it, any problems would have been more difficult to find because they could have been anywhere in the code. By writing a little, testing a little, and debugging a little along the way, we were gradually able to solve all the problems and come up with a procedure that works.

The only purpose of using `Debug.Print` in the code is to give yourself some feedback about what's going on behind the scenes as that code is running. After any problems are solved at a given point in a procedure, you can delete any `Debug.Print` statements that you don't need any more. After all, the `Debug.Print` statements aren't of any value to the users of your custom function. `Debug.Print` statements serve only as a programmer's debugging tool.

Testing Function and Sub procedures

The syntax for calling a `Sub` procedure from code, as well as from the Immediate window, is different from the syntax for calling a function. To run a `Sub` procedure from the Immediate window, just type the procedure's name (without the parentheses) and press Enter — for example, if your module contains a `Sub` procedure declared as `Sub`.

To test a custom `Sub` procedure from the Immediate window, just type the procedure's name without any quotation marks and then press Enter. To test a function from the Immediate window, use the syntax `? functionName (arguments)` where `functionName` is the name of your custom function and `arguments` represents any sample data that you want to pass to the function for testing. After the function runs, the Immediate window displays the value returned by your function.

Slowing down code

Using Debug.Print in code to get a little feedback about what's happening in your procedure is helpful, but when you run the procedure, it still executes in an eyeblink. To get things to slow down, you can set breakpoints in your code via the VBA Editor Code window. A *breakpoint* in your code doesn't make the code run in slow motion; rather, it forces the VBA Editor to suspend execution of the code at that point so that you can explore the values of variables or whatever in the Immediate window.

To set a breakpoint in a procedure, follow these steps:

1. **Make sure that the procedure you want to test is open and visible in the Code window.**

2. **Move the cursor to the line where you want to suspend code execution; then do whichever of the following is most convenient:**

   - Right-click the line and choose Toggle⇨Breakpoint from the short-cut menu.

   - Choose Debug⇨Toggle Breakpoint from the VBA Editor menu bar.

   - Press the F9 key.

   - Click in the gray area on the left side of the code window next to the line where you want to suspend the code's execution.

   - Click the Toggle Breakpoint button on the Debug toolbar.

     If the Debug toolbar isn't visible in your VBA Editor, choose View⇨Toolbars⇨Debug from the menu bar to make that toolbar visible.

After the breakpoint is set, test your code normally from the Immediate window. Your code executes at its usual blazing speed until execution reaches the line that you defined as a breakpoint. Rather than get compiled and executed, the breakpoint line of code gains a bright yellow highlighter in the Code window and doesn't execute until you press F8. Basically, you can then make your code slam on the brakes and go into *step mode,* where you miraculously take over all code execution yourself.

Of the several ways to use step mode, just take a look at the easiest and most common way to set a breakpoint and use step mode. Suppose that while creating the NumWord() procedure earlier in this chapter, you want to take a look at all your variables just before the line that reads strNum = Format(AmountPassed, "000000000.00") executes. In the Code window, you would right-click that line and choose Toggle⇨Breakpoint. Then you would run the function and pass some huge number to it, as a test, by entering something like **? NumWord(123456789.00)**.

The procedure would run at its usual blazing speed up to the breakpoint line and then slam on the brakes. If you wanted to take a quick look at some variable defined in the code before the breakpoint line executes, you could ask the Immediate window by typing **?** *variableName*. For example, if you enter **? strNum** into the Immediate window while the code is suspended, you get nothing in return because `strNum` is empty before the breakpoint line executes. Still, getting nothing in response to the `? strNum` expression is confusing. The following section presents a much quicker and easier way to check out the contents of your procedure's variables: the *Locals window*.

Using the Locals window

While your code is suspended in a breakpoint and in step mode, you can easily check the value and data type of every variable defined in your code up to that breakpoint. This saves you from having to type a bunch of `? variableName` statements in the Immediate window. To see an overview or all the variables in the procedure, just choose View➪Locals Window from the VBA Editor menu bar or click the Locals Window button on the Debug toolbar.

The Locals window opens, showing the name, value, and data type of every variable defined to that point in your code. Figure 12-9 shows an example where we opened the Locals window while code was suspended in the sample `NumWord()` procedure. There you can see the name, value, and data type of every variable that exists in `NumWord()` just before the breakpoint line executes.

Debug toolbar   Immediate window

Figure 12-9:
Checking
out the
locals in
step mode.

Code suspended at breakpoint   Locals window

Moving and sizing editor windows

As with all windows in the VBA Editor, you can anchor the Locals window to any edge of the program window. While it's anchored, you can change its height or width by dragging the border just above its title bar. You can also drag it by the title bar toward the center of the screen to make it a free-floating window. To put the Locals window back into hiding, click the Close (X) button on its title bar.

To get the Immediate and Locals windows to stack up as they're shown in Figure 12-9, first make sure that both windows are open. Drag one window's title bar right to the middle of the other's title bar and then release the mouse button. To resize them, drag the border line that separates the two panes up or down or drag the leftmost border to the right. To reverse the stack order of the two panes, drag the bottom pane's toolbar up to the middle of the top pane's window.

In the Locals window, you can easily see the strNum variable that you previously checked on in the Immediate window. The Locals window lets you know that the variable contains "123456789.00" as its value and String as its data type. That's all true and correct because a Dim statement near the top of the procedure has already declared strNum a string variable.

The Locals window shows the name, value, and data type of every variable created before the highlighted line of code. And knowing about all your variables at an exact moment can be a great aid to debugging your code. Keep reading because things really get good when you learn to use step mode.

Stepping through code in step mode

Suppose that you set your breakpoint, code execution stops at the breakpoint line, and you're looking at variables in the Locals window. The real question is "What next?" The answer is that you basically have four choices:

✔ **To execute the highlighted line of code (only) or step through a procedure being called by the current line:** Press F8 or choose Debug➪Step Into.

✔ **To execute the highlighted line of code and not step through another procedure being called by the current line:** Press Shift+F8 or choose Debug➪Step Over.

✔ **To execute all lines of code up to — but excluding — a specific line of code:** First click the line to which you want execution to run. Then press Ctrl+F8 or choose Debug➪Run to Cursor from the menu bar.

✔ **To bail out of break mode:** Press Ctrl+Shift+F8 or choose Debug➪Step Out.

The best way to use step mode (as a beginner, anyway) is to just press F8 to execute the selected line of code. When you do so, the line executes. Any changes to variables made by executed statements appear in the Locals window.

Even better, you can sit there and just tap the F8 key to watch the procedure execute one line at a time. You can see how code execution jumps over If...End If statements and how it goes around in circles in a loop. If the Locals window is open, you can watch variables appear and receive values just as they do when the code is really executing. It's code execution in super-slow motion, where you control the speed of things by tapping the F8 key.

If the code that you're debugging affects an open form in Access, you might notice the Access program window flash on-screen as the code executes. If you want to take a look at that open form — without losing your place in the VBA Editor — just click the Access taskbar button or press Alt+F11 to switch back and forth between Access and the VBA Editor.

Getting back to normal in the Code window

When you finish debugging or just want to start over with a clean slate, do one of the following:

- ✔ **To get out of step mode:** Press Ctrl+Shift+F8 or choose Debug➪Step Out. Code execution continues, and things go back to normal.

- ✔ **To remove a breakpoint:** Right-click the line and choose Toggle➪ Breakpoint from the shortcut menu.

- ✔ **To clear all breakpoints from your code:** Choose Debug➪Clear All Breakpoints.

- ✔ **To clear the Locals window of its value:** Right-click any text within the window and choose the Reset option from the shortcut menu.

Closing the VBA Editor window also terminates step mode. For instance, if you choose File➪Close and Return to Microsoft Office Access while in step mode, you see the prompt This command will stop the debugger (see Figure 12-10). If you click OK, the Visual Basic Editor then closes, step mode is terminated, and you return to the Access program window. (Clicking Cancel closes the dialog box without doing anything to the code. Clicking Help shows some confusing information about the dialog box.)

Figure 12-10:
Exit options when closing in step mode.

Microsoft Visual Basic

⚠ This command will stop the debugger.

[OK] [Cancel] [Help]

Wrestling Runtime Errors

Some VBA errors are caused by environmental conditions rather than anything that's wrong with the logic of the code or a compile error. As an extreme example, take a look at an environmental condition that could prevent code from executing. Say you drag and drop some icons from a folder to the icon for your floppy drive in My Computer. If no floppy disk is in the drive when you release the mouse button, you create an environmental condition in which no program could complete its task. There's just no way that any program in the world can copy files to an empty floppy disk drive!

In your VBA code, environmental conditions can be much more subtle than the missing floppy disk example. A more common example is a line of code that attempts to move the cursor to a specific control when the form isn't even open. For example, the following line of code attempts to move the cursor (`SetFocus`) to a control named `StateProv` on an open form named `Customers` (`Forms![Customers].SetFocus`).

```
Forms!Customers.[StateProv].SetFocus
```

The preceding line of code executes just fine as long as the form named `Customers` is open in Form view when the line executes. If the form named `Customers` is open in Design view when that line executes, a runtime error like the one shown in Figure 12-11 occurs.

Figure 12-11:
Sample
runtime
error
message.

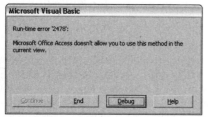

```
Microsoft Visual Basic

Run-time error '2478':

Microsoft Office Access doesn't allow you to use this method in the
current view.

     Continue        End        Debug        Help
```

Responding to a runtime error

When your code generates a runtime error and you're given the choices shown in Figure 12-11, you can choose to click one of these buttons:

- ✔ **Continue:** If code execution was suspended when the error occurred, resumes execution at the next line of code in the procedure. This option is disabled (not available) in most cases.
- ✔ **End:** Terminates code execution and takes you back to the Code window without going into step mode.

✔ **Debug:** Stops code execution and takes you back to the Code window. The line of code that generated the error is highlighted, and you're in step mode.

✔ **Help:** Provides brief help with debugging VBA code.

Most often, you just click End to get back to your code normally or click Debug to get back to your code with the faulty line highlighted and in step mode. If the problem is something that you can fix in that particular line, you can just modify the line and try again although it often takes a little more brain power than that to figure out what's really wrong.

For example, after inspecting the code that caused the runtime error, you discover that the line above the faulty line opens the Customers form in Design view (acDesign) rather than in the normal Form view, as shown here:

```
DoCmd.OpenForm "Customers", acDesign
Forms!Customers.[StateProv].SetFocus
```

Even though the error message was generated by the second line, the real problem is in the first line. The fix is to change acDesign to acNormal in the top line, as follows, so that the second line can do its job of moving the cursor to the StateProv control of that form:

```
DoCmd.OpenForm "Customers", acNormal
Forms!Customers.[StateProv].SetFocus
```

After you make the correction, you can just run the entire procedure again to test it.

If seeing the error is difficult, you can still use step mode to watch what's going on in your code and in Access. For example, in your code, you can set a breakpoint a few lines above the line that's causing the error. Then press the F8 key to step through your code one line at a time. After you press F8, you can press Alt+F11 to see what (if anything) happened in Access as a result of that statement's execution. Then press Alt+F11 again to return to VBA, press F8 to execute the next statement, and then press Alt+F11 again to see that statement's effect on Access. Just keep doing that, and eventually you'll discover which statement is really causing the situation that's making the faulty line fail.

Unfortunately, not all runtime errors are the kind that you can fix by correcting your existing code. Some runtime errors are caused by peculiar situations in the environment, like the missing floppy disk in the copy-to-floppy example, and there's really no way to write code to fix that error. The best that you can do with those kinds of errors is to trap them and give the user some kind of more friendly feedback and options than the VBA runtime error message box would provide.

Trapping runtime errors

As you can see in the preceding example, when a runtime error occurs, you get two pieces of information in the message box that appears (see Figure 12-12). Note the error number (referred to as `Err.Number` or *the Number property of the Err object* in programmer lingo). That number is of no value to a typical user, but can be handy for a programmer. The other piece of information that the error message provides is the error description, referred to as `Err.Description` in VBA. The error description is the text that (vaguely) describes why the error occurred.

Err.Number

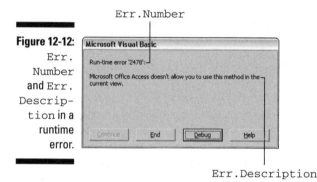

Figure 12-12: Err. Number and Err. Description in a runtime error.

Err.Description

When you see a runtime error on your screen, two things have happened. The obvious first thing is the message on-screen. But behind the scenes, VBA has raised a runtime error, and the `Err` object has also received two values that describe that error. Those values are stored in the `Number` and `Description` properties of the `Err` object (expressed as `Err.Number` and `Err.Description` in VBA code). Just like you can see the number and description of an error by looking at the message on-screen, VBA can "see" that same information by looking at the contents of the `Err.Number` and `Err.Description` properties.

Trapping runtime errors is basically a matter of anticipating which runtime errors might occur when the code runs, and also writing code to gracefully handle each type error without causing the whole procedure to crash. The code that you write to deal with runtime errors is often referred to as an *error handler* because that's exactly what the code does — it handles the error in some way without causing the whole procedure to crash.

To create an error handler, you first need to add an `On Error` statement to your code, preferably just after the `Sub` or `Function` statement that marks the beginning of the procedure. Use one of the following three different ways to create an `On Error` statement:

✔ `On Error GoTo` *label*: When an error occurs as a statement runs, code execution jumps to the section of code identified by label within the same procedure.

✔ `On Error Resume Next`: If an error occurs as a statement runs, that statement is ignored, and processing just continues with the next line of code in the procedure.

✔ `On Error GoTo 0`: Disables any previous `OnError GoTo` or `On Error Resume Next` statements so that future runtime errors are handled by VBA rather than by your own code.

The `Resume` statement can be used in any error-handling code to tell VBA exactly where to resume code execution after the runtime error occurred. The syntax for the `Resume` statement can take any of the following forms:

✔ `Resume`: Causes VBA to reexecute the statement that caused the error. You want to use this statement only if the error-handling code fixed the problem that caused the error in the first place. Otherwise, executing the same statement again just causes the same error.

✔ `Resume Next`: Causes execution to resume at the first statement after the statement that caused the error. The statement that caused the error doesn't execute.

✔ `Resume` *label*: Causes execution to resume at the label that's specified.

Code created by Control Wizards in Access 2003 and earlier and macro conversions might already have error-handling code written into it. For example, if you create a macro named `CloseCustForm` to close a Customers form, you can convert this macro to VBA by highlighting it in the Navigation pane and then clicking the Convert Macros to Visual Basic command in the Macro group of the Database Tools tab. In the dialog box that appears, make sure to check the box to add error handling to the generated functions, and then click Convert. Access creates a module with a function named `CloseCustForm()`. The macro and the VBA function are shown in Figure 12-13.

In the `CloseCustForm()` procedure that the conversion created, only the line `DoCmd.Close acForm, "Customers"` closes the form. Technically, the code would work just fine if `DoCmd.Close acForm, "Customers"` were the only statement in the entire procedure, but the conversion adds error handling to the code that it generates if you tell it to. And most of the lines in the procedure are there to handle errors in case some problem arises that prevents the form from closing.

Near the top of the procedure, you see the statement `On Error GoTo CloseCustForm_Err`. When executed, that statement tells VBA, "If a runtime error occurs while this procedure is executing, don't 'crash.' Instead, stop what you're doing and resume execution at the `CloseCustForm_Err` label."

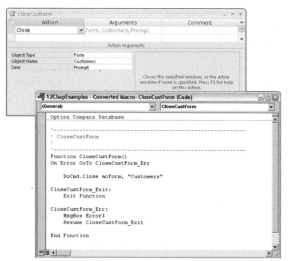

Figure 12-13:
Macro
(top) and
converted
function
with error
handling
in VBA
(bottom).

Then the code tries to execute the next statement, `DoCmd.Close acForm, "Customers"`. If VBA can close the form when executing that statement, no runtime error occurs. Instead, the code execution drops to the next actual statement in the procedure, `Exit Function`, which ends the procedure. In other words, if no error occurs when `DoCmd.Close acForm, "Customers"` executes, the code runs and ends normally without calling on any error-handling code.

However, if a runtime error does occur when VBA tries to execute the `DoCmd. Close acForm, "Customers"` statement, the procedure doesn't crash. Rather, it passes control to the first statement under the `CloseCustForm_Err:` label. There, the `MsgBox Error$` statement shows the description of the error in a simple message box, and code execution drops to the line that reads `Resume CloseCustForm_Exit`, which tells the procedure to go to the `CloseCustForm_Exit:` label and resume execution. The first statement under that label reads `Exit Function`. When executed, that statement just ends the procedure normally.

A key component of understanding how error handling works is realizing that any line that ends with a colon is a label in code. A label is different from a regular line of code in that it's not an instruction to the computer to do something. Rather, its just a placeholder in code to which `GoTo` and `Resume` statements can pass control. The sample `CloseCustForm` function has two labels, which are pointed out in Figure 12-14.

A label text can be any text at all, as long as it starts with a letter and contains no blank spaces. Using the words `Err` or `Exit` somewhere in the label is customary but not required. However, the colon at the end of the label is mandatory because it's the only character that lets the compiler know that the line is a label rather than a regular VBA statement.

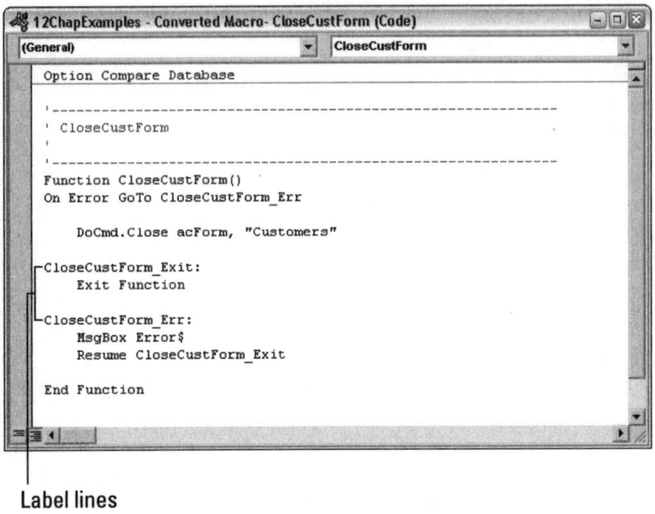

```
12ChapExamples - Converted Macro- CloseCustForm (Code)
(General)                                    CloseCustForm

Option Compare Database

' ---------------------------------------------------
' CloseCustForm
'
' ---------------------------------------------------
Function CloseCustForm()
On Error GoTo CloseCustForm_Err

    DoCmd.Close acForm, "Customers"

CloseCustForm_Exit:
    Exit Function

CloseCustForm_Err:
    MsgBox Error$
    Resume CloseCustForm_Exit

End Function
```

Figure 12-14:
Lines ending
with a colon
(:) are
labels, not
statements.

Label lines

Writing your own error handlers

When writing your own code and your own error handlers, it's not realistic to assume that you can anticipate every possible environmental condition that might cause the procedure to crash. For starters, you can just write the basic code to trap the error, display the error number and description in a simple message box, and then exit the procedure gracefully.

Assume that you've already written a procedure, and now you want to add some error-handling to that procedure. Exactly what the procedure does is irrelevant, so rather than show a bunch of VBA statements here, we just refer to the existing statements as the main body of code below. First, you need to add an On Error... statement at or near the top of the procedure so that any runtime error that occurs during execution branches control to some label.

Next, you need to define the label to which the On Error statement refers. Typically, you can add an Exit Sub or Exit Function statement just above the End Sub or End Function procedure that's currently in the code. That ensures that if the code runs without generating an error, code execution doesn't fall through to the error handler and make you think that there's an error when there isn't.

Finally, just above the Exit Sub or Exit Function statement at the bottom of the procedure, add whatever label you specified in your On Error statement. It's rarely possible to anticipate every conceivable error message. For starters, you just have the error handler display the error number and description in a standard message box. Here's the basic skeleton of what the starting error-handling code might look like in a Sub procedure (where the main body of code represents any number of VBA statements that define what the procedure does normally):

```
Sub anySub()
On Error GoTo MyErrorHandler

    Main body of code
    Main body of code
    Main body of code

    Exit Sub
MyErrorHandler:
    Dim Msg As String
    Msg = Err.Number & ": " & Err.Description
    MsgBox Msg
End Sub
```

The same skeleton structure works in a function. You just have to replace the Exit Sub with Exit Function, like this:

```
Function anyFunction()
On Error GoTo MyErrorHandler

    Main body of code
    Main body of code
    Main body of code

    Exit Function
MyErrorHandler:
    Dim Msg As String
    Msg = Err.Number & ": " & Err.Description
    MsgBox Msg
End Function
```

Take a look now at how even a simple generic handler like the preceding example can be adapted to deal with unexpected runtime errors. Suppose that somewhere in the main body of code is a statement that attempts to write some data from a query to an HTML file on a floppy disk. For instance, the following VBA statement copies data from a table named Customers to a file named Customers.html on a floppy disk:

```
DoCmd.OutputTo acOutputTable, "Customers", _
       acFormatHTML, "A:\Customers.html"
```

Figure 12-15 shows that code added to the main body of the basic skeletal structure for error handling. Once again, ...Main body of code... refers to any other numbers of statements in the same procedure.

Suppose that you run the procedure without a floppy disk in the floppy drive. Naturally, when VBA tries to execute the statement that tries to write to a floppy disk, the empty floppy drive causes a major environmental problem. That problem, in turn, raises an error message. However, by the time the DoCmd.OutputTo... statement executes, the On Error GoTo MyErrorHandler code has already been executed. So rather than just crash at the DoCmd.OutputTo... statement, execution gets passed down to the MyErrorHandler label.

The MyErrorHandler code then creates a little message string from the Number and Description properties of the Err object. That message is then displayed on-screen, as in Figure 12-16.

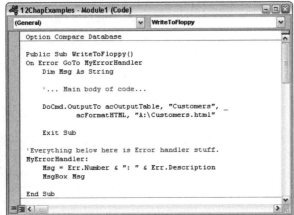

Figure 12-15: Procedure writes a file to a floppy.

Figure 12-16: Err. Number and Err. Description in a message box.

As a programmer, you just found out something very useful about your procedure. When a user tries to run this procedure without a floppy disk in the drive, Access raises Err.Number 2302 (the number at the start of the message). As a programmer, you also don't care about anything else, other than finding some graceful way of handling this situation that doesn't leave the poor user at a complete loss about what to do next. As a programmer, you click OK and get back to doing what programmers do — writing code.

You also know that when any error occurs in your code, execution always transfers to the MyErrorHandler label. To trap that 2302 error, you can place an If...End If statement right there under the label that reads, *If*

the error that got us here was error number 2302, then . . . *(handle it this way).*
Here we start (as we always do in real life) by just typing the If . . . End If
lines for trapping error 2302. These need to be inserted just under the label
MyErrorHandler:, as shown in boldface in the following example (we also
added a couple of comments to the code):

```
'Everything below here is Error handler stuff.
MyErrorHandler:

    'Trap "missing floppy" error (2302).
    If Err.Number = 2302 Then
        'Deal with missing floppy problem.
    End If

    'Just show error number and description, then end Sub.
    Msg = Err.Number & ": " & Err.Description
    MsgBox Msg

End Sub
```

So now you have an If . . . End If block of code in your handler that can
deal specifically with error 2302 when it arises. We suppose the smart thing
to do would be to show a message that tells the user to put a floppy in the
floppy drive, click an OK button, and let the code take another shot at copying to the floppy. The following code sample shows the appropriate code
added between the If . . . End If statements for error 2302:

```
'Everything below here is Error handler stuff.
MyErrorHandler:
    'Trap "missing floppy" error (2302).
    If Err.Number = 2302 Then
        'Deal with missing floppy problem.
        'Tell user what to do.
        Msg = "Please put a floppy disk in drive A:."
        Msg = Msg & " Then click OK. "
        MsgBox Msg

        'Re-execute line that copies to floppy.
        Resume
    End If

    'Just show error number and description, then end Sub.
    Msg = Err.Number & ": " & Err.Description
    MsgBox Msg

End Sub
```

Notice that now a block of code is executed if (and only if) error number 2302
is raised (If Err.Number = 2302 Then . . . End If). Within that block of
code is more code written specifically to handle that error. If the user runs
the procedure without a floppy in the drive, the user first sees the message
box defined in the code, which looks like Figure 12-17 on the user's screen.

Figure 12-17:
Custom error
message for
the missing
floppy (error
2302).

For starters, your custom error-handler has replaced the generic error message `Microsoft Office Access can't save the output data to the file you've selected` with a specific instruction telling the user exactly what to do. That's because the message being displayed now is the one defined by these lines of code within the `If Err.Number = 2302 Then...End If` block:

```
Msg = "Please put a floppy disk in drive A:."
Msg = ErrMsg & " Then click OK. "
MsgBox Msg
```

When the `MsgBox Msg` statement executes and displays the message on-screen, code execution halts until the user clicks OK (not because of anything special we did but rather because that's how `MsgBox...` statements always execute). When the user does as instructed and clicks OK, the next statement executed is

```
Resume
```

That statement forces execution to try the error-generating line again (`DoCmd.OutputTo...`). This time, because a floppy disk is in the drive, the statement runs just fine. Code execution then resumes normally under that line, and everything remains just as though the error never occurred.

That's what handling runtime errors gracefully is all about. By adding a general error-handler to the code, you can trap — and take a look at — whatever runtime errors that particular procedure might generate. When you find a specific runtime error, find some way of handling it that allows the code to keep running and keep working rather than just leave the user staring dumbfounded at the screen.

Part V
Reaching Out with VBA

The 5th Wave   By Rich Tennant

"Roger! Check the sewing machine's connection to the PC. I'm getting macros stitched across my curtains again."

In this part . . .

*E*ven though the focus of this book is on using VBA to program Microsoft Access, that doesn't mean that VBA works only in Access. VBA is a programming language for *all* the programs in Microsoft Office, including Word, Excel, and Outlook. In this part, you'll discover some tools and techniques for using VBA to automate transferring data among those programs — and even programs that aren't part of Microsoft Office.

Chapter 13

Using VBA with Multiple Databases

In This Chapter

▶ Importing data from external tables and queries

▶ Linking to external Access tables

▶ Creating recordsets from external data

▶ Importing, exporting, and linking to anything

*U*sually an Access database (an ACCDB file) contains all the tables, queries, forms, reports, and other objects that make up a single database. However, you find situations where it's to your advantage to split things into two or more database files. For example, you might want to put some tables for a database into a single ACCDB file that's located in a shared folder on a network and then put all the other stuff (queries, forms, reports, and code) in a separate database file. You can then distribute the front-end database to multiple users on the network, thus allowing several people to work with the same tables simultaneously from multiple computers.

Splitting a database into two allows you to set up a client-server relationship between the data in the tables and the queries, forms, reports, pages, macros, and modules that manage and access those tables. The computers that can get to the data are the *clients.* The computer that stores and serves the tables to the clients is the *server.* There are many ways to split up data into a client-server relationship. In this chapter, take a look at one of the most common methods — the Access Database Splitter.

Client-Server Microsoft Access

As you might (or might not) know, you can use Access's built-in Database Splitter to split any existing database into two separate databases (two separate ACCDB files). The Database Splitter is a wizard that takes you through the steps necessary to split the database. In the process, the wizard creates a database that contains only the tables. To open the Database Splitter, click the Database Tools tab, and then click the Access Database button in the Move Data group.

For example, you might want to split a database file named MOM.accdb by using the Database Splitter. Follow the instructions in the Database Splitter and click the Split Database button. In the Create Back-end Database dialog box, choose a filename for your database. In our example, we named the file MOM_be.accdb. After the database is split, you end up with a file named MOM_be.accdb, which contains all of that database's tables. You also still have your original MOM.accdb database containing all the original queries, forms, reports, pages, macros, and modules.

However, MOM.accdb doesn't contain any tables. Instead, the Navigation pane shows links to external tables. In the Navigation pane, each linked table has an arrow to the left of its icon, as in the example shown in Figure 13-1. Pointing to a linked table's icon or name displays the table's true location in a ScreenTip at the mouse pointer.

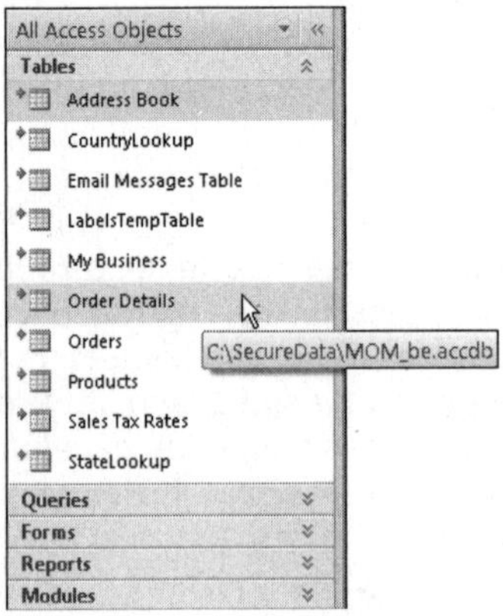

Figure 13-1:
Arrows next
to table
names
indicate
linked
tables.

Splitting the database in two lets you keep the back end separate from the front end. The back end is the database file that contains only the tables. On a network, you can place the back-end ACCDB file on any shared folder in a network so that all computers in the network can get to the tables.

When not to split a database

Splitting a database isn't something to be taken lightly, just for the heck of it. After you split a database file in two, changing or deleting a field in a table becomes a real headache. You have to open the back-end database table and change the field there. Furthermore, Name AutoCorrect can't propagate a field name change through other objects as it normally would. So you might have to manually change the same field name in several objects in the front-end database file.

Splitting a database across multiple computers also slows things down because now there's the extra step of transferring all data to and from tables over the network. To keep life simple and not slow things down while you're trying to create a database, keep your tables, queries, forms, reports, macros, and modules all in one ACCDB file. Don't even think about splitting things until you've created everything you need — and are sure that everything is working.

If you want to try it, start with a copy of a database (so that you still have the original unsplit database available to you). Open that database with Access in the usual manner, and then use the Database Splitter to split the database. For more information on the whole shebang, open Access Help go to or `http://search.microsoft.com` and search for the keywords **Database Splitter**, **Linked Table Manager**, and **Name AutoCorrect**.

After you place the back-end database in a shared folder, the next step is just a matter of opening the front-end database to make sure that it can find the linked tables. If you've changed the location of the back-end database since splitting the tables, you can use the Linked Table Manager — available in the Database Tools group on the Database Tools tab — to reestablish a link with those tables at any time.

Back in the `MOM.accdb` and `MOM_be.accdb` example, you might put `MOM_be.accdb` in a shared folder named MOMFolder on a computer named NetPC and then open the front-end database, `MOM.accdb`, on a computer other than NetPC. If the links to the back-end database fail, just click the Linked Table Manager button on the Database Tools tab and set the path for all of the tables to the new location. In this example, it's `\\NetPC\MOMFolder\MOM_be.accdb`.

After you reestablish the links, you can install the front-end database on any computer in the network that has Microsoft Access installed. For example, Figure 13-2 shows how the back-end database is installed on one computer, which acts as the server by serving table data to all who request it. Each of the other computers has a copy of the `MOM.accdb` front-end database installed, so each of those computers has access to exactly the same back-end tables.

Everything we discuss to this point in the chapter can be done without using any VBA. The Database Splitter and Linked Table Manager tools are both right on the Database Tools tab in Microsoft Access. After you establish a valid link between the front-end and back-end databases, everything else is automatic. As far as queries, forms, reports, macros, and modules go, a linked table is no different from a *local table* (a table that's actually in the current database, not just linked).

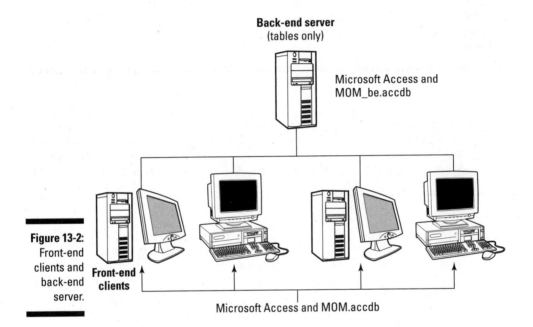

Back-end server
(tables only)

Microsoft Access and
MOM_be.accdb

Figure 13-2:
Front-end
clients and
back-end
server.

**Front-end
clients**

Microsoft Access and MOM.accdb

Here's a downside to the whole business of splitting the tables from the other objects: network traffic. It takes time to get things across a network. The heavier the traffic on the network, the longer it takes.

You might have situations where a certain external table needs to be accessed only occasionally. Perhaps only a snapshot of some data is all that's required. In such cases, you can use VBA to open and close external links as needed. For example, you can attach code to a form's On Load and On Unload event procedures to interact across the network only while that form is open or only at the moment when the data is required.

Changing linked tables back to local tables

To convert a linked table back to a local table, do the following:

1. **Right-click the linked table's icon in the Navigation pane and choose Cut.**

2. **Press Ctrl+V, or right-click some empty space in the Navigation pane and choose Paste.**

3. **In the Paste Table As dialog box that opens, type the original table name (same as the linked table's name), choose Structure and Data (Local Table), and then click OK.**

To illustrate the various techniques shown in this chapter, we use an example of a single Access ACCDB file named MOMSecure.accdb. To keep names short, this table is stored in a folder named SecureData on drive C:. Thus, the path to the database file is C:\SecureData\MOMSecure.accdb from any other Access database. (Most of the code that follows is copy-and-paste stuff. In most code, you need to change the path to reflect the actual location of your own external ACCDB file.)

If MOMSecure.accdb were in a shared folder named SecureData on a computer named Max in a local network, the path would be \\Max\Secure Data\MOMSecure.accdb from any Access database on the LAN.

To keep things relatively simple, say that MOMSecure.accdb contains only two objects: one table and one query. The table's name is CCSecure; its structure is shown in Design view on the top-left side of Figure 13-3. The figure also shows some sample data in the CCSecure table, in Datasheet view.

Disclaimer: All the names and credit card numbers shown in these figures are fictional, and any resemblance to real people or credit card numbers is purely coincidental. (So don't bother trying to use them to shop online.)

As you might have guessed already, the *CC* in the field names is short for *credit card.* Here's a quick overview of the purpose of each field in the CCSecure table:

✔ ContactID: A Long Integer that relates each record to a specific customer in a separate Customers table. ContactID is the foreign key here in the CCSecure table and the primary key in the Customers table.

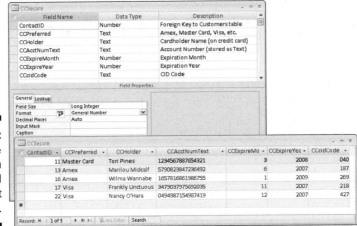

Figure 13-3:
CCSecure
table in
Design and
Datasheet
views.

✔ CCPreferred: Contains the name of a preferred credit card, such as AMEX, Master Card, or VISA.

✔ CCHolder: Contains the cardholder name as it appears on the card.

✔ CCAcctNumText: Stores the card account number as text: for example, 1234567898765432.

✔ CCExpireMon: The month when the card expires, as an integer (1–12).

✔ CCExpireYr: The year when the card expires, as an integer: for example, 2007 or 2008.

✔ CCcidCode: The three-digit CID code that appears on the back of the credit card.

The second object of MOMSecure is a query named CCSecureQry. For this example, we created a query named CCSecureQry. This query displays all records from the CCSecure table except the account number and CID fields. In place of the account number is a calculated field named CCHint, which is a calculated control based on the expression shown here:

```
CCHint: "xxxx-xxxx-xxxx-" & Right([CCAcctNumText],4)
```

Figure 13-4 shows the CCSecureQry query in both Design and Datasheet views. We omitted the CCcidCode field from the query for no particular reason other than to have an example of leaving fields out of a query. As you can see in Datasheet view, the CCHint field displays xxx-xxx-xxx-*1234*, where *1234* is the last four digits of the account number. Thus, the query is hiding some information from the CCSecure table.

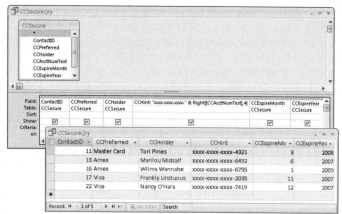

Figure 13-4:
CCSecure
Qry in C:
\Secure
Data\MOM
Secure.
accdb.

CCAcctNumText is a text field, so you use the expression
Right([CCAcctNumText],4) to refer to the last (rightmost) four
characters of that field's contents.

In a sense, you've turned the MOMSecure.accdb database into a little black
box from which you can zap some credit card info out of a query (or the
table, if need be) from any other Access database in the network. We suppose
you could call it your *customer credit card information server*. We also suppose
you can't call it your *secure server* right now because making it secure would
require some close encounters of the network administration kind, which has
nothing to do with Access or VBA.

How can any Access database on the network reach into MOMSecure.accdb
and grab data, even when that database is closed? Here are the three answers
to this question, and you can use whichever method seems most appropriate
to the occasion:

- ✓ **Import (a snapshot):** You can import a snapshot of a table or query, storing it as a table in the current database. The imported table becomes a
  local table and doesn't reflect any changes made to the source table
  since the snapshot was taken.

- ✓ **Link:** You can create a link to any table in any external database. This
  type of link is identical to that created by the Database Splitter. Changes
  made to the source table are reflected in the linked table.

- ✓ **Recordset:** You can create an ActiveX Data Objects Database (ADODB)
  recordset of any table or query from an external database. Recordsets
  are useful when you need only a brief snapshot of external data, such as
  when you're using that data for only a single VBA procedure.

Each of the methods has its pros and cons. Which method is most appropriate at any given time depends on the situation. If the situation calls for a quick snapshot of current data, you can import data. If the situation calls for an open link to the table, like when both tables need to be up-to-date with each other, you need either a link or a recordset. Start with the easiest scenario first — the quick-zap grab of a snapshot of current data.

Importing from External Databases

You can import data from any external Access table or query into a table in the current database. There are a couple of advantages to this approach. When you import, you create a table, within the current database, that contains an exact clone of the external table or query. Second, the imported data is stored in a normal, local Access table. After the table exists in the current database, all other objects in the database that depend on that table work just fine. No special handling is required.

The only disadvantage is that any changes made to the copy of the table in the current database don't carry over to the original table — or vice versa because the local table and external table are no longer connected in any way. So you want to import data from an external source whenever

- ✔ The external table is one that doesn't change much
- ✔ The current database needs the external table's data for only a short length of time

The `TransferDatabase` method of the `DoCmd` object is the easiest way to import an external table or query with VBA. The general syntax is shown here. Note that when typing your own code, you should type it in as one long line without the continuation characters (_). Or, if you want to break the statement into shorter lines, make sure that you end each of the first two lines with a blank space and an underscore, as shown here:

```
DoCmd.TransferDatabase acImport, "Microsoft Access", _
"pathToExternalDB", acTable, _
"externalTblQry", "localTableName"
```

where

- ✔ *pathToExternalDB* is the complete path and filename of the database file that contains the table or query.
- ✔ *externalTblQry* is the name of the table or query in the external database that contains the data you wish to import.
- ✔ *localTableName* is the name of the table in which the imported data will be stored.

Assume that at the moment when the MOM.accdb database is open in Access, C:\SecureData\MOMSecure\ACCDB does exist. When executed, the following statement creates a local table named CCSecureLocal, whose contents are a snapshot of the CCSecureQry query's Datasheet view, from the external database at C:\SecureData\MOMSecure.accdb:

```
DoCmd.TransferDatabase acImport, "Microsoft Access", _
    "C:\SecureData\MOMSecure.accdb", acTable, _
    "CCSecureQry", "CCSecureLocal"
```

After the preceding code executes, the MOM.accdb Navigation pane contains a new icon named CCSecureLocal. It's a normal table icon — not a link — because there's no link to the MOMSecure.accdb file. Opening the table shows a snapshot of the MOMSecure.accdb table's CCSecureQry, as shown in Figure 13-5.

If the current database already contains a table with the name specified in the *LocalTableName* argument, Access creates a new, separate table — a duplicate — with that name followed by a digit. There are easy ways to avoid that problem, as discussed in the section "Avoiding Multiple Tables and Links," a little later in this chapter.

Figure 13-5: Table contains data imported from an external query.

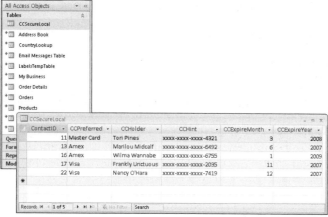

When VBA executes the preceding code, Access performs these tasks behind the scenes:

1. Opens the database named C:\SecureData\MOMSecure.accdb and then opens the query named CCSecureQry in Datasheet view

2. Creates a new, local table named CCSecureLocal as an exact clone of CCSecureQry

3. Closes CCSecureQry and C:\MOMSecure.accdb, breaking the connection between the two databases

The code for linking to an external table is almost the same as the basic syntax we show you and as our example of importing data from an external database's table or queries.

Linking to External Data through Code

The `TransferDatabase` method of the VBA `DoCmd` object also provides a syntax for linking to an external table (but not to a query). Note that the first argument after `TransferDatabase` is `acLink` rather than `acImport`. Other than that, the syntax is basically the same:

```
DoCmd.TransferDatabase acLink, "Microsoft Access", _
    "pathToExternalDB", acTable, _
    "externalTbl", "localTableName"
```

For example, the `DoCmd.TransferDatabase` (as shown here) sets up a link from the current database to an external table named `CCSecure` in the database file named `C:\SecureData\MOMSecure.accdb`. When the procedure executes, the Navigation pane gains a link icon named `CCSecureLinked`. That linked table contains the current contents of the external table:

```
DoCmd.TransferDatabase acLink, "Microsoft Access", _
    "C:\SecureData\MOMSecure.accdb", acTable, _
    "CCSecure", "CCSecureLinked"
```

After the preceding statement executes, the current database's Navigation pane displays a new link icon named `CCSecureLinked`. The arrow in the icon shows that this is a linked table, identical to the kind of linked tables that the Database Splitter creates. Opening the link shows the contents of the external table, as in Figure 13-6.

Figure 13-6: Result of linking to a `CCSecure` table in `C:\SecureData\MOMSecure.accdb`.

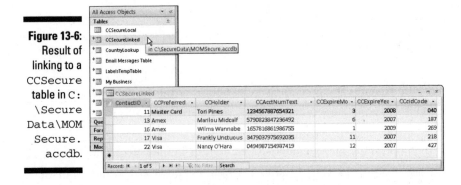

The advantage of the linked table over the imported table is that the linked table shows live data from the external MOMSecure.accdb file. Therefore, if somebody changes the table data, from any database, those changes are reflected in the linked table. The main disadvantage is that data access slows down because the link requires some network traffic between the actual table and the local link.

The other disadvantage — at least within the context of this example — is that you can't link to a query. You have to link to a table. So the only choice here is to link to the table, thereby making all the table's fields visible in Datasheet view. (However, a query in the local database that gets its data from the linked table could still hide any information within that table.)

Avoiding Multiple Tables and Links

One of the big tricks to using the TransferDatabase method is being aware of how it names the table or link that it creates. It doesn't overwrite an existing table. If the current database already contains a table or link with the name that you specify in the *localTableName* argument, Access creates a new table or link with a number added to the name.

For example, if CCSecureLocal already exists when you run the code to import its data, Access creates the new table as CCSecureLocal1. Run the code again, and you get CCSecureLocal2, then CCSecureLocal3, and so forth. The tables (or links) just keep piling up, which isn't good.

You can solve the piling-up problem by writing a general-purpose procedure that always deletes the existing table (if it exists) before creating the new table. You can set things up so that you just have to copy and paste the whole thing into any code that needs to import or link to an external table. Look at a couple of examples.

The procedure in Listing 13-1, named ImportQry, imports a query from an external database. It ensures that you don't end up with multiple linked tables by first deleting any previously imported copy of the table by the same name.

Listing 13-1:   Getting Data from an External Query

```
'Import a table snapshot from an external query.
Public Sub ImportQry(dbPath As String, extQry As String, _
       localName As String)
   'Loop through the AllTables collection.
   Dim tbl As AccessObject, thisDB As Object
   Set thisDB = Application.CurrentData
```

Listing 13-1 *(continued)*

```
For Each tbl In thisDB.AllTables
    'If the local table already exists...
    If tbl.Name = localName Then
        'If table is open...
        If tbl.IsLoaded Then
            '...close the table.
            DoCmd.Close acTable, localName, acSaveNo
        End If
        '...delete the local table.
        DoCmd.DeleteObject acTable, localName
    End If
Next tbl

'Local table gone, import the query now.
DoCmd.TransferDatabase acImport, "Microsoft Access", _
    dbPath, acTable, extQry, localName
'All done.
End Sub
```

You can just copy and paste this entire procedure into any standard module in your front-end database. Then, in any code that needs to import query results from an external database, call the procedure with the syntax

```
Call ImportQry("pathToDB","extQry","localName")
```

where

- *pathToDB* is the full path and name to your external database.
- *extQry* is the name of the query in that external database you want to import.
- *localName* is the name as it will appear in the current database.

For example, the following code imports data from the CCSecureQry in C:\SecureData\MOMSecure.accdb into a local table named CCSecureLocal. The whole procedure is bound to the On Click event property of a hypothetical button named ImportBttn:

```
Private Sub ImportBttn_Click()
    Call ImportQry( _
    "C:\SecureData\MOMSecure.accdb", _
    "CCSecureQry", "CCSecureLocal")

End Sub
```

Listing 13-2 shows a similar procedure for linking to external tables — a procedure named `LinkToTable` that can set up a link to any external Access database table. Before doing so, it deletes the existing link, if any, to avoid multiple links to the same table. It's basically the same code as the preceding `ImportQry()` procedure. However, it sets up a link to the external table by using `acLink` on the `TransferDatabase` method:

Listing 13-2:   Linking to a Table in an External Database

```
Public Sub LinkToTable(dbPath as String, extTbl as String, _
       localName As String)
   'Loop through the AllTables collection.
   Dim tbl As AccessObject, thisDB As Object
   Set thisDB = Application.CurrentData

   For Each tbl In thisDB.AllTables
      'If the local table already exists...
      If tbl.Name = localName Then
         'If table is open...
         If tbl.IsLoaded Then
            '...close the table.
            DoCmd.Close acTable, localName, acSaveNo
         End If
         '...delete the local table.
         DoCmd.DeleteObject acTable, localName
      End If
   Next tbl

   'Local table gone, import the query now.
   DoCmd.TransferDatabase acLink, "Microsoft Access", _
      dbPath, acTable, extTbl, localName

   'All done.
End Sub
```

Once again, you can just copy and paste the entire procedure, as-is, into any standard module in your database. When you want to set up a link to an external table, call the function by using the syntax

```
Call LinkToTable("extDB", "extTable", "localName")
```

For example, to link to a table named `CCSecure` in a database named `C:\SecureData\MOMSecure.accdb` — and ensure that you don't re-create the previous link — just call the procedure from your code by using the syntax

```
Call LinkToTable("C:\SecureData\MOMSecure.accdb", _
   "CCSecure", "CCSecureLinked")
```

Creating Recordsets from External Tables

You can also use VBA to create an ADODB recordset from any Access table, even one outside the current database. The basic idea is the same as in Chapter 7, where you need to define a connection to the table before creating a recordset. For example, the boilerplate code for defining a recordset from a local table starts out something like this:

```
Dim cnn1 As ADODB.Connection
Set cnn1 = CurrentProject.Connection
Dim myRecordSet As New ADODB.Recordset
myRecordSet.ActiveConnection = cnn1
<and so on...>
```

The only problem in that code is the `CurrentProject.Connection` is a reference to local tables. When the table from which you want to create a recordset exists outside the current database, you need to use a different connection. When the table is in an external Microsoft Access database (ACCDB) file, use the following syntax to define a local recordset, changing only the arguments shown in italics:

```
'Build a recordset from foreign .accdb database.
Dim CnnStr As String
CnnStr = "Provider=Microsoft.ACE.OLEDB.12.0;"
CnnStr = CnnStr & "User ID=Admin;"
CnnStr = CnnStr & "Data Source=path"

Dim MyRecordSet As New ADODB.Recordset
MyRecordSet.ActiveConnection = CnnStr
MyRecordSet.Open "Select * FROM [table/query]"
```

where *path* is the full path and filename of the external database file, and *table/query* is the name of a table or query within that table. For example, the following code creates, in the current database, a recordset named `MyRecordSet` that contains all the records from `CCSecureQry` in the external database `C:\SecureData\MOMSecure.accdb`:

```
'Build a recordset from foreign .accdb database.
Dim CnnStr As String
CnnStr = "Provider=Microsoft.ACE.OLEDB.12.0;"
CnnStr = CnnStr & "User ID=Admin;"
CnnStr = CnnStr & "Data
        Source=C:\SecureData\MOMSecure.accdb"

Dim MyRecordSet As New ADODB.Recordset
MyRecordSet.ActiveConnection = CnnStr
MyRecordSet.Open "Select * FROM [CCSecureQry]"
```

After this procedure executes, the current database contains an ADODB recordset named `MyRecordset` that contains the contents of the external `CCSecureQry` query. The recordset is invisible, as always. You need to use VBA code and ADODB recordset syntax to access data in the recordset.

See Chapter 7 for more information on creating and using ADODB recordsets.

Importing, Exporting, or Linking to Anything

As you might know, you can export data from Access to a variety of formats. You can do so *interactively* (without code). Here's how:

1. **In the Navigation pane, click the table, query, or other object that you want to export.**

2. **On the External Data tab, click a format in the Export group that is the type of data you want to export (for example, click Excel or Text File).**

3. **In the Export dialog box that appears, use the Browse button to navigate to a folder and enter a filename for the exported data file.**

4. **If available, choose a file format from the File Format drop-down list.**

   This option might not be available for certain types of exports. For example, if you're exporting to an Excel workbook, you can specify which version of Excel to export to.

5. **If available, specify any export options, such as**

   • Export Data with Formatting and Layout

   • Open the Destination File after the Export Operation Is Complete

   • Export Only the Selected Records

6. **Click OK.**

Using a macro to write the code

If you want to automate the export so that a user can do it with the click of a button, your best bet is to create a macro that uses the `OutputTo` action to export the data to a file. Here's how:

1. **Open the Access database that contains the database to export.**

2. **In the Other group on the Create tab, click the Macro button.**

3. **Choose OutputTo as the action argument, and then fill in the action arguments as summarized in Table 13-1.**

   Press F1 while the cursor is in any action argument for more information on that argument.

4. **Close and save the macro.**

Table 13-1	Action Arguments
Action Argument	*Description*
Object Type	Choose the type of object in your database you want to export (typically table or query).
Object Name	Choose the name of the object you want to export.
Output Format	Choose format, such as HTML or .xlsx (Excel Workbook), from the list of available options.
Output File	Enter the complete path and filename of the file you want to create from the exported data.
Auto Start	Choose Yes to have the exported object open automatically, or choose No to leave the exported object closed.
Template File	(Optional) Available only for HTML exports; specifies the name of a template file to use for formatting the HTML output.
Encoding	(Optional) Specifies a character set for the exported table. Leave blank for standard encoding used within the database.
Output Quality	Select the quality of the output, optimized for Screen or Print.

As an example, Figure 13-7 shows the selections needed to export a table named Products to an HTML page named FirstTest.htm in a folder named C:\SecureData on the current computer.

Figure 13-7: Macro to export a table to an HTML file.

ExportProducts		
Action	Arguments	Comment
OutputTo	Table, Products, HTML (*.htm; *.html), C:\SecureData\FirstTest.html, No, , 0, Print	Export Products table to HTML

Action Arguments

Object Type	Table
Object Name	Products
Output Format	HTML (*.htm; *.html)
Output File	C:\SecureData\FirstTest.html
Auto Start	No
Template File	
Encoding	
Output Quality	Print

Outputs the data in the specified database object to Microsoft Office Excel (.xls), rich-text (.rtf), MS-DOS Text (.txt), HTML (.htm) or Snapshot (.snp) format. Press F1 for help on this action.

For this example, we name the macro `ExportProducts`.

To test the macro, double-click its name in the Navigation pane. If all is well, the data should export without providing any feedback on-screen. To verify that the macro worked, go to the folder in which you placed the exported file and double-click its icon to open it. If the file contains data from the Products table, you're done: You've written the code necessary to export your data.

Because you used a macro to do the export, the code for exporting the data isn't visible, like it would be in VBA. However, you can get around that problem in a couple of ways. You can keep the macro as-is. Then, when you want to export data from some procedure, use the syntax

```
DoCmd.RunMacro "macroName"
```

where *macroName* is the name of the macro to run. For example, after creating the `ExportProducts` macro in a database, you could add the following statement to any procedure in the current database when you want code to export the query:

```
DoCmd.RunMacro "[ExportProducts]"
```

You can convert any macro to VBA code and then copy and paste the code into any VBA procedure. After you copy the converted code to a procedure, you don't need the macro or the `DoCmd.RunMacro()` statement any more. The code runs just like any code that you typed into the procedure yourself. Here's how to convert a macro to VBA:

1. **Click Macros in the Navigation pane, and then click the macro that you want to convert.**

2. **From the Macro group in the Database Tools tab, click the Convert Macros to Visual Basic button.**

3. **To convert without adding error-trapping to the exported code, clear (uncheck) the Add Error Handling to Generated Functions check box.**

4. **Click Convert, and then click OK when the conversion is finished.**

To get to your converted code, click Modules in the Navigation pane. The converted macro is in a module named `Converted Macro - yourMacroName` where *yourMacroName* is the name of the macro that you converted. Double-click that module name to see the converted code.

The converted code is inside a pair of `Function...End Function` statements, as in the example shown in Figure 13-8. There, you see the results of converting the macro shown in Figure 13-7 to VBA. (You can really get a sense here of how a macro is nothing more than VBA code that you create by filling in the blanks in action arguments rather than typing the source code in the VBA Editor.)

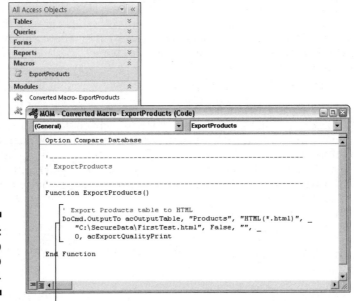

Figure 13-8:
Macro
converted to
VBA code.

Code to copy & paste

To use the converted code, copy everything between the `Function...End` and `Function` statements: that is, excluding the `Function` and `End Function` statements. Then paste that converted code into any class module or standard module, where you would otherwise have used `DoCmd.RunMacro()` to execute the macro.

Quick and easy import/export/link

The truth be told, the bit about creating a macro to import, export, or link to external data holds true for all kinds of transfers between Access and other files. The easiest way to solve any import/export/link problem is to create a macro to do the job. We've barely scratched the surface of all that's possible here.

In a macro, choose any action listed here to create a macro to do some sort of import, export, or link:

- ✔ CopyObject: Copy tables, queries, forms, reports, macros, and modules to the same or a different database (ACCDB file).

- ✔ OutputTo: Output an Access table, query, form, report, or module to one of these formats: Excel Workbook (*.xlsx), Excel 97- Excel 2003 Workbook (*.xls), text (*.txt), rich-text (*.rtf), or HTML (*.html, *.htm).

- ✔ SendObject: Send Access an Access table, query, form, report, or module via any e-mail server that supports Microsoft Mail Applications Programming Interface (MAPI).

- ✔ TransferDatabase: Import, link, or export data between two databases. Supports Access, dBase, Paradox, Windows SharePoint Services (WSS), and Open Database Connectivity (ODBC) formats.

- ✔ TransferSpreadsheet: Import, link, or export data between the current Microsoft Access database (ACCDB) or Access project (ADP) and a spreadsheet file. Import, export, or link to an Excel Workbook (*.xls). Import or export with a Lotus 1-2-3 worksheet (.wks). Some actions (linking, importing, and exporting) aren't supported with certain versions. Press F1 for more information on what's supported.

- ✔ TransferText: Import, link, or export a Microsoft Access database (ACCDB) or Access project (ADP) object with a text, HTML, or Word for Windows merge file.

After you choose an action, you can then choose options from the action arguments. The Help text to the right of the arguments describes the current argument. You can press F1 for more information on using the argument.

Create your macro, test it, and make sure that it works. If you just want to use the macro's VBA code, convert the macro to VBA, as described earlier in this chapter. Then copy all the code between the Function and End Function statements. It's a whole lot easier than trying to write the code from scratch!

The macro actions for importing, exporting, and linking correspond directly to various methods of the DoCmd object in VBA. If you're ever in the VBA Editor and need help with a DoCmd statement, click DoCmd in the Members column of the Object Browser, as in Figure 13-9. Then click any method name in the right column and click the Object Browser's Help button. The selected method's syntax appears at the bottom of the Object Browser.

Figure 13-9:
DoCmd
methods in
the Object
Browser.

Chapter 14

Integrating with Other Office Applications

. . . .

. . . .

*V*BA isn't just a programming language for Microsoft Access. VBA is a programming language for all the Microsoft Office application programs that support Automation. *Automation* (always with a capital *A*) refers to the ability of a program to expose itself to VBA so that VBA can control it behind the scenes, so to speak.

All the major applications in Microsoft Office — including Access, Excel, Outlook, PowerPoint, and Word — support Automation. You can write code to control any one of them. You can also write code to transfer information among programs. For example, you can automate pulling data from an Excel worksheet or sending data from an Access table to a Word document.

Accessing the Object Library

For VBA to manipulate a program — or a document within a program — VBA first needs to have access to that program's object library. You might envision VBA as sort of a steering wheel that can control any program to which it has access (through an object library), as in Figure 14-1.

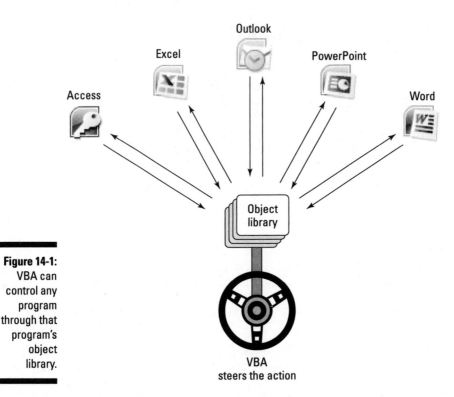

Outlook

Excel   PowerPoint

Access   Word

Object
library

Figure 14-1:
VBA can
control any
program
through that
program's
object
library.

VBA
steers the action

To write code for an Office application program, you first need to set a reference to that program's object library. To do so, starting from Microsoft Access, follow these steps:

1. **In Access, open the database that contains objects to share with other programs and open the VBA Editor.**

2. **Choose Tools⊏Reference from the VBA Editor menu bar.**

3. **From the list of available references, choose the libraries for the applications you want to program.**

For example, in Figure 14-2, we added references to Excel (Microsoft Excel 12.0 Object Library) and Word (Microsoft Word 12.0 Object Library).

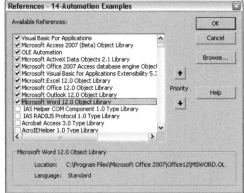

Figure 14-2:
Choose
object
libraries
in the
References
dialog box.

Exploring a program's object model

After you set a reference to a program's object model, you can explore its exposed objects, properties, and methods through the Object Browser. In the VBA Editor, just press F2 or choose View➪Object Browser. To limit the display to a given program's objects, choose that program's name from the Project/Library drop-down list. For example, in Figure 14-3, Excel is selected from the Project/Library drop-down list. The classes and members in the columns beneath this list refer to Microsoft Excel and any data that might be in the open Excel worksheet.

In the Object Browser, *classes* mean objects, collections, and such, whereas *members* mean properties, methods, and events of (whatever is highlighted in the Classes pane).

What if you don't have Word or Excel or Outlook?

Automation between Microsoft Office programs works with only the programs installed on your computer. If you don't have a given program (like Microsoft Outlook) installed, you can't load its object library or control it through VBA.

Things can get confusing when you copy a database (an ACCDB file) that contains VBA code to a different computer. Any code that refers to Word, Excel, Outlook, or PowerPoint fails if the current computer doesn't have those programs installed. In other words, VBA can't create those programs if they're missing. VBA can use those programs only if they already exist on the current computer.

For more goods on the Object Browser, see Chapter 2.

Each Office application exposes a lot of objects to VBA. Even if you limit the Object Browser to show just one program's model, you still end up with a zillion names of things. We don't have enough room in this book to define all those things. You just have to learn how to get the information you need (whatever that might be) when you need it. In the Object Browser, that generally involves clicking the name you need help with and then clicking the ? (Help) button.

Figure 14-3: Viewing classes and members of the Excel object library.

Meet the Application object

Different application programs expose different object models to VBA, but all programs have in common an `Application` object (with a capital *A*). The program's `Application` object exposes all that program's collections and objects to VBA.

If a document is open in the program, the document's objects are also exposed to VBA. For example, when VBA opens an Excel workbook, Excel exposes its own capabilities to VBA through its `Application` object. Every cell in the workbook is also exposed. Basically, VBA can do anything in the workbook that a person sitting at the workbook could do from the Excel Ribbon.

Connecting to other programs

After you set a reference to an external program's object library, you can create instances that you program in VBA. An *instance* is basically the same idea as an open program window. For example, when you start Microsoft Internet Explorer on your computer, you're creating an instance of Internet Explorer. If you right-click a link and choose Open in New Window, a new, separate Internet Explorer window opens to show the new page. Now you have two instances of Internet Explorer open, each showing a different Web page.

Before you can create an instance of a program, you have to declare an object variable that will become the name used by VBA to refer to the program. The object variable name can be any name you like. Just try to think of a short, simple name that's meaningful. The syntax for declaring an object variable that refers to an external open program is

```
Dim objectVariable As New program.Application
```

In the syntax, `objectVariable` is the object variable name, and `program` is a reference to one of the Office programs: Word, Excel, Outlook, or PowerPoint. The `.Application` part refers to the program's `Application` object of that program. The `New` keyword is optional but recommended because it ensures that the object creates a new instance of the program. Here are some examples of declaring object variables for each of the Office programs:

```
Dim XL As New Excel.Application
Dim Wrd As New Word.Application
Dim Olk As New Outlook.Application
Dim Ppt As New PowerPoint.Application
```

You must set a reference to a program before writing a `Dim` statement to declare an instance of the program.

After you declare an object variable to refer to an open instance of a program, you can then open that program (and any document) so that your VBA code has access to all the program's objects. The syntax for opening a program is

```
Set objectVariable As CreateObject("program.Application")
```

where `objectVariable` is the same as the name you specified in the `Dim` statement and `program` is the name of the application program: Excel, Word, PowerPoint, or Outlook. Referring to the earlier `Dim` statements, the `Set` statements that you use for each defined object variable are

```
Set XL = CreateObject("Excel.Application")
Set Wrd = CreateObject("Word.Application")
Set Olk = CreateObject("Outlook.Application")
Set Ppt = CreateObject("PowerPoint.Application")
```

We use short names for our object variables here: XL for Excel, Wrd for Word, Olk for Outlook, and Ppt for PowerPoint. You can use any names you want. We kept ours short just to save space here.

Anyway, that's the basic procedure for making the connection to an external program. To review and summarize, the basic procedure is

1. **Set a reference to the program's object library in the References dialog box.**

2. **In your code, use a Dim statement to create a variable with a name that you'll use in code to refer to the program.**

3. **After the Dim statement, use a Set statement with CreateObject() to open an instance of the program.**

You can see examples in the sections that follow, where we share data between Microsoft Access, Outlook, Word, and Excel.

Sending E-Mail via Outlook

Suppose you want to be able to send e-mail messages to people listed in a table named Customers in an Access database. You're absolutely certain that you can send and receive e-mail with Microsoft Outlook. (*Important:* None of the code described here works with Outlook Express or a Web browser.) For this example, you want to create a standard form-letter-type e-mail message to whatever customer a user chooses from a drop-down list, as in Figure 14-4. There, the controls named MsgAddress and MsgSubject are text, and MsgBody is a memo field.

Microsoft Outlook has built-in security to prevent you from sending huge mass mailings from Access. If you're thinking of using it to flood the Internet with some junk e-mail message, it doesn't work.

When the user clicks the Send button in Figure 14-4, you want VBA to create and display an e-mail message. Because you'll call on Outlook to do the job, the first step in the VBA Editor is to choose Tools⇨References from the menu bar and set a reference to the Microsoft Outlook 12.0 Object Library.

To write the procedure to create the message, create a procedure that's attached to the Send button. In our example, that button is named SendMailBttn. All the code for the procedure is shown in Listing 14-1.

Listing 14-1:   Sending Mail via Outlook

```
Private Sub SendMailBttn_Click()

    'Open an instance of Microsoft Outlook, name it Olk.
    Dim Olk As Outlook.Application
    Set Olk = CreateObject("Outlook.Application")

    'Create a new, empty Outlook e-mail message.
    Dim OlkMsg As Outlook.MailItem
    Set OlkMsg = Olk.CreateItem(olMailItem)

    'Put data from form into the new mail message.
    With OlkMsg
        'Make MsgAddress the "To" address of message.
        Dim OlkRecip As Outlook.Recipient
        Set OlkRecip = .Recipients.Add(Me![MsgAddress])
        OlkRecip.Type = olTo
        .Subject = Me![MsgSubject]
        .Body = Me![MsgBody]
        'Display the finished message.
        .Display
    End With

    'Clean up object variables, then done.
    Set Olk = Nothing
    Set OlkMsg = Nothing
    Set OlkRecip = Nothing
End Sub
```

MsgSubject

MsgAddress

Figure 14-4:
Controls on
a sample
e-mail form.

MsgBody

The procedure looks like a lot of code. Like all procedures, though, it's just a series of small, simple steps. The procedure reaches into Outlook and creates a new, empty e-mail message. The code then fills in that new message with data from the `MsgAddress`, `MsgSubject`, and `MsgBody` controls on the form and displays it — and that's the end of it. Take a look at the code one chunk at a time.

The first two statements under the first comment declare an object variable named `Olk` and set it to an open instance of Microsoft Outlook:

```
'Open an instance of Microsoft Outlook, name it Olk.
Dim Olk As Outlook.Application
Set Olk = CreateObject("Outlook.Application")
```

The `Application` object for Outlook lets you declare a `create` object variable of the type `Outlook.MailItem`, to which you can then assign a new, blank e-mail message. In the following code, we create a new, blank e-mail message named `OlkMsg`. (The name `OlkMsg` is one we just made up. The `Olk.` in `Olk.CreateItem(...` is a reference to the open Outlook program, and `olMailItem` is a constant from the Outlook object library.)

```
    'Create a new, empty Outlook e-mail message.
    Dim OlkMsg As Outlook.MailItem
    Set OlkMsg = Olk.CreateItem(olMailItem)
```

The `With...End With` block of code sets properties for the newly created e-mail message, `OlkMsg`:

```
With OlkMsg
...
End With
```

Within the `With...End With` block of code, the first three lines provide the recipient's e-mail address. The first line, as shown here, declares a new object variable named `OlkRecip` as an `Outlook.Recipient` object. This is a general object for e-mail addresses and can be a To, CC, or BCC (blind carbon copy) address field. The second line sets the `OlkRecp` value to whatever e-mail address is on the `MsgAddress` control on the form. The last line, `OlkRecip.Type=olTo`, turns the recipient address into the To address (where `olTo` is a constant from the Outlook object library):

```
'Make MsgAddress the "To" address of message.
Dim OlkRecip As Outlook.Recipient
Set OlkRecip = .Recipients.Add(Me![MsgAddress])
OlkRecip.Type = olTo
```

The next two lines copy the contents of the form's `MsgSubject` and `MsgBody` controls into the Subject line and body of the e-mail message:

```
.Subject = Me![MsgSubject]
.Body = Me![MsgBody]
```

The last line within the `With...End With` block displays the message, using the syntax `OlkMsg.Display`:

```
    'Display the finished message.
    .Display
End With
```

Note that all those properties are being applied to the new e-mail message named `OlkMsg`. The full syntax would be `OlkMsg.Subject=...`, `OlkMsg.Body=`, and `OlkMsg.Display`. But here you can omit the `OlkMsg` part of the name because the `With OlkMsg` statement means *All properties and methods from here to* `End With` *refer to the new e-mail message named* `OlkMsg`.

After the message is displayed, the job is done. Although it isn't absolutely necessary, we did a little housekeeping at the end of this procedure, by setting the object variable names we created to `Nothing`. Doing so breaks the link between the name and object and reclaims any memory that those things were using:

```
    'Clean up object variables, then done.
    Set Olk = Nothing
    Set OlkMsg = Nothing
    Set OlkRecip = Nothing

End Sub
```

When you run the procedure, you see why the Access-Outlook combination really isn't appropriate for any mass mailing. When you first run the procedure, you see a security warning, as at the top of Figure 14-5. You need to grant permission (for a maximum of ten minutes). The bottom half of the figure shows the displayed message in Outlook.

If you use the `OlkMsg.Send` method rather than the `OlkMsg.Display` method to send the message without first opening it in Outlook, the real torture sets in as it makes you wait a few seconds and then answer Allow before each sent message. If you were trying to send out hundreds or thousands of messages, you would click Allow over and over again for a long time.

Like all object libraries, Outlook's library is quite large and not something that we can discuss in detail here. It would take more pages than there are in this entire book to even list and briefly define each object, property, method, and event in the Outlook object library. After you set a reference to Microsoft Outlook in the VBA Editor References dialog box, you can get information from the Object Browser. Everything described in this example comes from Outlook's `Application` object (see Figure 14-6).

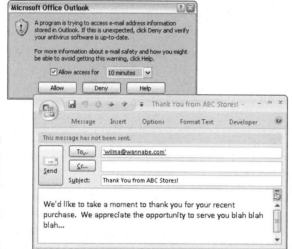

Figure 14-5:
Outlook
security
prevents
mass
mailings.

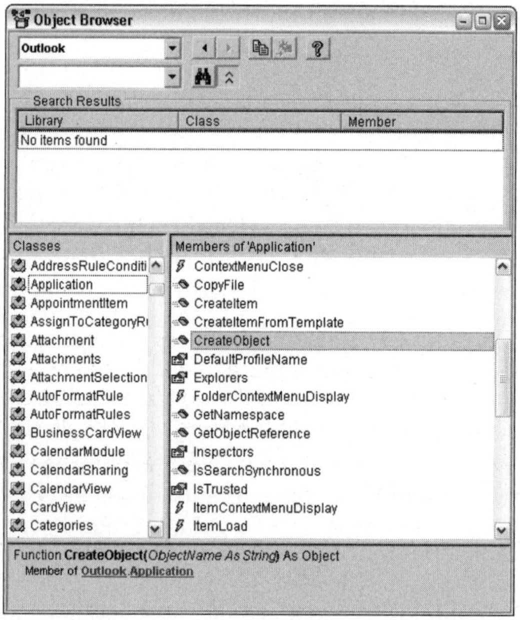

Figure 14-6:
The Outlook
`Appli-
cation`
object
selected in
the Object
Browser.

The Microsoft Web site is another good resource for getting more information on automating activity between Access and Outlook. To see what's available, go to `http://search.microsoft.com` and search for **Access Outlook Automation**.

Whenever you're searching the Microsoft Web site for information on programming interactions between Office programs, include both program names and the word *Automation* in your search.

Sending Data to Microsoft Word

You can print Access data in plenty of ways without getting into VBA. The usual method is to just create a report from the Create tab. You can also use the Microsoft Word Mail Merge Wizard to print form letters, envelopes, labels, and catalogs from any Access table or query. No VBA is involved in any of that. Just learn to use Word's Mail Merge feature, and you're on your way.

Yet a third approach would be to create a general Word template that contains *bookmarks* (placeholders) for data to be filled in later. Then use VBA in Access to replace the bookmarks with data from an Access table. This technique is particularly handy when you want to be able to click a button on a form in Access to print one Microsoft Word form letter.

Creating the Word template

The first step to merging data from Access into a Word document is to create a Word document template (DOTX file). Start with any blank Word document and type your form letter (or whatever you want) as you normally would in Word. You can use any and all Word features — fonts, pictures, tables, WordArt, or whatever.

Wherever you want VBA to insert data from an Access table, create a Word bookmark. A *bookmark* (in Word) is just a placeholder. Bookmarks are usually hidden, so before you add any bookmarks to the document, click the Microsoft Office button and choose Word Options. In the Word Options dialog box that opens, click Advanced, scroll to the Show Document Content section, select Show Bookmarks, and then click OK.

You can insert bookmarks however you want. Here's how we usually do it:

1. **Move the cursor to where you want VBA to insert data from Access.**

2. **Type a short, simple name for the bookmark.**

   The name cannot contain spaces or punctuation, and it *must* start with a letter.

3. **Select (double-click) the name you just typed and then press Ctrl+C to copy it.**

4. **Click the Insert tab, click Links, and then choose Bookmark from the menu that appears.**

5. Press Ctrl+V to paste the typed name as the bookmark name.

6. Click the Add button.

Go through those steps for each item of data that you want VBA to insert later. In the example shown in Figure 14-7, we add three bookmarks to the document. Note that the square brackets around each bookmark's name are visible because the Show Bookmarks option is enabled. We didn't type any of those square brackets.

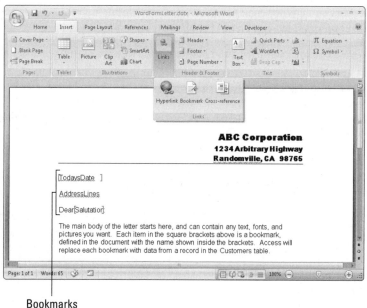

Figure 14-7:
Word
document
template
with
bookmarks
to later
accept
Access
data.

Bookmarks

The bookmark names in the sample document template get data from Access and VBA as follows:

- ✔ TodaysDate: VBA replaces this bookmark with the current date.
- ✔ AddressLines: VBA replaces this line with as many lines as necessary to show the recipient's address.
- ✔ Salutation: VBA replaces this with the customer's first name or just Sir or Madam if the first name is Null (empty) in the record being printed.

When you finish typing your document and all your bookmarks are in place, follow these steps to save the document as a Word template:

1. Click the Office button and choose Save As.

The Save As dialog box appears.

2. **From the Save As Type option at the bottom of the Save As dialog box, select Word Template (*.dotx).**

3. **Use the Save In drop-down list to navigate to the folder in which you want to store the document template.**

   Your best bet is to put it in the same folder as your database ACCDB file, but you can use any folder you want — as long as you know the full path to the document. For example, if you put the Word template in your Shared Documents folder, the path to that document is `C:\Documents and Settings\All Users\Shared Documents`.

4. **Name the document (but don't change the `.dotx` extension) and click the Save button.**

   We name our document template `WordFormLetter.dotx`, but you can name yours however you want.

5. **Close Microsoft Word.**

That takes care of the Word document. The rest of the action takes place in Access and VBA.

Creating the Access form

For this example, we create a simple form that's bound to a table named `Customers`, with the usual name and address fields that you would expect to find in such a table. Figure 14-8 shows a sample form in Form view. The controls that are relevant to the form letter start at the one containing the name *Tori*. Starting at that field and reading down and to the right, the names of the controls are

```
FirstName
LastName
Company
Address1
Address2
City
State
ZIP
```

In the VBA code to follow, you see the names referred to with square brackets — `[FirstName]`, `[LastName]`, and `[Company]`, for example. The e-mail address control, near the bottom, isn't really relevant to the topic at hand. The drop-down list near the top of the control provides the user with a means of choosing a customer. The Merge to Word Letter button is named `MergeBttn`.

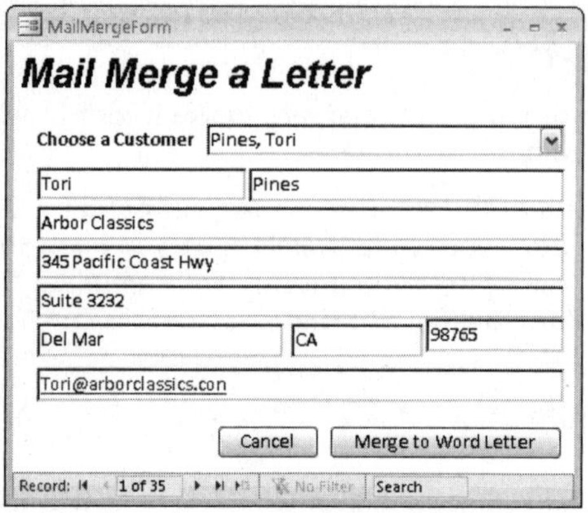

Figure 14-8:
Create a
form to
display one
customer's
name and
address
at a time.

To use the form, a person chooses a name from the Choose a Customer
combo box and then clicks the Merge to Word Letter button. That button
executes VBA code to open the document template, replaces each bookmark
with data from the current record in the form, prints the document, and then
closes Word.

Writing the merge code

For this example, we place the code in the form shown in Figure 14-8 by
attaching it to the `MergeBttn` control's `On Click` event. The VBA code is
shown in its entirety in Listing 14-2.

Listing 14-2: Merging Data with a Word Document

```
Private Sub MergeBttn_Click()

    'Declare variables for storing strings (text).
    Dim AddyLineVar As String, SalutationVar As String

    'Start building AddyLineVar, by dealing with blank
    'LastName and Company fields (allowed in this table).
    If IsNull([LastName]) Then
        AddyLineVar = [Company]
        'Just set SalutationVar to generic "Sir or Madam".
        SalutationVar = "Sir or Madam"
    Else
        AddyLineVar = [FirstName] & " " & [LastName]
        'If the Company isn't blank, tack that on after
            name.
```

```
        If Not IsNull([Company]) Then
            AddyLineVar = AddyLineVar & vbCrLf & [Company]
        End If
        'Salutation will be customer's first name.
        SalutationVar = [FirstName]
    End If

    'Add line break and Address1
    AddyLineVar = AddyLineVar & vbCrLf & [Address1]

    'If Address2 isn't null, add line break and Address2
    If Not IsNull([Address2]) Then
        AddyLineVar = AddyLineVar & vbCrLf & [Address2]
    End If

    'Tack on line break and then City, State, Zip.
    AddyLineVar = AddyLineVar & vbCrLf & [City] & ", "
    AddyLineVar = AddyLineVar & [State] & "   " & [ZIP]

    'Declare an instance of Microsoft Word.
    Dim Wrd As New Word.Application
    Set Wrd = CreateObject("Word.Application")

    'Specify the path and name to the Word document.
    Dim MergeDoc As String
    MergeDoc = Application.CurrentProject.Path
    MergeDoc = MergeDoc & "\WordFormLetter.dotx"

    'Open the document template, make it visible.
    Wrd.Documents.Add MergeDoc
    Wrd.Visible = True

    'Replace each bookmark with current data.
    With Wrd.ActiveDocument.Bookmarks
        .Item("TodaysDate").Range.Text = Date
        .Item("AddressLines").Range.Text = AddyLineVar
        .Item("Salutation").Range.Text = SalutationVar
    End With

    'Letter is ready to print, so print it.
    Wrd.ActiveDocument.PrintOut

    'All done. Close up (no need to save document)
    Wrd.ActiveDocument.Close wdDoNotSaveChanges
    Wrd.Quit

End Sub
```

Like all procedures, this one is just a series of small steps carried out in a specific order to achieve some goal. The first line tells you that this procedure executes whenever a user clicks the MergeBttn button:

```
Private Sub MergeBttn_Click()
```

The next two lines declare two string variables named AddyLineVar and SalutationVar. Each of those variables becomes a string of text to be substituted into the document template in place of the AddressLines and Salutation bookmarks:

```
'Declare variables for storing strings (text).
Dim AddyLineVar As String, SalutationVar As String
```

In the Customers table we use for this example, the Address1, City, State, and ZIP code fields are required, but the user can leave the FirstName, Company, and Address2 fields empty (Null). The code that follows builds the variable AddyLineVar as needed for whatever information is available in the current record. The first big If...End If block, shown next, starts out by saying "If the LastName field for this record is empty, make the first line of the AddyLineVar the company name and make SalutationVar into the general title, Sir or Madam:."

```
'Start building AddyLineVar, by dealing with blank
'LastName and Company fields (allowed in this table).
If IsNull([LastName]) Then
    AddyLineVar = [Company]
    'Just set SalutationVar to generic "Sir or Madam".
    SalutationVar = "Sir or Madam"
```

If the LastName field for this record is not null, the following code adds the customer's first and last names to AddyLineVar. Note that vbCrLf is the Access VBA constant for a carriage return or linefeed. Each vbCrLf in AddyLineVar translates to the end of the line in the Word document. Note, too, that SalutationVar gets its value from the FirstName field in the following code:

```
Else
    AddyLineVar = [FirstName] & " " & [LastName]

    'If the Company isn't blank, tack that on after name.
    If Not IsNull([Company]) Then
       AddyLineVar = AddyLineVar & vbCrLf & [Company]
    End If

    'Salutation will be customer's first name.
    SalutationVar = [FirstName]
End If
```

Because `Address1` is a required field, you can assume that it is not null. The following code adds a `vbCrLf` and the contents of the `Address1` field to `AddyLineVar`:

```
'Add CRLF and Address1
AddyLineVar = AddyLineVar & vbCrLf & [Address1]
```

The next `If...End If` block adds a line break and the contents of the `Address2` field to `AddyLineVar` but only if the `Address2` field isn't empty:

```
'If Address2 isn't null, add CRLF and Address2
If Not IsNull([Address2]) Then
    AddyLineVar = AddyLineVar & vbCrLf & [Address2]
End If
```

Because the `City`, `State`, and `ZIP` fields are required in the `Customers` table, the next lines of code just add another `vbCrLf` to `AddyLineVar`, followed by the `City`, a comma and blank space (`, `), the `State`, two blank spaces, and then the `ZIP`:

```
'Tack on line break and then City, State, Zip.
AddyLineVar = AddyLineVar & vbCrLf & [City] & ", "
AddyLineVar = AddyLineVar & [State] & "  " & [ZIP]
```

At this point in the code, the `AddyLineVar` and `SalutationVar` variables both contain the data to be plugged into the form letter. Now you can start writing the code to open Word and replace its bookmarks with some actual data. First, use the standard syntax described earlier in this chapter to declare and open an instance of Microsoft Word:

The VBA Editor doesn't accept the statements that follow if you haven't already selected the Microsoft Word 12.0 Object Library in your References dialog box:

```
'Declare an instance of Microsoft Word.
Dim Wrd As New Word.Application
Set Wrd = CreateObject("Word.Application")
```

From this point in the code, the object variable named `Wrd` refers to an open instance of Microsoft Word (and its entire `Application` object, which exposes all of Microsoft Word to VBA).

The next step is to open the document template that contains the bookmarks and text. The syntax for opening a Word document from Access VBA is *objVar*`.Documents.Add` *path*. The *objVar* must match the object variable used in the `Dim` and `Set` statements (`Wrd` in this example).

The path must be the complete path to the Word document. In our example, we place the Word document in the same folder as the database ACCDB file (which makes it easy to find). In Access, you can use `Application.CurrentProject.Path` to get the path to the open database. We named our Word document `WordFormLetter.dotx`. The following statements create a string variable named `MergeDoc` that contains the full path and filename of that Word document template:

```
'Specify the path and name to the Word document.
Dim MergeDoc As String
MergeDoc = Application.CurrentProject.Path
MergeDoc = MergeDoc & "\WordFormLetter.dotx"
```

If `WordFormLetter.dotx` were in some other folder, we couldn't use `Application.CurrentProject.Path` to get its path. We would have to specify the path literally in the code. For example, in Windows, if your user account name is Bobo and your form letter is named `MyFormLetter.dotx` and is stored in your My Documents folder, the following statement works just fine as long as you type it into the Code window as one long line:

```
Wrd.Documents.Add "C:\Documents and Settings\Bobo\My
               Documents\MyFormLetter.dotx"
```

Normally, when VBA opens an instance of Word, the program window is invisible, and all activity takes place behind the scenes. For testing and debugging purposes, though, you probably want to make Word visible so that you can see what's happening. To make the window visible, set its `Visible` property to `True`, as shown here:

```
Wrd.Visible = True
```

When Word and a document are both open, VBA can refer to the document as *objVar*.`ActiveDocument` (where, once again, *objVar* matches the object variable name, which is `Wrd` in this example). The `ActiveDocument` object, in turn, contains a `Bookmarks` collection, which contains a list of all bookmarks in the document.

This statement begins a `With...End With` block that defines the current document's `Bookmarks` collection (`Wrd.ActiveDocument.Bookmarks`) as the item to which all properties to follow (up to `End With`) are applied:

```
'Replace each bookmark with current data.
With Wrd.ActiveDocument.Bookmarks
```

Within the `With...End With` block, you can refer to any bookmark by name by using the syntax `.Item(`*bookmarkName*`)` where *bookmarkName* is the name of the bookmark as defined in the Word document. Each bookmark has a `.Range` property, which refers to everything that's contained within the bookmark. The `.Range` property in turn has a `.Text` property, which refers specifically to the text within the bookmark. Thus, the statement

```
.Item("AddressLines").Range.Text = AddyLineVar
```

says "Change whatever text is currently in the bookmark named `AddressLines` to whatever is currently in the variable named `AddyLineVar`."

In the following code, we change the `TodaysDate` bookmark to the current date, the `AddressLines` bookmark to the contents of the `AddyLineVar` variable, and the `Salutation` bookmark to whatever is in the variable named `SalutationVar`:

```
    .Item("TodaysDate").Range.Text = Date
    .Item("AddressLines").Range.Text = AddyLineVar
    .Item("Salutation").Range.Text = SalutationVar
End With
```

On-screen, the document template now contains the complete form letter with all the right information. This next statement prints the form letter:

```
'Print the letter.
Wrd.ActiveDocument.PrintOut
```

The following statement closes the letter without saving it. (You don't need to save the letter after it's printed because you always have the document template to work with.)

```
'All done. Close up (no need to save document)
Wrd.ActiveDocument.Close wdDoNotSaveChanges
```

These two lines close Microsoft Word and end the procedure:

```
    Wrd.Quit

End Sub
```

Figure 14-9 shows an example of using the procedure. There we chose a customer named Tori Pines from the Access form and then clicked the Merge to Word Letter button. The form letter that you see in the background is the result, with the date, address lines, and salutation all in place. The code is written to print the letter, so you would never see the form on top of the Word document. (We had to superimpose the form there.) However, you would get a printed copy of the letter shown in the figure.

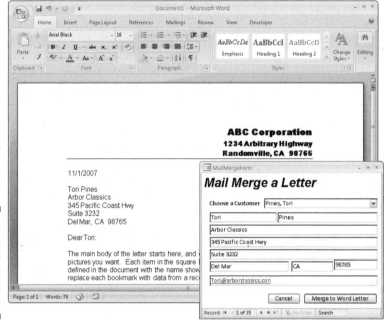

Figure 14-9:
Record from
the form
merged into
a form
letter.

Interacting with Microsoft Excel

Microsoft Excel is a great program for playing what-if scenarios with data because it lets you plug data and formulas into cells in whatever manner you want. Excel isn't good, however, at managing large volumes of data. For large volumes of data, you need a database like Microsoft Access.

Microsoft Access can certainly do any math calculations that Excel can do. Playing with what-if scenarios with data in Access isn't so easy, though, because you need to get queries and/or forms involved. It's just plain difficult to experiment with what-if scenarios in Access.

Sometimes, the data you need for your worksheet might come from an Access database. For example, you might manage all your orders in an Access database. Every now and then you want to grab the total sales from all your orders into a worksheet and use that value to play around with your data.

You could, of course, just open Excel and type in the total sales value — or even copy and paste it from some form in Access. Optionally, you could automate the whole thing by creating a button on some Access form that opens the worksheet and plugs in the total sales amount for you. Look at an example of Automation that does just that.

Creating the worksheet

The first step is to create an Excel worksheet that contains a blank cell that gets its values from Access. Give the cell a name so that you can refer to that cell by name in VBA code. For example, in Figure 14-10, we create a worksheet named `MySheet.xlsx`. Cell B3 in that worksheet is named `FromAccess`.

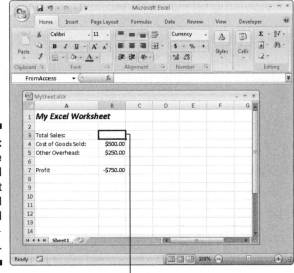

Figure 14-10:
Sample
Excel
worksheet
with a cell
named
From-
Access.

Cell named `FromAccess`

To name a cell or range in Excel, click the cell or select the cells that you want to name. Then type a name into the Name box (where `FromAccess` appears in Figure 14-10) and press Enter. For more information, search the Excel Help for **name cells**.

For the sake of example, we save that worksheet in the root of our C: drive with the name `MySheet.xlsx`. The complete path to that worksheet is

```
C:\MySheet.xlsx
```

That's important to know because VBA can't find the worksheet without the complete path and filename. When you're creating files that you'll open from VBA, make sure that you know where they're located.

Creating a query and a form

After you create and save the worksheet, you can close Excel and open Access. In Access, you need to create a query that can do the calculations and also create a form that can display the appropriate value to copy to the Excel sheet. For this example, we create a totals query in Access that totals all the sales for each product from tables named `Products` and `Order Details` in a sample database. Figure 14-11 shows that query, named `Order Summary Totals Qry`, in Design view (left) and Datasheet view (right).

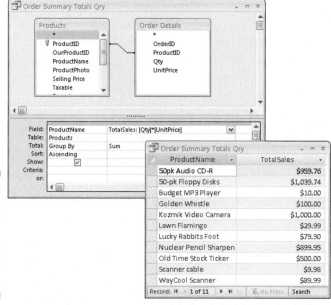

Figure 14-11: Sample query to total sales from orders in a database.

Next, we create a form that's bound to `Order Summary Totals Qry`. In Design view, we set the Form's `Default View` property to `Continuous Forms` so that the detail band displays all the records from the underlying query. In the Form Footer of that form, we add a calculated control named `GrandTotal` that contains the expression `=Sum([TotalSales])` to display the grand total of all the `TotalSales` values. We also create a button named `ExportBttn` (the Export To Excel button, as shown in Figure 14-12). Figure 14-12 shows the form in Design (left) and Form (right) views.

As always, when using external applications, you must choose the Excel object library (`Microsoft Excel 12.0 Object Library`) in the References dialog box before writing the code that follows.

Figure 14-12:
Sample
form named
`Order-`
`Summary-`
`Form.`

Writing the Excel code

With the query and form squared away, the next step is to write VBA code that can open the Excel sheet and copy the value in the control named `GrandTotal` to the cell named `FromAccess` in the `MySheet.xlsx` worksheet. You can attach that to the `ExportBttn On Click` event. The entire procedure is shown in Listing 14-3.

Listing 14-3:   Copying Access Form Data to an Excel Worksheet

```
Private Sub ExportBttn_Click()

    'Declare a variable named MySheetPath as String.
    Dim MySheetPath As String

    'Note: You must change the path and filename below
    'to an actual Excel .xlsx file on your own computer.
    MySheetPath="C:\MySheet.xlsx"

    'Set up object variables to refer to Excel and objects.
    Dim Xl As Excel.Application
    Dim XlBook As Excel.Workbook
    Dim XlSheet As Excel.Worksheet

    'Open an instance of Excel, open the workbook.
    Set Xl = CreateObject("Excel.Application")
    Set XlBook = GetObject(MySheetPath)

    'Make sure everything is visible on the screen.
```

(continued)

Listing 14-3 *(continued)*

```
    Xl.Visible = True
    XlBook.Windows(1).Visible = True

    'Define the topmost sheet in the Workbook as XLSheet.
    Set XlSheet = XlBook.Worksheets(1)

    'Copy GrandTotal to FromAccess cell in the sheet.
    XlSheet.Range("FromAccess").Locked = False
    XlSheet.Range("FromAccess") = Me!GrandTotal

    'Boldface the new value (optional).
    XlSheet.Range("FromAccess").Font.Bold = True

    'Save the sheet with the new value (optional).
    XlBook.Save

    'Close the Access form (optional).
    DoCmd.Close acForm, "OrderSummaryForm", acSaveNo

    'Clean up and end with worksheet visible on the screen.
    Set Xl = Nothing
    Set XlBook = Nothing
    Set XlSheet = Nothing
End Sub
```

Even though the procedure is just an example, it illustrates many techniques for manipulating Excel and worksheets from Access VBA. Taking it one bit at a time, the first line, as always, names the procedure. In this case, the procedure is tied to the On Click event property of ExportBttn, so the procedure name is ExportBttn_Click():

```
Private Sub ExportBttn_Click()
```

In this example, the code changes the contents of an Excel workbook named MySheet.xlsx, stored in the computer's C:\ folder. The following statements create a string variable named MySheetPath and store the pathname, C:\ MySheet.xlsx, in that variable. (The only reason we split it into multiple lines was to get the code to fit within the margins of this book):

```
'Declare a variable named MySheetPath as String
Dim MySheetPath As String

'Note: You must change the path and filename below
'to an actual Excel .xlsx file on your own computer.
MySheetPath = "C:\MySheet.xlsx"
```

Opening Excel and a workbook

The next step in this sample procedure is to open Excel and the workbook. First, you need to declare some object variables so that you have short names to use for these objects later in the code. An Excel workbook is actually two objects: The workbook as a whole is a `Workbook` object; each sheet (page) in the workbook is a `Worksheet` object. So you can set up three object variables:

- ✔ One for Excel (of the type `Excel.Application`)
- ✔ One for the workbook (of the type `Excel.WorkBook`)
- ✔ One for a specific sheet within that workbook (of the type `Excel.Worksheet`)

In the following lines of code, we assign each of these object types named `Xl`, `XlBook`, and `XlSheet`:

```
'Set up object variables to refer to Excel and objects.
Dim Xl As Excel.Application
Dim XlBook As Excel.Workbook
Dim XlSheet As Excel.Worksheet
```

With the object variables declared, you can start assigning specific objects to them. The following statement opens an instance of Microsoft Excel and makes the object variable name `Xl` refer specifically to that open instance of Excel:

```
'Open an instance of Excel, open the workbook.
Set Xl = CreateObject("Excel.Application")
```

After Excel is open, you can use the `GetObject()` function to open a specific file and assign it to the workbook object. The syntax is

```
Set objectVarName = GetObject(filePathName)
```

where *objectVarName* is the object variable name declared as an `Excel.Workbook` (`XlBook` in this example), and *filePathName* is the complete path and filename of the worksheet to open (previously stored in the variable named `MySheetPath` in this example). The next statement in the procedure uses `GetObject()` to open the `MySheet.xlsx` workbook:

```
Set XlBook = GetObject(MySheetPath)
```

One thing that you always need to be aware of is that when you use Automation (that is, VBA) to open an instance of a program, the program usually isn't visible on-screen. In the case of Excel, even an open workbook isn't necessarily visible. You have to specifically tell Excel to make its first document window (referred to as `XlBook.Windows(1)` in VBA) visible. The following lines of code ensure that Excel and the workbook are visible on-screen:

```
'Make sure everything is visible on the screen.
Xl.Visible = True
XlBook.Windows(1).Visible = True
```

The code still needs to set a reference to the first sheet on the open workbook. You can use the workbook's `Worksheets` collection with a subscript to refer to a specific sheet by number. For example, `.Worksheets(1)` refers to the first (topmost) page of a workbook — the one that's automatically visible when you first open the workbook. In the following statement, that topmost sheet is assigned to the object variable `XlSheet`:

```
'Define the topmost sheet in the Workbook as XLSheet.
Set XlSheet = XlBook.Worksheets(1)
```

Referring to worksheet cells from VBA

After you set a reference to the worksheet, you can use its `.Range` property to refer to any cell in the worksheet. There are several ways to use the property. You can refer to a single cell by its address in the worksheet. For example, assuming that the following object variable name `XlSheet` refers to an open worksheet, the following expression refers to cell A1 in that sheet:

```
XlSheet.Range("A1")
```

You can also specify a range by using the syntax *objectVarName*`.Range` (*startCell*:*endCell*) where *startcell* and *endCell* are both cell addresses. For example, the following expression refers to the range of cells extending from cell B3 to cell F20:

```
XlSheet.Range("B3:F20")
```

If you previously named a cell or range in the worksheet, you can use that name in place of a cell address. For example, this statement refers to a cell or range named `FromAccess`:

```
XlSheet.Range("FromAccess")
```

To change the contents of a cell in a worksheet, follow the cell reference by an = sign and the value that you want to store in that cell. For example, this statement stores the words *Howdy World* in cell C2:

```
XlSheet.Range("C2") = "Howdy World"
```

This statement stores the number 100 in cell C3:

```
XlSheet.Range("C3") = 100
```

To put a literal date in a cell, enclose the date in # symbols. For example, this expression stores the date 12/31/07 in cell C4:

```
XlSheet.Range("C4") = #12/31/2007#
```

To put the current date into a cell, use the built-in `Date()` function without the parentheses, as shown here, where cell C5 receives the current date as its value:

```
XlSheet.Range("C5") = Date
```

To place a formula in a cell, use the standard Excel syntax but place the whole formula inside quotation marks. For example, the following statement places the formula =Sum(D4:D10) in cell D11 of the worksheet:

```
XlSheet.Range("D11") = "=Sum(D4:D10)"
```

Note that you must still precede the formula with an = sign, inside the quotation marks, to ensure that the new cell content is treated as a formula rather than as a string of text.

Getting back to the sample procedure, the worksheet is open and visible at this point in the procedure. The next step is to copy the value displayed in the `GrandTotal` control on `OrderSummaryForm` into the cell named `FromAccess` in the worksheet. To play it safe, the following statements first make sure that the cell isn't locked (`XlSheet.Range("FromAccess").Locked = False`). Then the next statement makes the content of the cell named `FromAccess` equal to the values stored in the form's `GrandTotal` control:

```
'Copy GrandTotal to FromAccess cell in the sheet.
XlSheet.Range("FromAccess").Locked = False
XlSheet.Range("FromAccess") = Me!GrandTotal
```

At this point, the job is complete. The procedure could end right there with an `End Sub` statement. Just to illustrate a technique for formatting cells from VBA, we added the following statement to boldface the `FromAccess` cell in the worksheet:

```
'Boldface the new value (optional).
XlSheet.Range("FromAccess").Font.Bold = True
```

You see other techniques for formatting spreadsheet cells in a moment. For now, continue with the sample procedure. The next statement simply saves the worksheet with the new data in place. Again, this step is entirely optional:

```
'Save the sheet with the new value (optional).
XlBook.Save
```

Now that the spreadsheet is open and the `FromAccess` cell has its new value, it's really not necessary to keep `OrderSummaryForm` open. This statement closes that form:

```
'Close the Access form (optional).
DoCmd.Close acForm, "OrderSummaryForm", acSaveNo
```

At this point, the procedure has finished its job, and there's really nothing left to do. Just to keep things tidy, the following statements break the bonds between the object variables and Excel objects. Think of this as the programming equivalent of tying up loose ends. Then the procedure ends.

```
    'Clean up and end with worksheet visible on the screen.
    Set Xl = Nothing
    Set XlBook = Nothing
    Set XlSheet = Nothing
End Sub
```

It's worth noting that only one statement in the whole procedure, `XlSheet.Range("FromAccess") = Me!GrandTotal`, copies the value from the form control to the Excel worksheet. All the code preceding that statement is just getting things open and on-screen so that the statement can execute. All that code is boilerplate code for opening an instance of Excel and a workbook. As you see in the next example, you can use most of that code, as-is, to do something different — copy an entire table, or the results of any query, to a worksheet.

Copying a table or query to a worksheet

To copy a table or query results to an Excel worksheet, you first need to create a recordset. You can use the general techniques described in Chapter 7 to create a `Select` query that produces the records you want to export. Then you can copy and paste its SQL statement into code to create a recordset in code. Then, thanks to the Excel `CopyFromRecordset` method, the code can copy the whole recordset to any place in the worksheet with a single command.

For example, the hefty-looking chunk of code in Listing 14-4 copies all records produced by `Order Summary Totals Qry` (refer to Figure 14-11) to a worksheet named `RecordsetSheet.xlsx` (for lack of a better name). As intimidating as it all looks, it's mostly a bunch of copy-and-paste code that we just lifted from other procedures.

Listing 14-4:   Copying a Recordset to an Excel Worksheet

```
'We'll start by creating a recordset named MyRecordset.
Dim cnn As ADODB.Connection
Set cnn = CurrentProject.Connection
Dim MyRecordset As New ADODB.Recordset
MyRecordset.ActiveConnection = cnn

'Build the SQL statement (swiped from a query).
Dim MySQL As String
```

```
MySQL = "SELECT [ProductName], Sum([Qty]*[UnitPrice])"
MySQL = MySQL & " AS TotalSales FROM [Order Details]"
MySQL = MySQL & " INNER JOIN Products ON"
MySQL = MySQL & " [Order Details].ProductID ="
MySQL = MySQL & " Products.ProductID"
MySQL = MySQL & " GROUP BY Products.[ProductName]"
MySQL = MySQL & " ORDER BY Products.[ProductName]"

MyRecordset.Open MySQL
'Now MyRecordset contains records to be exported.

'Now for the Excel rigmarole.
'Define the path to the workbook, save it as MySheetPath.
Dim MySheetPath As String
'Note: You must change the path and filename below
'to an actual Excel .xlsx file on your own computer.
MySheetPath = "C:\RecordsetSheet.xlsx"

'Set up object variables to refer to Excel and objects.
Dim Xl As Excel.Application
Dim XlBook As Excel.Workbook
Dim XlSheet As Excel.Worksheet

'Open an instance of Excel, open the workbook.
Set Xl = CreateObject("Excel.Application")
Set XlBook = GetObject(MySheetPath)

'Make sure everything is visible on the screen.
Xl.Visible = True
XlBook.Windows(1).Visible = True

'Define the topmost sheet in the Workbook as XLSheet,
Set XlSheet = XlBook.Worksheets(1)

'Copy the recordset to worksheet starting at cell B3.
XlSheet.Range("B3").CopyFromRecordset MyRecordset

'Clean up and end with worksheet visible on the screen.
MyRecordset.Close
Set cnn = Nothing
Set Xl = Nothing
Set XlBook = Nothing
Set XlSheet = Nothing
```

We didn't put the preceding code between Sub...End Sub statements. You could just attach the code to any command button's On Click event to run it when you want it run. To show how the code isn't as intimidating as it looks, let us tell you how we wrote it.

First, before we even wrote any code, we created an Excel worksheet, added a heading in cell A1, did a little formatting, and saved it in our C:\ drive as `RecordsetSheet.xlsx` (for lack of a better name). So we want our VBA code to open that workbook.

We also created a query in Access that defines the records we wanted to copy to the worksheet. We made sure that query was working and also that its Datasheet view showed the exact data we wanted to copy to Excel. Then we closed and saved that query.

With the worksheet and query in place, we started writing the code. We knew that we would need two major chunks of code here: one chunk to create the recordset and another to open the worksheet. We already had boilerplate code (from Chapter 7) for creating an ADODB (ActiveX Data Objects Database) recordset, so we just did a quick copy-and-paste of that code into a new procedure.

Most of the copy-and-paste code was fine. We just had to delete all the `MySQL =` statements so that we could build a new SQL statement. To get that new statement, we opened our previously defined and tested query in SQL view and copied its SQL statement (minus the semicolon at the end) into the Code window.

In the Code window, we set about breaking that lengthy SQL statement into smaller chunks. (*Note:* We did that only to make it all fit within the margins of this book.) In the following code fragment, italics indicate the lines that we had to change. All other lines are straight from a copy-and-paste operation:

```
'We'll start by creating a recordset named MyRecordset.
Dim cnn As ADODB.Connection
Set cnn = CurrentProject.Connection
Dim MyRecordset As New ADODB.Recordset
MyRecordset.ActiveConnection = cnn

'Build the SQL statement (swiped from a query).
Dim MySQL As String
MySQL = "SELECT [ProductName], Sum([Qty]*[UnitPrice])"
MySQL = MySQL & " AS TotalSales FROM [Order Details]"
MySQL = MySQL & " INNER JOIN Products ON"
MySQL = MySQL & " [Order Details].ProductID ="
MySQL = MySQL & " Products.ProductID"
MySQL = MySQL & " GROUP BY Products.[ProductName]"
MySQL = MySQL & " ORDER BY Products.[ProductName]"

MyRecordset.Open MySQL
'Now MyRecordset contains records to be exported.
```

That takes care of the recordset problem. Now move on to opening Excel and the workbook. This was another copy-and-paste job, this time from the procedure shown in Listing 14-3. The path and filename to the workbook are different in this procedure, so we had to change those lines of code (again shown in italics here), but the rest is exactly what we pasted into the procedure:

```
'Now for the Excel rigmarole.
'Define the path to the workbook, save it as MySheetPath.
Dim MySheetPath As String
'Note: You must change the path and filename below
'to an actual Excel .xlsx file on your own computer.
MySheetPath = "C:\RecordsetSheet.xlsx"

'Set up object variables to refer to Excel and objects.
Dim Xl As Excel.Application
Dim XlBook As Excel.Workbook
Dim XlSheet As Excel.Worksheet

'Open an instance of Excel, open the workbook.
Set Xl = CreateObject("Excel.Application")
Set XlBook = GetObject(MySheetPath)

'Make sure everything is visible on the screen.
Xl.Visible = True
XlBook.Windows(1).Visible = True

'Define the topmost sheet in the Workbook as XLSheet,
Set XlSheet = XlBook.Worksheets(1)
```

At this point in the code, we have our recordset and we have our open worksheet. Because this procedure copies a recordset, the next statement is brand new, but it's not too terribly difficult to figure out what it's doing even if you just read it and take a wild guess:

```
'Copy the recordset to worksheet starting at cell B3.
XlSheet.Range("B3").CopyFromRecordset MyRecordset
```

The preceding statement is all that you need to copy a recordset to an open Excel worksheet. The `B3` in the statement just moves the cursor to cell B3. Then `CopyFromRecordset MyRecordset` copies the recordset, starting at cell B3, into the worksheet. Nothing to it!

The rest of the code is just cleanup, but that code is just a straight copy-and-paste job from the other two procedures as well. So you see, as big and intimidating as the procedure looks, it really required very little typing or programming on our part. We used boilerplate code — that we know already works — to write at least 90 percent of the procedure! That's the way you write code: Use what already works, when you can. Create new stuff only when you have to.

Running Excel macros from Access

Speaking of writing code by using what works and creating only what you have to, consider formatting an Excel worksheet. When you write a procedure that copies data from Access to Excel, you might be tempted to write some code to format the worksheet as well, but that would be tedious and unnecessary. That's because in Excel, you can just record a macro while you're formatting the sheet. Then save that macro, and run it from your Access VBA program.

For example, rather than add a bunch of code to either of the procedures in the preceding section to format the worksheet, you could just open the worksheet and move the cursor to some known starting point — cell A1, for example. Then do the following:

1. **On the Developer tab in Excel, click the Record Macro button in the Code group.**

2. **Give the macro an easily remembered name (like Format Sheet) and then click OK.**

3. **Format your worksheet using whatever techniques you want.**

   For example, you might

   • Click a column heading (like B), click the Home tab, and choose Format⇨AutoFit Column Width in the Cells group to size the column to its contents.

   • Click a column heading (like C) and click the button with the dollar sign to format the selected column as Currency.

   • Move the cursor to a cell and type a formula.

While recording a macro, try to use the Name box as much as possible to move the cursor to a specific cell. That way, if you move the cell or range later, the macro goes to its new location rather than to the old location.

4. **Keep doing whatever you have to do to make the sheet look right, and then click the Stop Recording button.**

To test the macro, choose Macros from the Code group on the Developer tab. Click the macro name and choose Run. The macro executes. If all is well, you're done. To run macros in Excel 2007, you have to save your file as an Excel Macro-Enabled Workbook (*.xlsm) and place it in a trusted location.

The recorded macro is also VBA code. If you choose Macros from the Code group on the Developer tab, click a macro name, and then click Edit, the macro opens in the VBA Editor. Each step in the procedure that you see was recorded while you were recording the macro.

Back in your Access VBA procedure, you most likely want to run the macro after your code copies new content to the worksheet — for example, just under the `XlSheet.Range("FromAccess") = Me!GrandTotal` statement in Listing 14-3, or under `XlSheet.Range("B3").CopyFromRecordset MyRecordset` in Listing 14-4. The syntax for running a macro in the open workbook, from Access, is

```
objVar.Run ("macroName")
```

where *objVar* is the object variable to which you assigned the Excel application (`Xl` in previous examples), and *macroName* is the name of the macro in the worksheet that you want to run. For example, from any Access VBA procedure, the following statement runs the macro named `FormatSheet` in the open worksheet (assuming that the open worksheet contains a macro named `FormatSheet`):

```
Xl.Run ("FormatSheet")
```

If you want to put the cursor in a specific field before the macro executes, use the syntax `objVar.Range("Address").Select` before running the macro. For example, the following code positions the cursor to cell A1 and then executes the macro named `FormatSheet` in the open workbook:

```
'Go to cell A1.
XlSheet.Range("A1").Select

'Run macro named FormatSheet.
Xl.Run ("FormatSheet")
```

You also need to change the worksheet's extension from `.xlsx` to `.xlsm` because you created a new file. If you moved the file to a trusted location, make sure that you also update the path to the workbook file.

Automating interaction between Access and other Office programs can be cumbersome. This chapter only touches the surface of what you can do. By adding references to Outlook, Word, PowerPoint, and Excel, you can explore the various objects, methods, and properties available for you to control.

Part VI
The Part of Tens

The 5th Wave   By Rich Tennant

"I'm sure there will be a good job market when I graduate. I created a virus that will go off that year."

In this part . . .

No *For Dummies* book would be complete without a Part of Tens. Ten is such a nice number to work with, given our ten fingers and all. Chapter 15 covers the main strategies that you should adopt to avoid going crazy trying to get VBA to do something. Then Chapter 16 lists the top ten nerdy programming tasks that you're most likely to want to do from Day 1 of using VBA.

Chapter 15

Ten Commandments of Writing VBA

- -

*E*very programmer makes a mistake or two (or a million) while figuring out how to write code. This chapter lists ten common errors that programmers make — heed these commandments, and you'll make fewer mistakes when you're writing your own code.

1. Thou Shalt Not Harbor Strange Beliefs about Microsoft Access

VBA is a programming language for manipulating objects in Microsoft Office application programs. This book describes using VBA to manipulate objects and their properties in Access. Before you can write code to manipulate objects programmatically, you must first understand the objects themselves.

Therefore, you really have to understand the purpose of tables, queries, forms, reports, macros, controls on forms, expressions, and other Access concepts before you can even think about tackling VBA. If you try to use VBA without first knowing Access, you will surely break the tenth commandment for all your programming days.

11. Thou Shalt Not Use VBA Statements in Vain

Or, to put this another way, thou shalt not attempt to make up thine own programming language.

You need to know the exact spelling and syntax of every VBA keyword and every Access object that you name. If the correct line to type is

```
DoCmd.OpenForm "myForm", acNormal, , , acFormEdit
```

don't assume that something reasonably close, like any of these examples, will work:

- ✔ Do Cmd.OpenForm "myForm", acNormal, , , acFormEdit
- ✔ DoCmd.Open Form "myForm". acNormal..acFormEdit
- ✔ DoCmd.OpenForm "myForm", acNormal, , , acFrmEdit
- ✔ DoCmd.Open Form "myForm", acNormal, , , acFormEdit
- ✔ DoComnd.OpenForm "myForm", acNormal, , , acFormEdit
- ✔ DoCmd.OpenForm "myForm", "acNormal", , , "acFormEdit"

After casual observation, you might think that any of these six lines would work in place of the original example. In fact, each of these six statements contains a syntax error (additional spaces, misspelled words, missing commas, and so forth) that would cause the line to fail.

III. Remember to Keep Holy the VBA Syntax

Every VBA statement has strict rules of syntax that define the exact spelling, punctuation, and order of items in that statement. They're not suggestions: They're *rules* that must be obeyed if you expect your code to work. (Okay, so we're still harping on the second commandment.)

If you don't have a clue what that shaded box in Figure 15-1 is about, or why **FormName** is in boldface there, study in earnest how to understand syntax in Chapter 3. Woe be to those who don't heed this warning, for surely they will live their remaining programming days breaking the tenth commandment.

Figure 15-1: Don't be clueless.

IV. Honor Thy Parens and Quotation Marks

Punctuation marks count big-time in all programming languages. Many marks come in pairs. For example, you will never find a VBA function or statement that uses only one parenthesis. Every open parenthesis must have exactly one corresponding closed parenthesis.

Do yourself a favor by getting in the habit of always typing both punctuation marks immediately when you know that two are required. For example, when you have to type something like **IsNull([Last Name])**, you can type it like a programmer rather than like a normal person. First type this line:

```
IsNull()
```

The syntax of `IsNull()` requires both parentheses, so now both parentheses are typed. If you don't type both of them when you're thinking about them, you might forget to type the closing parenthesis later. (That's a compile error!)

Next, a programmer types the square brackets inside the parentheses, like this:

```
IsNull([])
```

Once again, if you type the opening bracket, you know that you need a closing bracket, so just type it while it's fresh in your mind. Finally, type the part in the middle of it all:

```
IsNull([Last Name])
```

The same goes for quotation marks. For example, to type `MyText = "Hello World"`, first type

```
MyText = ""
```

You can't forget to type the closing quotation mark now because it's already there. Then type the stuff that goes inside the quotation marks:

```
MyText = "Hello World"
```

The abbreviated version of the fourth commandment is "Thou shalt not type like a normal person."

V. Thou Shalt Not Guess

When it comes to anything having to do with computers, guessing rarely works. When it comes to database management or programming, guessing *never* works. Woe be to those who attempt to create a database or code by guessing, for surely they will end up in green padded cells, breaking the tenth commandment for all their remaining days.

VI. Thou Shalt Not Commit Help Adultery

Microsoft Access is a computer program that has its own, built-in Help system. The VBA Editor is a separate program that has its own built-in Help system. They are not one and the same. For help on Access matters, use Access Help (see the top of Figure 15-2). For help with VBA, use VBA Help (see the bottom of the figure). If you're in doubt, try both. Don't just try one and give up. Don't guess!

Access Help

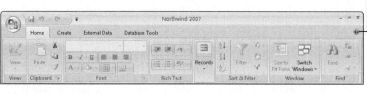

Figure 15-2:
Seek
relevant
facts by
using the
correct Help
system.

VBA Help

Use the taskbar buttons or press Alt+F11 to switch between Access and the VBA Editor program windows.

When all else fails, go to `http://search.microsoft.com` and search for more information. Make sure to include relevant words, like *Access VBA,* in all searches, or you may end up with 196,342 irrelevant links to sift through.

If you use Google, or any other whole-Web search engine, to search for help, be sure to include even more relevant words, like *Microsoft Office Access VBA.* Otherwise, you might end up with more links than you could view in 100 lifetimes.

VII. Thou Shalt Steal Whenever Possible

The more you type, the more likely you are to make typographical errors. Whenever you have an option to choose rather than type (as in Figure 15-3), always choose. Don't ignore the options, make up your own words, or choose options at random.

Figure 15-3: Thou shalt not ignore options or choose options cluelessly.

If you can find the code on some Web page somewhere, or any place from which you can copy and paste, go ahead and copy and paste. Don't be afraid to copy and paste code, especially when you're starting out with VBA. You have to learn to crawl (use a computer) before you learn to pole-vault (program a computer).

VIII. Thou Shalt Not Bear False Witness against Thy Object Browser

Everything in an Access database is an object. VBA exists to manipulate those objects programmatically. The Object Browser leads you to code that actually works. It helps to remind you that `Forms!` and `Reports!` refer to open objects and that `AllForms` and `AllReports` work with closed objects.

For example, the Object Browser helps you to discriminate between the `DoCmd` *object* and the `DoCmd` *property*. It takes you to the land of truth and facts, and gives you names and words that work in VBA.

The Object Browser is always available in the VBA Editor: Just press F2. Learn to use the Object Browser successfully — it makes writing code much easier.

If you don't know an Object Browser from a Web browser, or a property from pastrami, see Chapter 5, which covers objects and collections.

IX. Thou Shalt Not Covet Thy Neighbor's Knowledge

Nobody was ever born already knowing how to use a computer or do database management, and no one was ever a fresh-out-of-the-womb VBA programmer. Everyone who already knows this stuff went through the same learning curve you're faced with. Don't feel stupid for not knowing VBA from birth. You acquire skills like everyone else — by learning, doing, and knowing how to get the information you need when you need it.

X. Thou Shalt Not Scream

Screaming doesn't help. Nor do wishes, hopes, guesses, opinions, beliefs, anger, envy, wrath, sloth, gluttony, or sadness. Only facts matter. Anything else is a futile waste of time and energy.

We were tempted to add that *prayers* don't help. Because we're listing the Ten Commandments of VBA, we figured we would leave that one off the list of futile strategies. In the interest of keeping things practical, here's a 21st century tenth commandment amendment:

Thou shalt press F1 after every prayer.

Chapter 16

Top Ten Nerdy VBA Tricks

. . . .

Access and VBA are both huge products in the sense that you can do about a bazillion different things with either one of them. However, when it comes to learning VBA, having a zillion options to choose from doesn't help. It only creates the unanswerable question "Where do I start?"

From a big-picture point of view, you have to know Access before you even attempt to work in VBA. You also need to get your bearings in how and where VBA fits into the whole Microsoft Access picture. We cover the getting-your-bearings endeavor in Part I of this book. Eventually, you'll get to the point where you're typing real VBA code.

After you start typing code, you return to the problem of having a zillion different things that you *could* type and figuring out where to start. Well, if you were to ignore the zillion things that you *could* type and keep only the top ten things that you *most likely* want to type, you would end up with the sections in this chapter.

Open a Form from VBA

When you want a procedure to open an Access form in Form view — so that the user can see and use the form — use the OpenForm method of the DoCmd object, like this:

```
DoCmd.OpenForm "yourFormName", acNormal
```

and replace *yourFormName* with the name of the form that you want to open. For example, if your database contains a form named Products and you want VBA to open that form in Access, use the statement

```
DoCmd.OpenForm "Products", acNormal
```

See Whether a Form Is Already Open

Sometimes it's useful for a procedure to know whether a form is open or closed. The CurrentProject.AllForms collection contains the name of every form in the current database. Each form has an IsLoaded property that's True if the form is open or False if the form is closed. The syntax for using IsLoaded is

```
CurrentProject.AllForms("formName").IsLoaded
```

where *formName* is the name of a form in the current database. For example, the following expression returns True if the form named Customers is open or False if the form is closed:

```
CurrentProject.AllForms("Customers").IsLoaded
```

A practical example is an If...End If block that closes the form named NewCust only if that form is open:

```
If CurrentProject.AllForms("NewCust").IsLoaded Then
    DoCmd.Close acForm, "NewCust", acSaveYes
End If
```

Refer to an Open Form

VBA keeps track of all open forms in the Forms collection. To refer to an open form from a standard module, use the syntax

```
Forms![formName]
```

where *formName* is the name of the open form. For example, when the Products form is open, use

```
Forms![Products]
```

in VBA to refer to that form as a whole. However, you typically want to refer to a specific control on the open form or perhaps a property of the form as a whole. To refer to a form property, use the syntax

```
Forms![formName].[propertyName]
```

where *propertyName* is the name of the property. For example, every form has a RecordSource property that contains the name of the table or query to which the form is bound. The following example refers specifically to the RecordSource property of the open form named Products:

```
Forms![Products].RecordSource
```

Use an exclamation point (!) (sometimes called a *bang*) in front of any name that you create yourself, such as the name of a form, report, field, or control on a form. Use a period (.) to precede property names and method names that are built into Access (names that you didn't make up yourself).

To refer to a specific control on an open form, use the syntax

```
Forms![formName]![controlName]
```

where *controlName* is the name of a control on the open form. For example, the following statement refers specifically to the value stored in a control named `Product Name` on an open form named `Products`:

```
Forms![Products]![Product Name]
```

To refer to a property of a control, use the syntax

```
Forms![formName]![controlName].propertyName
```

where *propertyName* is a valid property for the control. For example, just about every control type has a `Value` property that refers to the current contents of the control. To refer to the Value property of the `Product Name` control on the open `Products` form, use

```
Forms![Products]![Product Name].Value
```

Move the Cursor to a Control

To move the cursor to a specific control on an open form (from within a standard module), use this syntax:

```
Forms![formName]![controlName].SetFocus
```

For example, the following VBA statements open a form named `NewCust` and move the cursor to a control named `TaxExempt` on that form:

```
'Open my NewCust form in Form view.
DoCmd.OpenForm "NewCust", acNormal

'Move the cursor to the Tax Exempt control.
Forms![NewCust]![Tax Exempt].SetFocus
```

Change the Contents of a Control

To change the contents of a control on an open form, use the syntax

```
Forms![formName]![fieldName].Value = newValue
```

where *newValue* is the value to assign to the control.

For example, the following statement sets the value of a field named Credit Limit on an open form named NewCust to 10,000. The syntax assumes that Credit Limit is bound to a Number or Currency field:

```
Forms![NewCust]![Credit Limit].Value = 10000
```

The following example sets the field named CustStatus on the open form named NewCust to Approved. The syntax assumes that CustStatus is bound to a Text or Memo field:

```
Forms![NewCust]![CustStatus].Value = "Approved"
```

The following statement changes the value of a Date/Time control, named DateEntered on an open form named NewCust, to the current date:

```
Forms![NewCust]![DateEntered].Value = Date
```

The following statement changes the contents of the Date/Time field named DateEntered specifically to the date January 1, 2008:

```
Forms![NewCust]![DateEntered].Value = #1/1/2008#
```

The following statement sets the value of a Yes/No field named PrintedYet to True on an open form named NewCust:

```
Forms![NewCust]![PrintedYet].Value = True
```

Update a List Box or Combo Box

ListBox and ComboBox controls can show lists of data from tables or queries. A common problem with such controls occurs when the row source for the list changes while the control is open and visible on the form. List boxes and combo boxes don't recheck their recordsources after the form is open, so it's easy for a list to get out of sync with what's in its source table or query.

VBA can force a list box or combo box to update its list immediately, via the syntax

```
Forms![formName]![controlName].Requery
```

where *formName* is the name of the open form, and *controlName* is the name of the ListBox or ComboBox control on that open form. For example, the following statement updates a ComboBox or ListBox control named CustID on an open form named Customers:

```
Forms![Customers]![CustID].Requery
```

It's not necessary (or possible) to requery a control on a closed form. If the preceding statement executes when the form named Customers isn't open in Form view, the statement generates an error message.

To prevent such a statement from executing when the specified form isn't open, place the Requery statement in an If...End If block that executes the statement only if the form is open, as in this example:

```
If CurrentProject.AllForms("Customers").IsLoaded Then
    Forms![Customers]![CustID].Requery
End If
```

Show a Custom Message

You can use VBA to display a simple message and an OK button on the screen. The syntax for doing so is

```
MsgBox "yourMessage"
```

where *yourMessage* is the *prompt* (the text to show), as shown in Figure 16-1.

Figure 16-1:
A simple
custom
message
with an OK
button.

For example, the following VBA statement displays the exact message box shown in Figure 16-1:

```
MsgBox "Your message here."
```

The following statement shows the text Thank you. in a message box:

```
MsgBox "Thank you."
```

Ask the User a Question

If you want your VBA code to ask the user a question and then perform some action based on the user's answer, use the more complex MsgBox function syntax and an If...Else...End If block of code with the general syntax, as shown here:

```
Dim variableName As Integer
variableName = MsgBox("prompt",buttons,"title")
If variableName = vbYes Then
    'Code to execute if user clicked Yes goes here.
Else
    'Code to execute if user clicked No goes here.
End If
```

where

- ✔ *variableName* is a name of your own choosing (such as *Answer*).
- ✔ *prompt* is the text of the question that the box displays.
- ✔ *buttons* is any VBA constant or sum of constants. (For a question like the one shown in Figure 16-2, use vbYesNo+vbQuestion.)
- ✔ *title* is the title of message box.
- ✔ *'Code to execute if...* represents any number of VBA statements.

Figure 16-2:
A question
on the
screen with
Yes and No
buttons.

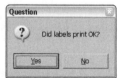

In the following example, the statement

```
Answer = MsgBox("Did labels print OK?", vbYesNo+vbQuestion, "Question")
```

displays the message box shown in Figure 16-2. The question mark icon and Yes/No buttons are in the box courtesy of the vbQuestion+vbYesNo expression in the *buttons* argument:

```
Dim Answer As Integer
Answer = MsgBox("Did labels print OK?", vbQuestion+ vbYesNo, "Question")

If Answer = vbYes Then
      MsgBox "You clicked Yes"
Else
      MsgBox "You clicked No"
End If
```

In the preceding code example, when a user clicks a button, he just sees a little message specifying which button he clicked, which serves no practical purpose. In real life, replace MsgBox "You clicked Yes" and MsgBox "You clicked No" with code that does something useful.

Print a Report

If you want VBA to print a report from the current database, use the syntax

```
DoCmd.OpenReport "reportName", acViewNormal
```

where *reportName* is the name of any report in the current database. For example, the following statement prints a report named MyLabels:

```
DoCmd.OpenReport "MyLabels", acViewNormal
```

In case you hadn't noticed, the DoCmd (pronounced "do command") object shows up quite a few times in this chapter. That's because the DoCmd object lets you do lots of useful things with the tables, queries, forms, and reports in your database. In fact, now that we think of it, we suppose that our tenth nerdy trick should be. . . .

Get to Know the DoCmd Object

The DoCmd object is one of your most potent programming allies because it can do virtually anything you can do in the Access program window. When you type **DoCmd.** into the Code window, the hefty list of items that appears on the little menu (see Figure 16-3) represents various methods of the DoCmd object. Each method, in turn, represents something that the DoCmd object can do.

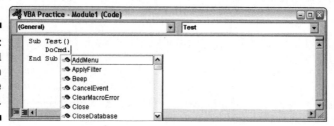

Figure 16-3:
DoCmd
methods in
the Code
window.

The DoCmd methods that you're most likely to use, especially as a beginning programmer, are summarized in Table 16-1. As with any Access object, you can use the Object Browser to get more information on any DoCmd method.

Table 16-1	DoCmd Methods Worth Getting to Know
Goal	*DoCmd Method*
Close a form or report	DoCmd.Close
Open a form	DoCmd.OpenForm
Move to a specific record	DoCmd.GoToRecord
Open a report	DoCmd.OpenReport
Export data	DoCmd.OutputTo
Print data	DoCmd.PrintOut
Rename an object	DoCmd.Rename
Run a macro	DoCmd.RunMacro

Goal	DoCmd Method
Run an action query	DoCmd.RunSQL
Save an object	DoCmd.Save
Select an object	DoCmd.SelectObject
E-mail an object	DoCmd.SendObject
Import/export spreadsheet	DoCmd.TransferSpreadsheet

You can read about the Object Browser in Chapter 2. As a quick head start, in case you're already familiar with the Object Browser, you can find the DoCmd object in the Classes column. When you click the object, you see its methods in the Members column (see Figure 16-4). The bottom of the window shows a summary of the syntax for using the method. For details, though, click the Object Browser's Help button.

Figure 16-4:
DoCmd
selected in
the Object
Browser.

Index

Notes

Notes

BUSINESS, CAREERS & PERSONAL FINANCE

0-7645-9847-3

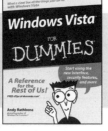

0-7645-2431-3

Also available:
- Business Plans Kit For Dummies
  0-7645-9794-9
- Economics For Dummies
  0-7645-5726-2
- Grant Writing For Dummies
  0-7645-8416-2
- Home Buying For Dummies
  0-7645-5331-3
- Managing For Dummies
  0-7645-1771-6
- Marketing For Dummies
  0-7645-5600-2

- Personal Finance For Dummies
  0-7645-2590-5*
- Resumes For Dummies
  0-7645-5471-9
- Selling For Dummies
  0-7645-5363-1
- Six Sigma For Dummies
  0-7645-6798-5
- Small Business Kit For Dummies
  0-7645-5984-2
- Starting an eBay Business For Dummies
  0-7645-6924-4
- Your Dream Career For Dummies
  0-7645-9795-7

HOME & BUSINESS COMPUTER BASICS

0-470-05432-8

0-471-75421-8

Also available:
- Cleaning Windows Vista For Dummies
  0-471-78293-9
- Excel 2007 For Dummies
  0-470-03737-7
- Mac OS X Tiger For Dummies
  0-7645-7675-5
- MacBook For Dummies
  0-470-04859-X
- Macs For Dummies
  0-470-04849-2
- Office 2007 For Dummies
  0-470-00923-3

- Outlook 2007 For Dummies
  0-470-03830-6
- PCs For Dummies
  0-7645-8958-X
- Salesforce.com For Dummies
  0-470-04893-X
- Upgrading & Fixing Laptops For Dummies
  0-7645-8959-8
- Word 2007 For Dummies
  0-470-03658-3
- Quicken 2007 For Dummies
  0-470-04600-7

FOOD, HOME, GARDEN, HOBBIES, MUSIC & PETS

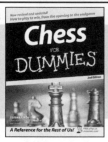

0-7645-8404-9

0-7645-9904-6

Also available:
- Candy Making For Dummies
  0-7645-9734-5
- Card Games For Dummies
  0-7645-9910-0
- Crocheting For Dummies
  0-7645-4151-X
- Dog Training For Dummies
  0-7645-8418-9
- Healthy Carb Cookbook For Dummies
  0-7645-8476-6
- Home Maintenance For Dummies
  0-7645-5215-5

- Horses For Dummies
  0-7645-9797-3
- Jewelry Making & Beading For Dummies
  0-7645-2571-9
- Orchids For Dummies
  0-7645-6759-4
- Puppies For Dummies
  0-7645-5255-4
- Rock Guitar For Dummies
  0-7645-5356-9
- Sewing For Dummies
  0-7645-6847-7
- Singing For Dummies
  0-7645-2475-5

INTERNET & DIGITAL MEDIA

0-470-04529-9

0-470-04894-8

Also available:
- Blogging For Dummies
  0-471-77084-1
- Digital Photography For Dummies
  0-7645-9802-3
- Digital Photography All-in-One Desk Reference For Dummies
  0-470-03743-1
- Digital SLR Cameras and Photography For Dummies
  0-7645-9803-1
- eBay Business All-in-One Desk Reference For Dummies
  0-7645-8438-3
- HDTV For Dummies
  0-470-09673-X

- Home Entertainment PCs For Dummies
  0-470-05523-5
- MySpace For Dummies
  0-470-09529-6
- Search Engine Optimization For Dummies
  0-471-97998-8
- Skype For Dummies
  0-470-04891-3
- The Internet For Dummies
  0-7645-8996-2
- Wiring Your Digital Home For Dummies
  0-471-91830-X

* Separate Canadian edition also available
† Separate U.K. edition also available

Available wherever books are sold. For more information or to order direct: U.S. customers visit www.dummies.com or call 1-877-762-2974.
U.K. customers visit www.wileyeurope.com or call 0800 243407. Canadian customers visit www.wiley.ca or call 1-800-567-4797.

SPORTS, FITNESS, PARENTING, RELIGION & SPIRITUALITY

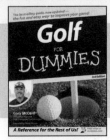

0-471-76871-5

0-7645-7841-3

Also available:

- Catholicism For Dummies
  0-7645-5391-7
- Exercise Balls For Dummies
  0-7645-5623-1
- Fitness For Dummies
  0-7645-7851-0
- Football For Dummies
  0-7645-3936-1
- Judaism For Dummies
  0-7645-5299-6
- Potty Training For Dummies
  0-7645-5417-4
- Buddhism For Dummies
  0-7645-5359-3

- Pregnancy For Dummies
  0-7645-4483-7 †
- Ten Minute Tone-Ups For Dummies
  0-7645-7207-5
- NASCAR For Dummies
  0-7645-7681-X
- Religion For Dummies
  0-7645-5264-3
- Soccer For Dummies
  0-7645-5229-5
- Women in the Bible For Dummies
  0-7645-8475-8

TRAVEL

0-7645-7749-2

0-7645-6945-7

Also available:

- Alaska For Dummies
  0-7645-7746-8
- Cruise Vacations For Dummies
  0-7645-6941-4
- England For Dummies
  0-7645-4276-1
- Europe For Dummies
  0-7645-7529-5
- Germany For Dummies
  0-7645-7823-5
- Hawaii For Dummies
  0-7645-7402-7

- Italy For Dummies
  0-7645-7386-1
- Las Vegas For Dummies
  0-7645-7382-9
- London For Dummies
  0-7645-4277-X
- Paris For Dummies
  0-7645-7630-5
- RV Vacations For Dummies
  0-7645-4442-X
- Walt Disney World & Orlando
  For Dummies
  0-7645-9660-8

GRAPHICS, DESIGN & WEB DEVELOPMENT

0-7645-8815-X

0-7645-9571-7

Also available:

- 3D Game Animation For Dummies
  0-7645-8789-7
- AutoCAD 2006 For Dummies
  0-7645-8925-3
- Building a Web Site For Dummies
  0-7645-7144-3
- Creating Web Pages For Dummies
  0-470-08030-2
- Creating Web Pages All-in-One Desk
  Reference For Dummies
  0-7645-4345-8
- Dreamweaver 8 For Dummies
  0-7645-9649-7

- InDesign CS2 For Dummies
  0-7645-9572-5
- Macromedia Flash 8 For Dummies
  0-7645-9691-8
- Photoshop CS2 and Digital
  Photography For Dummies
  0-7645-9580-6
- Photoshop Elements 4 For Dummies
  0-471-77483-9
- Syndicating Web Sites with RSS Feeds
  For Dummies
  0-7645-8848-6
- Yahoo! SiteBuilder For Dummies
  0-7645-9800-7

NETWORKING, SECURITY, PROGRAMMING & DATABASES

0-7645-7728-X

0-471-74940-0

Also available:

- Access 2007 For Dummies
  0-470-04612-0
- ASP.NET 2 For Dummies
  0-7645-7907-X
- C# 2005 For Dummies
  0-7645-9704-3
- Hacking For Dummies
  0-470-05235-X
- Hacking Wireless Networks
  For Dummies
  0-7645-9730-2
- Java For Dummies
  0-470-08716-1

- Microsoft SQL Server 2005 For Dummies
  0-7645-7755-7
- Networking All-in-One Desk Reference
  For Dummies
  0-7645-9939-9
- Preventing Identity Theft For Dummies
  0-7645-7336-5
- Telecom For Dummies
  0-471-77085-X
- Visual Studio 2005 All-in-One Desk
  Reference For Dummies
  0-7645-9775-2
- XML For Dummies
  0-7645-8845-1

HEALTH & SELF-HELP

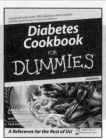

0-7645-8450-2

0-7645-4149-8

Also available:
- Bipolar Disorder For Dummies
  0-7645-8451-0
- Chemotherapy and Radiation
  For Dummies
  0-7645-7832-4
- Controlling Cholesterol For Dummies
  0-7645-5440-9
- Diabetes For Dummies
  0-7645-6820-5* †
- Divorce For Dummies
  0-7645-8417-0 †

- Fibromyalgia For Dummies
  0-7645-5441-7
- Low-Calorie Dieting For Dummies
  0-7645-9905-4
- Meditation For Dummies
  0-471-77774-9
- Osteoporosis For Dummies
  0-7645-7621-6
- Overcoming Anxiety For Dummies
  0-7645-5447-6
- Reiki For Dummies
  0-7645-9907-0
- Stress Management For Dummies
  0-7645-5144-2

EDUCATION, HISTORY, REFERENCE & TEST PREPARATION

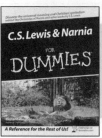

0-7645-8381-6

0-7645-9554-7

Also available:
- The ACT For Dummies
  0-7645-9652-7
- Algebra For Dummies
  0-7645-5325-9
- Algebra Workbook For Dummies
  0-7645-8467-7
- Astronomy For Dummies
  0-7645-8465-0
- Calculus For Dummies
  0-7645-2498-4
- Chemistry For Dummies
  0-7645-5430-1
- Forensics For Dummies
  0-7645-5580-4

- Freemasons For Dummies
  0-7645-9796-5
- French For Dummies
  0-7645-5193-0
- Geometry For Dummies
  0-7645-5324-0
- Organic Chemistry I For Dummies
  0-7645-6902-3
- The SAT I For Dummies
  0-7645-7193-1
- Spanish For Dummies
  0-7645-5194-9
- Statistics For Dummies
  0-7645-5423-9

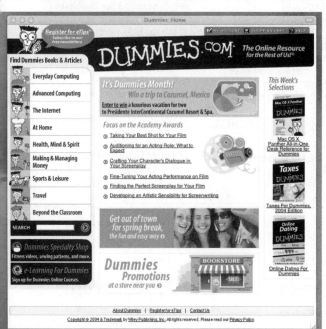

Get smart @ dummies.com®

- **Find a full list of Dummies titles**
- **Look into loads of FREE on-site articles**
- **Sign up for FREE eTips e-mailed to you weekly**
- **See what other products carry the Dummies name**
- **Shop directly from the Dummies bookstore**
- **Enter to win new prizes every month!**

* Separate Canadian edition also available
† Separate U.K. edition also available

Available wherever books are sold. For more information or to order direct: U.S. customers visit www.dummies.com or call 1-877-762-2974.
U.K. customers visit www.wileyeurope.com or call 0800 243407. Canadian customers visit www.wiley.ca or call 1-800-567-4797.